National Identities

The Constitution of the United Kingdom

D0974420

National Identities

The Constitution of the United Kingdom

Edited by
Bernard Crick

Blackwell Publishers

Copyright © The Political Quarterly Publishing Co. Ltd.

ISBN 0–631–18213–6

First published 1991

Blackwell Publishers
108 Cowley Road, Oxford, OX4 1JF, UK.

and
3 Cambridge Center,
Cambridge, MA. 02142, USA.

British Library Cataloguing in Publication Data
National identities: the constitution of
the United Kingdom.   I. Crick, Bernard
327.415041
ISBN 0–631–18213–6

Library of Congress
Cataloguing in Publication Data applied for

Typeset by Joshua Associates Ltd., Oxford
Printed in Great Britain by Whitstable Litho, Kent.

CONTENTS

FOREWORD

THIS book emerges from a small conference arranged by *The Political Quarterly* in conjunction with the Coleg Harlech in September 1990. Those attending were given the brief:

> To consider the government of the United Kingdom and relationships with Ireland in light of: (i) the essential sense of identity of each of the nations; (ii) the extent to which this receives satisfactory institutional expression; (iii) whether these institutions need reform, both internally in each case and in the totality of relationships and interrelationships; and (iv) the impact of 1992 and moves to European integration.

And it quickly became clear that regional identities and regional policy needed discussing, both in the context of these islands and of Europe as a whole.

In a long sentence the conference and book try to bring together two things that have run in parallel, but have not hitherto been thought about together in any depth: the arguments that the constituent nations of these islands need more appropriate, specifically national institutions (such as the Campaign for a Scottish Assembly); and the arguments for reform of the UK constitution (such as those associated with Charter 88) which have usually been put in somewhat (or overwhelmingly) English terms of ideas and machinery for ensuring civil liberties and good government, among which is 'devolution', but not a devolution that measures up to what Welsh and Scots mean by national parliaments, nor for power-sharing parliamentary government in Northern Ireland.

But this book is not an assemblage of conference papers written before the event, as too often happens, to be sternly defended from behind prepared positions and left unchanged unless they suffered exceptionally heavy damage. We took preventive action to avoid this by not asking participants for papers, but only to speak from notes; and we equivocally dangled only a possibility of publication. So people discussed and argued in an open-minded and friendly way, and then wrote their chapters later after reflecting on what others had said. In only one case did the preventive action fail to stop, only damage, a pre-programmed missile.

That it was a friendly exchange is not entirely accidental. The people who came had nearly all been thinking about these themes as a common problem, and if not federalist, all turned out to be broadly pluralist; and if not all had rejected the concept of 'sovereignty', none saw it in the traditional manner of the English lawyers. Though all the participants had a strong sense of national identity, we were spared and did not seek the kind of nationalist who has all the answers already packed and trundles round the conference or conciliation circuit stating his or her unbending the case. But neither did we seek spokesmen for the very familiar view that United Kingdom is a simple unitary state and that any encouragement of antique national sentiments (except British or English) threatens its breakdown. In other words, partly by luck and partly by design, it was a thoughtful and thinking-together gathering, not confrontational, acceptive of change and wanting it, and all exploring the contemporary implications of the United Kingdom being a multi-national state, and one with a close and exceptional relationship to Ireland.

Not all the present authors could be present at Harlech. Hugh Kearney was not able to come, but a paper of his was circulated as an historical focus, together with the remarkable *Guardian* editorials as a political focus. Jim Ross's paper 'The Road to Constitution' has been added, as has Garret Fitzgerald's 'The British and the Irish in Europe'. We had asked him to be the keynote speaker on that very theme, but he was away. By serendipity he chose it for the Mackintosh Memorial lecture in Edinburgh.

I have edited this volume because I was the conference's convener. I thank the editors of *The Political Quarterly* for this trust, particularly David Marquand for being so active at Harlech and Colin Crouch for supervising the final publication.

Above all to thank Joe England, Warden of Coleg Harlech, and Neil Evans, a tutor in history, for making all the conference arrangements so smooth. No-one meeting there can but be moved by the diversity of the British Isles and the integrity of the component nations of the United Kingdom. Coleg Harlech is dedicated to full-time adult education. So are we. Neil Evans had recently edited the proceedings of a stimulating symposium, *National Identity in the British Isles* (Coleg Harlech Occasional Papers in Welsh Studies, No. 3, 1989) which we gave to all participants.

We thank *The Guardian* for permission to reproduce the two editorials.

B.C.
Edinburgh, January 1991

FOUR NATIONS OR ONE?

MOST readers, I take it, live in a political unit termed 'the United Kingdom'. We all agree that our school children should learn something about its history. But how are we to characterise this unit? Some historians seem to see it as a single nation. They refer to 'the story of our nation'. 'In my opinion', states Norman Stone, 'it is essential for school children to know the elements of our national past'. Jonathan Clark tells us that 'history is national property and the decisions to be taken on the history curriculum will be intimately connected with our national self-image, sense of heritage and purpose'.

But what is this nation to which they refer? It is here that we begin to run into difficulties. Mrs Margaret Thatcher declared that 'children should know the great landmarks of British history'. But, is there a British nation? and if there is one today does it have a history stretching back beyond the early twentieth century?

Perhaps we do not have a single national history. Historians have taught us to see the rise of the nation-state as one of the signs of modernity. But suppose that the United Kingdom is not a nation-state like, say, France, but a multi-national state like Belgium, Switzerland, Yugoslavia, the Soviet Union—in fact like the great majority, perhaps, of so-called 'nation-states'. In that case we will be distorting the complexity of our history if we speak of a single 'national past' and a single 'national image'. The 'we' and 'our' of all this are rather a mixed bunch.

The notion that we have several national pasts has been obscured by the understandable dominance of England, particularly since the industrial revolution and the concomitant urbanisation and population rise. In terms of current population England with 46.3 million is by far the largest segment of the UK, Wales having 2.7 million, Scotland 5.1 million and Northern Ireland 1.5 million. (In 1801 English preponderance was much less marked.) As a result it became convenient for many in dealing with the history of the United Kingdom to equate it with the history of England. Thus Mrs Thatcher stated when Prime Minister that 'it was absolutely right' for the new national curriculum to concentrate on the kings and queens of England, while almost in the same breath declaring that 'children should know the great landmarks of British history'. British history, it would appear is in essence English history. 'We' look back to the Tudors, for example, and forget that Scotland had no Tudor dynasty.

---

* The author was born in Liverpool and has taught at University College Dublin, Sussex, Edinburgh and since 1975 at the University of Pittsburgh. Among his works are *Strafford in Ireland*, *The Origins of the Scientific Revolution*, *Scholars and Gentlemen*, and recently *The British Isles: A History of Four Nations*.

1

Does it matter? After all the Oxford history school, our leading nursery of historians, got along quite well for a century unrepentantly teaching English history. If, like Stubbs, we concentrate our attention upon political and constitutional history perhaps the distortion is less. The view from Buckingham Palace, Westminster and the Home Counties easily leads to the assumption that Britain can be safely equated with England and that the histories of Wales, Scotland and Ireland can be dismissed, more or less, under the heading of 'Celtic fringe'. Unfortunately the further one moves away from W.1. the more of a strait-jacket a merely Anglo-centric history becomes. The British Empire was more than an expansion of England. It was also, even in the colonial period, an expansion of the multi-national British Isles.

Emphasis on unity?

If we accept that we live in a multi-national state, we are able to make sense of many phenomena which are otherwise unintelligible. Concentration on political or constitutional history (whose importance I do not wish to downplay) may lead to an emphasis upon the unity of our historical development as exemplified in the Acts of Union of 1536–43 (Wales), 1707 (Scotland) and 1800 (Ireland). Crown and Parliament symbolise the political unity of the United Kingdom. Outside this political framework however we immediately encounter diversity. Unlike any other state we have no national team in any sport apart from the fiction of the 'British Lions' in rugby, which allows 'southern Irish' to count as 'British' (or, alternatively, permits Irish citizens to accept an affront to their republicanism for the sake of the oval ball). We have an established church in England but none in Wales, Scotland or Ireland. We have differences between the common law of England and Wales (and Ireland) and Scots Law. We have a British Army which divides into English, Welsh, Scottish and Irish regiments. We have linguistic divisions between English, Scots Gaelic, and Welsh (Scots Gaelic being derived from Irish). We have distinctive educational systems, with Scotland and Northern Ireland and to a large extent Wales being markedly different from that of England.

It might have seemed in the twentieth century that these national differences were moving towards a common 'British' denominator. Ireland apart, the experiences of the two world wars led towards a common national 'British' identity. The rise of the Labour party led to the playing down of national differences. Aneurin Bevan was not alone in setting his face against what he regarded as separatism. A process of 'nation-building' seemed to be underway. The concept of 'Brit' appeared.

In the neighbouring island the Republic was forging a new largely Catholic national identity, while in Northern Ireland attempts were made to introduce the concept of a province of Ulster into regular usage. All three trends towards 'Britishness', 'Irishness' and 'Ulsterness' were reflections of current political realities. They provide a poor guide however to our history before the twentieth century.

Where does all this leave us? One senses a certain nostalgia for traditional English history. Why can't we return to the basic verities of '1066 and all that' as the present government seems to want? 'England' is undoubtedly the most powerful national grouping within the United Kingdom and the history of the Kings and Queens of England should form part of a sound education in history. But England is part of a wider story. For better or worse the history of England became involved with that of the rest of the British Isles. As Norman Stone remarks 'Great swaths of a country's literature and architecture are incomprehensible without a knowledge of it' (i.e. history). But 'English' literature includes Scott and Burns, Swift, Burke and Yeats, Joyce and O'Casey, Gerard Manley Hopkins and Dylan Thomas as well as Shakespeare and Milton. We simply cannot understand 'our' literature if we confine ourselves to a narrow view of 'Englishness'. We have a multi-national history.

However, I myself am not wholly happy with the term 'nation'. The concept of 'nation' has powerful emotional overtones which make detachment difficult. Questions of loyalty quickly arise. How are we to recognise fellow members of our nation? Are they blonde and blue-eyed? Are they Christian? Do they support the national cricket team (if the MCC is a national cricket team)? I prefer to lower the emotional temperature of our concepts and see our history as 'multi-cultural' rather than 'multi-national'. The question 'Four nations or one?' need not then arise. Since 1920 there have been as a matter of historical fact two sovereign states within the British Isles but there are many urban cultures—Brummagen, Geordie, Glaswegian, Cockney, Scouse (*quorum pars magna fui*). Class, gender and religion form part of our cultures. There are cultural antagonisms (hence ethnic jokes). Since the end of World War II, new ethnic cultures have made their appearance within the United Kingdom, not always without controversy. In this, our experience is not unique. France, Germany, and the Soviet Union are all affected by similar changes. To see our history in narrowly English (or Scottish, Welsh or Irish) terms is to surrender ourselves to nationalist mythology. It is time to move on to a nearer approximation to the truth about our history.

Britishness

To describe the United Kingdom as a 'multi-national' state makes a good deal of sense both of past and present. It is however not a complete description, since it ignores the unifying factor of 'Britishness'. All but a small proportion of the inhabitants of the United Kingdom accept the term 'British' when applied to them even if they do not apply it to themselves without some thought. 'British' is thus a convenient shorthand to apply to the inhabitants of Great Britain and Northern Ireland. There has been a 'British' history over and above our 'multi-national' history. We speak of 'the Battle of Britain', the British Army, the British Navy, the British Empire, the British Parliament, the British Constitution. Americans and others regularly refer to 'the Brits' as we might refer to 'the Yanks', a term of amused tolerance rather than condescension. To outsiders the term 'British' means 'us' or most of us, even if we have not totally internalised the description ourselves. It may be that 'Britain' is a national equivalent of 'Oxford University' which, famously, does not exist apart from the colleges. Visitors to Oxford, asking 'where is the University' are mystified when they cannot be directed to it. But 'Oxford university', as in gaining an Oxford degree or an Oxford blue, clearly has some kind of existence over and above the colleges. In much the same way Britain seems to exist over and above our multi-national structure. The answer to our original question 'four nations or one' should be perhaps 'four nations and one'.

For most of the inhabitants of these islands their primary self description, which first comes to their lips, will be English, Irish (or Northern Irish), Welsh or Scottish rather than British. But a majority of the inhabitants of Northern Ireland would describe themselves first as 'British' and only secondly as from 'Ulster'. This is true also of the children of recent immigrants from Asia, Africa or the West Indies. Mr. Peregrine Worsthorne, the son of a recent immigrant, is perhaps an exception in describing himself as 'English' not 'British'.

Scots, irritated at being called 'English', seize upon the description 'British' with relief, as do the Welsh. It is the English, or the most self-consciously WASP inhabitants of England, who gibe at the term 'British' and accept it with some reluctance. If they do use it they do so as a shorthand for 'English'. Such are the complexities of national self-descriptions within the United Kingdom.

The 'so what?' question cannot be avoided now. Does all this matter? I think it does if we are looking to the future of the United Kingdom. Since we are now a multi-cultural as well as a multi-national society, it is important to make assimilation towards a generally accepted national identity as easy as possible for those who wish to do so. It is for this reason that we should aim at teaching a wider 'British' history in our schools, which has some reference to the history of the British Empire. The Irish-oriented inhabitants of Kilburn should also be able to see themselves as having a place in 'our' history, if they wish to do so.

Of equal importance are the political and constitutional implications of a multi-national approach. As it stands at present the United Kingdom is a unitary state administered from Westminster with some gesture towards local interests in the form of secretaries of State for Wales, Scotland and Northern Irleand. The resurgence of nationalist or quasi-nationalist sentiment in Scotland however suggests that the establishment of a 'Home Rule' Scottish Assembly may be only a matter of time. We now seem to be returning to the political pattern of the 1880s when 'Home Rule all round' was a political possibility. As someone who has lived many years in the United States I do not look upon federalism as some exotic growth. To me, the United States federal constitution seems to strike a nice balance between national interests and local interests. Federalism is not of course a political utopia. Corruption can exist in Harrisburg Pa. as well as in Washington. But federalism is clearly workable and where national feelings are as strong as they seem to be in Scotland it seems desirable. Clearly also a federal solution seems equally desirable in Northern Ireland, at least in the long run. Wales is perhaps a special case. It may be that Wales is so closely integrated with England, while allowing for a high degree of local autonomy in language and education, that the present solution is regarded as reasonably satisfactory by most of its inhabitants.

In the United States constitution, the House of Representatives may be seen as the equivalent of the House of Commons. But there is also a Senate, the equivalent of the British House of Lords. If we are intending to provide a federal dimension to the British constitution it may be that the House of Lords provides the best opportunity of bringing this about. As a second chamber elected according to a time frame different from the Commons, every ten years for example, the Lords could provide appropriate representation for Wales, Scotland and Northern Ireland as well as for various ethnic groups including the 'Southern Irish' (more peers like, or unlike, the Earl of Longford). Membership of the Lords would have symbolic resonance as well as political influence.

There remains the Crown, a symbol of great national significance but one which occupies a paradoxical position in a society which aims, in John Major's words, to be 'classless' and 'meritocratic'. The Crown seems to symbolise a vanished imperial era. David Cannadine has shown how the myth of monarchy was built up in Britain during the late nineteenth and twentieth centuries. It may be that a move in the opposite direction would now be appropriate, on the lines of the Swedish, Dutch and Danish monarchies which seem more in the nature of presidencies. A move away from Buckingham Palace to a more modest establishment would better reflect the reduced status and power of the United Kingdom. Buckingham Palace could then be opened to the public as is the case with Holyrood Palace (or Dublin Castle) save when state occasions make this impossible. The 'Home Counties' tone of monarchy might also be changed in some way.

What then remains of the question with which we began: 'four nations or one?' If we accept Benedict Anderson's view that nations are 'imagined communities', the concept of 'nation' itself is problematic. Of the nations we have been discussing, however, it is the British nation which is most problematic since it seems to be made up of four other nations. A prime minister appealing to 'the British people' is appealing to a sense of national identity which may have been stronger in the heyday of the British Empire than it is today. A government centred upon Westminster which aims at preserving the United Kingdom needs to think long and hard about the

5

nature of 'British identity'. That there is confusion in high places emerged in Mrs Thatcher's speeches when she happily intermingled 'British' and 'English' history. There was also uncertainty in the setting up of a national history curriculum, which turned out to be not 'national' in the sense of 'British' but more narrowly national in the sense of Welsh, English and 'Northern Ireland'. Scotland was not even included. Small wonder if immigrants from Pakistan or Bangladesh are confused about their identity if the British people have not yet made up their minds.

THE BRITISH AND THE IRISH IN THE CONTEXT OF EUROPE

GARRET FITZGERALD*

THE impact of European Community membership has been quite disparate, of course, in the two states of the United Kingdom and the Republic of Ireland. Even where the aspects of social, economic or political life that have been affected are similar in the two countries the effects of membership seem to me to have been often quite different. And because of the striking divergences between the Irish and British states and societies there are some aspects of life and attitudes in Britain that have been or are beginning to be affected by closer involvement with the rest of the European Community but in respect of which one can trace no similar effect in Ireland. This is because certain aspects of the Irish political structure and culture are, whether for historical reasons or by chance, closer to those of the European Community than in the case of Britain, with the result that in these particular respects Ireland has not experienced the same shock effects as has the neighbouring island. On the other hand in at least one respect Britain is closer than Ireland to our EC partners, viz. its involvement with NATO.

Let me at the outset summarise the matters to which I propose to refer. First both Ireland and Britain have been faced with the need to re-think their attitudes towards national sovereignty. Second both our countries have also faced a substantial psychological reorientation, away from a more familiar external English-speaking environment to which both of us have been informally linked in the past, and towards a continental European environment which for linguistic and cultural reasons is less familiar. Third, the role of our currencies—which is of fundamental political as well as economic importance—has had to be re-thought. And, fourth, at a more speculative level, traditional complexes—of superiority in the case of Britain and of inferiority in the case of Ireland—have been challenged and have in each case, I feel, begun to be modified.

Britain, however, is having to face other adjustments in attitudes from which for one reason Ireland is exempt. These include, first, the realisation that Parliament is no longer sovereign save in the highly theoretical sense of having the legal capacity to denounce the Rome Treaty, but at a political and economic cost that would be so intolerable as to render such an action inconceivable in practice. Second, attention has begun to be directed to

* The author was Minister of Foreign Affairs, then Taoiseach, of the Republic of Ireland, Leader of Fine Gael, and author of *Towards a New Ireland*, *inter alia*. This is an edited version of the John P. Mackintosh Memorial Lecture given at the University of Edinburgh in October 1990.

the possibility of an important juridical change logically associated with the *de facto* disappearance of parliamentary sovereignty: this is the concept of individual human rights being protected by the Courts. I believe this makes increasing sense as people in Britain come to be seen and to see themselves legally as citizens rather than as subjects of that constitutional fiction, the Crown in Parliament. Third, there is a growing realisation that the British electoral system is much more of an anachronism than had previously been realised. And finally Conservatives have been faced with the fact that the concept of the Social Charter is common to both the Socialist and Christian Democratic streams of political thought in continental Europe; so that their opposition to it isolates them from all other political forces in Europe. None of these latter problems of adjustment affect Ireland which is, however, faced with the need in the light of membership of a rapidly developing Community to re-assess popular attachment to military neutrality.

This list of ways in which Community membership has affected our two societies is not, of course, exhaustive; it is, however, sufficiently long, and some of the items in it sufficiently important, to indicate that for both countries, although perhaps for Britain more than for Ireland, membership of the Community involves a number of fundamental adjustments in political concepts and attitudes, some at least of which are potentially divisive within our national polities.

The national sovereignty issue

Transfers of sovereignty required by membership of the Community have posed potentially greater problems for Britain and for Ireland than was the case with the original members of the Community or with the new member states of the 1980s.

For Ireland this problem derived from her sovereignty being so newly acquired. Ireland became an independent State in 1922 but did not secure recognition of its sovereign independence until the Statute of Westminster in 1931. Moreover, because for historical reasons Commonwealth membership continued even after that time to carry with it for many Irish people an implication of continued dependence on Britain—however unwarranted this may have been—it was not until 1949 that most Irish people felt that they had achieved sovereignty in the form in which it had originally been sought: as a Republic outside the Commonwealth.

Countries that have recently acquired sovereignty naturally attach a special value to it. It is scarcely a coincidence that the only country which negotiated membership of the Community but was finally forced by its own public opinion to withdraw its application was Norway, which with Ireland is the only Western European State to have achieved independence in the current century—albeit with much less trauma than in the case of Ireland!

8

Britain's sovereignty problem is in a sense the opposite one: a feeling that British sovereignty has such deep roots in the past that anything impinging upon it challenges, almost denies, history itself. It is relevant in this connection that whereas Ireland had never found that its insular situation offered much protection against external invasion or conquest, Britain's insularity is deeply rooted in a conviction that being an island has given to its sovereignty an important additional dimension of security. This has been believed despite the fact that Danish, Norman, Welsh and Dutch dynasties were installed at different periods as a result of successful invasions of Britain—not to speak of a fifth invasion that led to the installa-tion of the House of Lancaster in 1399!

Moreover despite the frequency and cost in terms of blood as well as money of Britain's historical interaction with continental Europe, this involvement has always been seen in Britain as action at a distance. The loss of considerable British territory on the Continent—whatever effect it may have had on the heart of Queen Mary I of England—was never seen as impinging on the sovereignty of England iteself.

The ways in which Ireland and Britain have handled the psychological problem of the post-1973 sharing of sovereignty have differed signi-ficantly. In Ireland, partly bcause the economic benefits of membership of the Community have been so obvious, sharing of sovereignty came to be accepted with much greater equanimity than might have been expected in view of the historic strength of Irish nationalist feeling. What may perhaps have facilitated this has been a practical realisation that the sovereignty of a small country like Ireland has severe limitations; so that in terms of Irish interests, the acquisition of a role, however small, in the exercise of power by its European partners could bring far more benefits than could have been secured by the maintenance of a theoretical, but in the external forum largely unexercisable, Irish sovereignty.

Nevertheless, I think it is fair to add that what has happened in the Irish case has involved something much more positive than a reluctant acquiescence in an inevitable process. There was at the outset of Irish membership not merely an unambiguous intellectual decision that Irish interests would best be served by not merely accepting with reluctance the sovereignty-sharing involved in membership, but by going well beyond this to *advocate* more and more rapid economic integration within the Community as being in the long-term interest of a small country like Ireland.

This positive support for European integration derived from two separate considerations. One was a belief that the interests of a small country are best protected by a more fully integrated Community with a strong institutional structure capable of inhibiting possible abuse by larger member States of their greater economic and political strength. The other has been a realistic calculation that for a country that was bound to be a major beneficiary of membership, but would not be contributing to the defence of the Community it was joining, a positive approach to integration

9

would provide a safeguard—a safeguard against possible recrimination by countries contributing to Ireland through the Community budget but who see no return in terms of a contribution to European defence.

The reason why Ireland was bound to be a major beneficiary of membership is that alone among member States it benefits *both* from the Common Agricultural Policy, designed to assist the farming communities of Northern European countries, and *also* from the social and regional policies, designed primarily to assist the poorer peripheral areas which are otherwise all in the southern part of the Community.

The Referendum in 1972 on entry to the EC elicited a vote of five to one in favour of membership in a 70 per cent poll. That result was, however, secured on the basis of almost exclusively economic arguments, particularly relating to the agricultural sector. Far from extolling the merits of European integration in its own right, those arguing for membership—myself included—tended in presenting the economic arguments to leave this issue on one side—in some instances even expressing a minimalist view of the implications of membership for national sovereignty. Moreover, although Ireland's original application for membership in 1961 had clearly assumed a willingness to accept ultimate political union and eventual participation in European defence, during this referendum campaign stress tended to be laid rather on the fact that membership of the Community involved no obligation to join NATO or WEU and that European defence was unlikely to arise as a practical issue for a long time to come. Thus support for Irish membership on the striking scale shown in this Referendum carried with it no implications as to public attitudes with regard to further economic and political integration of the Community.

The decision immediately after entry to pursue an integrationist policy within the Community was not, therefore, a logical corollary of the support given to Irish membership in the recently-held referendum; rather it represented a rational decision at Government level to set on one side in the perceived national interest the instinctive emotional attachment to sovereignty. The capacity to take such a decision in this way and to carry it through effectively derived from the coherence of the decision-making process in the small Irish Government structure. This has always seemed to me to contrast with the relative incoherence of the much larger British political and administrative machine.

Was this key policy decision contested within the Irish political system? There was certainly a measure of criticism from the political Opposition in the mid-1970s but this tended to be concentrated upon one limited aspect of the policy pursued by the Government: its stated attitude to the desirability of moving from decision-making by unanimity to qualified majority decision-making—with the consequent loss of the so-called veto exercisable by the Irish Government. But this Opposition argument was not very strongly pressed because of a realisation, at least in political circles if not in popular opinion, that the 'veto' had a very limited potential application in the case of a small country. If attempts had been made by

Ireland, as a major net beneficiary of membership of the Community, to block progress in key areas where unanimity was required, the penalty in terms of negative reactions to future Irish needs could have been highly dangerous to the national interest. In practice, therefore, it was only in a small number of cases where a genuine major Irish national interest was at stake, such as the Community fishery regime in the mid-1970s or the milk super-levy in the early 1980s, that threats to veto progress could in practice be plausible and usable.

The contrast with the situation in Britain with regard to the impact of European integration on national sovereignty has, therefore, been marked. Because in Britain's case the net economic and political advantages of membership were less clear-cut, the sovereignty issue tended from the outset to loom much larger. The opening up of new markets on the Continent to British exporters was less clearly advantageous than in the Irish case because the competitiveness of British industry *vis-à-vis* Continental producers was doubtful, and in terms of the Community Budget Britain would be a net contributor on a scale that almost from the outset caused deep concern in that country. The concept of the proceeds of customs and excise revenue as Community Own Resources never received easy acceptance in Britain where the allocation of these funds to the Community budget was represented as taking resources from Britain. This complaint made little sense on the Continent where many of the imports reaching, say, Germany came through Dutch or Belgian ports. The effective extension of the customs frontier of Germany to Rotterdam and Antwerp, involving the collection of tariffs and levies on goods for Germany at these ports rather than at the frontier of the German State, could not readily be accepted by Germans as entitling the Dutch or Belgians to regard this revenue as thenceforth belonging to them—nor would the Dutch or Belgians so claim it.

Moreover the purpose to which a very large proportion of the Community Budget was put, that is support for the Common Agricultural Policy, had little attraction for a country like Britain in which barely 3 per cent of the population—the lowest in Europe—were engaged in agriculture. Thus contributions to the Community Budget were bound to be more resented in Britain. The greater part of the first decade of British membership was in fact devoted to two attempts to renegotiate the financial arrangements of membership so as to minimise the proportion of the Community's Budget derived from the United Kingdom. This prolonged argument contributed simultaneously to the growing unpopularity of Britain among its EC partners and to the growing unpopularity of the Community with British voters.

More surprising, perhaps, was the clear failure of British politicians as well as of British public opinion to appreciate and take advantage of the political role that membership of the Community made possible. Britain's refusal to join the Community at the outset, and the attempt made at that time by British diplomacy to persuade Germany against joining, led to the

11

development of a purely continental Community with France and Germany as clearly the leading powers. Thereafter these two States could not have been dislodged from this position without difficulty, but it was open to British diplomacy, after the United Kingdom's eventual adherence to the Rome Treaty, to secure a share in this Community leadership. From time to time there were opportunities to exploit differences between France and Germany. No serious attempt ever seems to have been made to undertake sustained diplomatic action of this kind, however. This was at least partly because the single-minded pre-occupation of the British government with reducing its financial contribution—marginal though that was to the United Kingdom budget as a whole—effectively deprived that government of any capacity to operate a positive diplomacy during the first ten or eleven years of membership.

Even more fundamental, perhaps, was the fact that British governments, both Conservative and Labour, notably failed to make the psychological leap from thinking of Britain as being still a great power to seeing the opportunity for Britain to play once again a leading role in world affairs *through* the European Community. French governments have consistently sought to do just this while at the same time preserving and exercising their autonomy of action in sectors of particular interest to them. Throughout much of this century there would appear to have been a paralysis of British policy-making deriving from a deep-seated reluctance, particularly amongst politicians, to face the realities of changing power relationships. That this was complicated by a remarkable capacity for self-delusion, as for instance in the manner in which the essentially humiliating dependent relationship of Britain on the United States—which Britain could have broken out of to some degree at least by means of an active participation in a dynamic Europe—was transmuted in the British mind during the post-war period into a 'special relationship'; something regarded as so valuable as to be hung onto at all costs.

What seems most striking about this post-War period has been the persistent failure of the British political system to carry through successfully the process of objective analysis of the character of British interests and of the optimal means of pursuing them. I am aware that at the administrative level of the British Government the capacity to undertake this task certainly exists and has, within certain limits, been effectively deployed. But little encouragement to this kind of exercise has been given by the British political elite, unwilling to face realities and apparently incapable of a coherent 're-think' of underlying British interests. They have frustrated such efforts as have been made by the civil service to initiate such a process.

An outsider can only be struck, indeed bemused, by the contrast throughout this period between, on the one hand, the scale of the British policy-making structure and the personal capacity and commitment of many of those involved in it and, on the other hand, the dismal results of the political direction of British policy towards the achievement of Britain's essential interests.

Re-orientation of trade and other external links

Now let me turn to several other ways in which the European Community has had a profound effect on the orientation of the trade and external links of both the United Kingdom and Ireland. In the case of both our states, the expansion of trade with other European Community countries at the expense of more traditional links has been striking, but it has certainly been more dramatic in the case of Ireland than in the case of the United Kingdom. (Nevertheless the share of UK exports going to traditional Commonwealth markets has fallen by over three-quarters in the past three decades, while the EC share of the UK exports has more than doubled.)

For historical reasons Ireland's export trade was traditionally dominated by Britain. As late as 1958 almost 80 per cent of Irish exports went to the British market and barely 5 per cent to the other countries that now form the European Community. During the thirty-odd years since that time total Irish exports have grown about thirteen times in volume terms, but the rate of growth has been very disparate as between the United Kingdom, the rest of the EC and other countries. During this period exports to Britain have risen about five-and-a-half times; exports to the world outside the EC over twenty times; and exports to continental EC countries almost one hundred times! As a result Irish exports to continental European countries now constitute well over two-fifths of total Irish exports, with barely one-third going to the United Kingdom.

Much of this trade diversification, of course, reflects the export pattern of newly-established foreign-owned firms in Ireland which now account for almost 45 per cent of employment and well over half of the total net output of Irish manufacturing industry. However, even the domestically-owned manufacturing sector now exports over half of its output to countries other than the UK, although it is still the case that only a minority of these non-UK exports by domestic Irish firms go to Continental European countries.

It is, incidentally, worth commenting that the dynamic that membership of the European Community provided for the Irish economy and the resulting attraction of many foreign enterprises to Ireland as a manufacturing centre have made Ireland today the most export-orientated economy in the industrialised world. Last year the ratio of Irish exports to GNP at just under 70 per cent exceeded for the first time the Belgian figure—Belgium having always been the most open and export-orientated economy in Europe. (Most of the more open industrialised economies have export ratios of 20–30 per cent of GNP, with figures as low as 12–17 per cent in the case of the more protectionist economies such as France, Italy and Spain.)

This far greater change in Ireland's external orientation compared to Britain's is not, however, confined to the area of exports. To a striking degree Brussels has replaced London as *the* external centre towards which Ireland looks, although in part at least this reflects the relative importance of agriculture, and therefore the CAP, in the life of Ireland as against Britain. Even today following the thirty-fold expansion of Irish industrial exports in the last three decades, agricultural exports represent one-sixth of the Irish export total.

The greater relative importance of resources from the regional and social funds in the case of Ireland than in the case of Britain is, of course, another factor directing Irish attention towards Brussels. The fact that almost since the time Ireland joined the Community the net flow of resources under these various headings from the Community Budget to the Irish Exchequer has been the equivalent of more than 5 per cent of Irish GNP, is alone sufficient to explain the extent to which Brussels has come to loom large in the Irish psyche.

The currency issue

Currency is another aspect of economic life which has significantly affected Britain and Ireland in quite different ways. Ireland joined the Exchange Rate Mechanism of the EMS when this system was launched. The benefits that were expected to derive from the *de facto* linkage of the Irish pound to the Deutschmark rather than with sterling were, however, a little slow to emerge. The early period of the EMS was in any event a somewhat disturbed one with a number of significant currency realignments involving devaluations of the French franc in particular, especially in the immediate aftermath of a socialist government coming to power in France in 1981. These events coincided with a period in Ireland when inflationary pressures were allowed to get out of control, fuelled by massive increases in public spending, an increase of over 50 per cent between 1977 and 1982. Nevertheless during the years from 1983 onwards when a greater measure of stability was secured within the EMS, Ireland's participation in it provided an important additional incentive to bring these inflationary pressures under control; during the years 1982 and 1987 inflation was in fact reduced from over 20 per cent to 3 per cent.

Throughout these first eight years of membership of the EMS the Irish currency remained in the centre of the band during several realignments, although twice it moved down with the French franc. On only one occasion was it unilaterally devalued. This was in 1986 at the end of the period of domestic adjustment when, as the country approached at last a period of low inflation, high growth, and reasonably balanced budgets, I judged that a single unilateral devaluation of 8 per cent would place the Irish pound in a position to withstand any likely future pressures and so thereafter be able to remain firmly linked to the Deutschmark. As a result

Irish interest rates have since 1986 been much closer to the German than the British level. Moreover the Irish pound has during the past four years been one of the hardest currencies in Europe.

The prolonged economic difficulties in Ireland of the period 1980 to 1986 means that there has as yet been only a relatively short experience of the full benefits of linkage with the continental EC rather than Britain in terms of currency as well as trade; but there are already signs that this realignment may be contributing to an acceleration of the underlying growth rate. During the past four years the Irish growth rate has in fact exceeded that of the rest of the European Community.

Despite the fact that the beneficial effects of EMS membership and participation in the ERM were slow to emerge in Ireland because of problems of domestic mismanagement in the late 1970s, historians will, I think, see the 1979 shift from parity with sterling to something very close to parity with the Deutschmark as an event of fundamental importance in the economic history of Ireland. The maintenance of sterling parity for almost sixty years after Irish independence both reflected and in part contributed to an excessively close linkage with what has been throughout the twentieth century the slowest growing economy in Europe, the United Kingdom. This relationship clearly inhibited the development of the Irish economy in the aftermath of political independence.

One cannot but be struck by the contrast between the beneficial manner in which EMS membership has, after a period, affected Ireland and the manner in which Britain has seemed to refuse to accept the potential benefits of participation in the ERM during these years. Here, as in other aspects of its relationship with the EC, Britain has seemed to have persistent difficulty in identifying clearly its own interests and in making the necessary clear-cut decisions to pursue these interests. This is, of course, a value judgement and there will be those who will defend the eleven-year delay in British membership of the ERM; but I doubt if such a defence will be validated by the judgement of history.

Moreover, very strikingly, Britain's recent belated decision to join the ERM has yet to be accompanied by a recognition of the vital importance to Britain of full participation in the impending Economic and Monetary Union. Once again to the outsider this reticence is difficult to understand on rational grounds. Here, as in so many other key decisions, emotion has seemed to replace reason as the determining factor in decision-making. It appears to me, indeed, that British reticence about participation in Economic and Monetary Union is rationally explicable only on the basis of a belief that such a Union will not in fact come into existence: the same kind of belief that led Britain to opt out of participation in the European Community itself in 1955 to 1956. For if, as to most people now seems inevitable (however uncertain the time-scale), a full Economic and Monetary Union including a single currency is going to take place at some point during the 1990s, British self-exclusion from such a union would strike at what appears to be one of Britain's most crucial national interests—some would say its biggest single national interest at least in the economic sphere: the preservation and enhancement of the City of London as Europe's major financial centre.

Countries sometimes fail, usually for reasons of irrelevant emotion and more rarely for idealistic motives, to pursue in a clear-sighted way their national interests. But it must be almost unique for a government to select one of its major national interests as an object effectively to be undermined rather than preserved.

There can be, and will be, many arguments as to *how* the Community should move towards its goal of a single currency, but this is now the self-evident and clear-cut objective of almost all EC member governments, and of industrial, financial and public opinion within the European Community. With such a degree of unanimity as to the objective to be achieved, only the time-scale and the technical details of how we are to arrive at that point now seem to be seriously in doubt. Whatever the explanation for the current resistance in Britain to the idea of a single European currency, it seems to me that no British government could survive an attempt to keep Britain outside such a structure as and when it emerges. The visible damage to Britain through such self-exclusion as the City of London's key activities moved to Frankfurt would simply not be tolerated by public and political opinion.

Thus while both governments during the period subsequent to the establishment of the EMS can be criticised for the manner in which they managed their economic affairs, there is a striking contrast between the manner in which they have handled their long-term currency strategies.

Impact on self-esteem

Another quite different area in which the Community has impinged differently on both countries is that of their individual self-esteem. Traditionally Britain, seen from outside at any rate, has seemed to have something of a superiority complex, deriving from its remarkably successful history until this century. As the leading manufacturing country and the dominant imperial power at the beginning of the century it would have been surprising if the British did not at that time have a high degree of self-esteem—an inclination to consider their country's performance and their own role in the world as superior in many respects to those of other States.

By contrast Ireland, after many centuries of incomplete colonisation, and placed in what seemed to be a permanently inferior role *vis-à-vis* its larger neighbour, had little on which to base self-esteem, save for some memories of a millennially distant past of high cultural attainment and the exercise in those Dark Ages of a significant role in the re-Christianising of north-western Europe after the barbarian invasions—as well, of course, as the conversion of Scotland to the Christian faith!

For many centuries divergent psychological attitudes have bedevilled the the practical relationships between the two peoples and, after 1922, between the two States. A superiority complex usually carries with it a certain incapacity to understand and empathise with others. And an inferiority complex frequently carries with it an enduring sense of paranoia and a deep-seated belief that failures of understanding, or of incompetence in handling relationships, by the dominant neighbour actually reflect Machiavellianism and malevolence. The resultant mis-understandings can make relations between peoples and States extremely difficult.

To what extent have these attitudes—which I recognise of course to be stereotypes inapplicable to very many people in both countries—been modified by the joint experience of our two States within the European Community? I cannot judge the extent to which traditional British attitudes have been modified by its European experience—although I suspect that a process of readjustment is under way which will lead in time to a more realistic assessment of Britain's role in Europe and the world and of its relationship with its European partners.

A perceptible change in Irish attitudes has, I think, taken place during the past two decades. Despite the deep tensions created between our two States and peoples by the situation in Northern Ireland, the multi-lateralisation of Ireland's external relationships during this period has, I believe, had beneficial effects on Irish attitudes towards Britain. It can never be healthy for any country to feel itself dominated in economic or political or cultural terms by one larger neighbour, and the anglo-centrism of Ireland in the post revolutionary period—compounded of a large dose of anglophobia and a smaller dose of anglophilia!—was clearly unhealthy.

Another aspect of Anglo-Irish relations that merits consideration in this context is the extent to which after 1931 the scale and frequency of contacts between Irish and British governments was much reduced. And this was even more the case in the post-War period, apart from limited and occasional contacts at Foreign Minister level at the United Nations or at the Council of Europe. Thus a succession of British governments between 1949 and 1965 found no occasion for any significant direct contacts with Irish governments; these were the governments of Churchill, Eden, Macmillan and Douglas-Home.

Following the two countries' joint adherence to the European Com-munity in 1973, however, Irish and British ministers began to find them-selves once again meeting together often, this time in the relative intimacy of the different formats of the Council of Ministers. And in these councils they were no longer engaged in an over-intense and inherently unbalanced bilateral relationship, but found themselves working with others, some-times for common objectives but often pursuing different interests. In this more relaxed atmosphere both sides became able to make a more objective evaluation of each other and to shed preconceptions inherited from a receding past. On the Irish side these close contacts contributed to the disappearance of elements of paranoia and inferiority complex which had afflicted Irish attitudes towards Britain for so long.

Hitherto I have been discussing ways in which Ireland and Britain have reacted differently to aspects of their relationship with the European Community that were basically common to both. But part of the reason for Britain's greater difficulty in adjusting to membership has lain in the fact that in several respects Britain has faced problems which Ireland, for one reason or another, has been fortunate enough to avoid.

The sovereignty of the British parliament

Perhaps the most fundamental of these is the problem posed by Britain's unwritten constitution based upon the theory of the sovereignty of the Crown in Parliament, in relation to which the people of the United Kingdom are subjects rather than citizens. No other European country has a constitution of this type. This has influenced profoundly the psychology of both politicians and people in Britain, although perhaps somewhat more in England than in Scotland where for some people the Treaty of 1707 must represent in certain respects an approach to a written constitution—although whether this is recognised in England is another matter.

The contrast between Britain and Ireland could not be more striking. For while all other members of the European Community have written constitutions into the framework of which the written constitution of the treaties of the European Community have been fitted in ways appropriate to each country's constitutional tradition and laws, it is in Ireland more than in any other member State that such a written constitution most tightly limits through the courts the power of the legislature and executive.

The Irish courts can strike down any law or part of any law which is regarded by the judges as infringing the constitution—most often as infringing aspects of the constitution designed to protect individual human rights. The Irish constitutional system could indeed be described as a conventional European parliamentary democracy incorporating, however, an American-type supreme court. In Ireland the idea of parliamentary sovereignty is more often seen as a potential threat to individual rights than as something to be admired or extolled. Irish people value the power of the courts to protect their rights against what in practice have been unintentional—but not infrequent—intrusions by the executive or legislature. (The role of the Irish courts is, then, in contrast to Britain, essentially an anti-Establishment one.)

The courts can, of course, interpret these rights in ways that may sometimes be unpopular with a majority of the population. An instance of this occurred some fifteen years ago when a Supreme Court decision about the rights of a natural mother in relation to a child who had been legally adopted some years earlier was rejected by public opinion. The decision was shortly afterwards overturned by a referendum of the people initiated by the executive in parliament.

Thus once the Irish people had accepted the idea of a sharing of sovereignty with other states and the role of the European institutions, by an overwhelming majority in a constitutional referendum, the concept of regulations enacted by the Council of Ministers having *direct* effect and superseding Irish law created no serious psychological problems. When such issues were brought to the European Court in Luxembourg and decided there, against Ireland in certain instances, this was taken as quite normal, being in line with the Irish experience of the role of the Irish Supreme Court in relation to domestic legislation.

In other words, the sharing of sovereignty with other states was accepted as involving not merely the joint actions of governments in the Council of Ministers and of elected members in the European Parliament, but also of the European Court of Justice.

In Britain by contrast the relationship between the theoretically sovereign national parliament and the European institutions established by the Paris and Rome treaties has clearly posed immense psychological problems, particularly for some politicians. Although there have already been many instances in which decisions at European level, including decisions of the European Court, have effectively by-passed or even over-turned decisions of the British parliament, there has been an extra-ordinary unwillingness to accept that these events have in fact occurred. The reaction to the recent case in which the European Court held that not only *its* decisions but also decisions of *British* courts *applying European law* over-turned British parliamentary legislation has demonstrated the extent of the incomprehension that seems to exist on this subject. There was something rather ironic, I felt, about the fact that concern for parliamentary sovereignty in Britain seemed to involve even greater objections to British courts over-turning parliament than to the European Court doing so!

Judicial protection of human rights

There is another aspect of this problem. No direct protection for human rights exists in Britain when parliament implements legislation proposed by the executive, except to the extent that the courts might on occasion find that through some legislative defect action taken infringing upon some human right was inadequately backed by the relevant legislation and was consequently *ultra vires*. It is, however, now arguable that a small start may have been made with the introduction of judicial protection of human rights in Britain by virtue of the fact that in deciding cases involving European Community law, the European Court of the Community in Luxembourg has regard to the European Code of Human Rights of the Council of Europe. Thus paradoxically a British citizen may find his rights protected where the law impinging upon him is a European one rather than a British one!

There has, however, been a growing interest in recent years in the concept of introducing direct protection of human rights by the courts in Britain, possibly through the enactment into British law of the European Code of Human Rights—even if support for this still seems to come only from a minority of public and parliamentary opinion. Earlier this year I found myself discussing this matter with a senior member of the British cabinet. I found that *my* incomprehension of his resistance to the idea of human rights being protected by the courts was matched by *his* incomprehension as to how such a system could conceivably work without creating political chaos! The example he gave to me was an interesting one. What, he asked, would have happened if in the immediate post-war period the courts had struck down as involving unconstitutional interference with property rights some of the 1945–51 socialist government's legislation, e.g. on nationalisation? Would this not have created an intolerable conflict between the courts and the democratic political system in Britain?

Such a conflict had never previously struck me as possible and when I came to reflect on why this was a problem in Britain but had never occurred to me, or, I think, to anyone in Ireland, as being a possible difficulty, I could only come to the conclusion that this difference reflects the exceptional strength of ideological attitudes in British politics. This ideological divide may, I believe, be intensified and preserved both by the British electoral system and by the shape of the House of Commons. There is a striking contrast between the adversarial British approach and the more consensual approach to politics that is characteristic not merely of Ireland but many other EC countries.

The British electoral system

The British first-past-the-post electoral system is another aspect of the system which may require reconsideration as a result of membership of the European Community. So long as Britain remained apart from Europe and felt itself closer to the United States and its former overseas dominions, which for reasons specific to their own political structures, a number of which are federal in character, had retained the British first-past-the-post electoral system, it was possible for people in Britain to feel that this system was almost divinely ordained. If it was good enough for most other English-speaking people, apart from the eccentric Irish, why should Britain not retain it? It has certainly been widely felt that this system contrasts favourably with various forms of PR practised by other European countries which are known as a result to end up frequently with coalition governments—something generally seen in Britain as being inherently undesirable. But now that Britain is part of the European Community, and has drifted much further away from its former colonies overseas (including the United States!), the proposition that the first-past-the-post system is inherently better than PR is, perhaps, less self-evident.

There is, I think, a growing realisation in Britain that during this century the countries in Europe which operate some form of proportional representation have in fact been strikingly more successful economically than Britain—by a margin of about 1 per cent per annum cumulative, which over such a long period amounts to quite a lot! (Forms of PR seem to have been introduced in most Western European countries during the first quarter of this century as part of the movement towards universal suffrage.) A case can certainly be made that these two features of most Western European countries—PR and economic success—are not entirely coincidental but may to some degree be related to each other. For societies within which the electoral system requires an accommodation of views, mitigating the asperities of ideological conflict, may well provide a political climate more conducive to economic growth than ones in which ideological conflict is politically elevated and ritualised. Such ideological conflicts can lead to alternating governments operating reversals of policy that create conditions of uncertainty and discourage investment and innovation.

Of course there is no proof of this proposition; but the contrast in economic performance between Britain and its continental neighbours in this century has been sufficiently striking to put in question the traditional British thesis that strongly marked alternations in the ideological composition of governments are good for growth.

There are, of course, arguments other than ones based on economic performance in favour of different electoral systems. And to put it mildly, not all of these other arguments point clearly to the superiority of the first-past-the-post system. Thus, for example, where, as in the case of Britain, a smaller third political party exists, and at certain times secures significant minority support from the electorate, the operation of the first-past-the-post system may bring into office not infrequently a party to which the electorate would, if given the real choice, prefer *not* to give its consent.

However, the real point that I wish to make is simply that the growth of support for changes in the British electoral system may at some level owe a certain amount to a greater recognition of the possible merits of other electoral systems, and that this has come about through the closer involvement with the other democracies of the EC.

The European Social Charter

The European Social Charter is another area where British participation in the EC is bringing that country face to face with new concepts potentially important for its social and economic life. The unique British opposition to this Charter has highlighted for the first time the extent to which the political right in Britain and the political right in other EC countries have quite different perceptions of the most appropriate relationship between what are known in many countries as the 'social partners'. Of course, there is a very clear political divide in other EC countries between the two main streams, Christian Democrats and Social Democrats, although in some countries, including my own, the two parties have at times co-existed in government reasonably comfortably. But while these two parties differ in important respects in their approach to social issues, and can place a different emphasis upon the relative importance in politics of encouraging enterprise or ensuring social equity, they have one belief in common: that the relationship between management and workers should as far as possible be organised constructively as a partnership rather than adversarially.

Germany provides a good model of this. The tension between Christian Democrats and Social Democrats is probably more acute in Germany than elsewhere. Many Christian Democrats, not to speak of members of the Christian Social Union in Bavaria, are bitterly anti-socialist. But both favour a partnership of management and workers in supervisory boards of companies—to give but one example. Such, indeed, is the relationship between management and workers and such is the social climate there in terms of various welfare provisions, that it is the German CDU who have been most concerned to secure a European Charter that would require other countries to make similar social provisions. For without this some of these countries might, in the German view, be unfairly competitive with German industry. The contrast between this approach and that of the British Conservative government, seeking to minimise social provisions, could hardly be more striking.

These differences in attitudes between the British Conservative government on the one hand and European Christian Democrats on the other, explain the remarkable political isolation of the British Conservatives within the European Parliament. Their views on issues of social partnership make them unacceptable to many Christian Democrats and this, rather than any British Conservative hang-ups about the Christian element in Christian democracy, seems to explain why they have not been admitted to the Christian Democratic Group at Strasbourg. By contrast, in the Irish case my own Party, Fine Gael, fits reasonably comfortably within the Christian Democratic framework in the European Parliament because, like the the other political parties in Ireland and most of those in Continental Europe, we accept and advocate the idea of social partnership. Fine Gael tends, however, to find itself on the left wing of the Christian Democratic movement, closer to the Belgians, Dutch, Luxembourgers and some at least of the French than to the Germans and the majority of the Italians.

Irish neutrality

Thus the European experience impinges in a number of ways upon British political ideas and practices in a way that has not been the case with Ireland. By contrast there is one way in which involvement in Europe impinges on Irish politics in a manner that does not apply in the case of Britain. This, of course, is the issue of neutrality. Ireland is the only member state of the Community that is not a member of a military alliance—either NATO or the WEU. The reasons for this are historical and need not detain us here. However, it was made clear to the Irish government at the time when Ireland first sought membership of the EC in 1961 that while membership did not involve any commitment to join either of these two military alliances, it *did* imply a willingness to accept the 'finality' or expressed goal of the Community: the creation of a political, economic and monetary union which in time would have a common foreign policy and a common defence policy. This was accepted in the White Paper on membership published at that time and the point has been reiterated by the leader of every Irish government since that time.

Until recently, however, the Community had made little progress in the direction of a common foreign or defence policy. For many member states a European defence concept was one that for long seemed to carry a risk of weakening NATO. It might suggest to the United States that Europe was becoming self-sufficient and might no longer need the participation of American forces on the European continent or the benefit of the American nuclear umbrella. Britain, Germany and Denmark have been among the countries which were the most concerned about these possible negative implications of European defence. Accordingly the issue of Irish neutrality has not been of great significance during the first seventeen years of Irish membership of the Community.

Recently, however, there have been signs of a change. The radical transformation of the European security scene within the last twelve months, combined since August last with the emergence of a major security problem in the Middle East demanding a coherent European response, has raised in a much more concrete way than in the past the issue of a possible common European foreign and defence policy.

It is clearly too soon to say what shape any such development may take. However, very recently there have been signs of the Irish government starting to recognise that the calling of a conference on political union in parallel to the conference on economic and monetary union necessitates further reflection on the Irish position with regard to neutrality. From comments made in the latter part of 1990 by the Taoiseach, Charles J. Haughey and the Minister for Foreign Affairs, Gerard Collins, it would appear that, while rejecting participation in the WEU, the Irish Government is now prepared to consider participation in the formulation of foreign and security policy, and possibly at a later stage in defence policy within the framework of the EC.

Thus Ireland like Britain has been forced to reconsider an important aspect of traditional policy which, whatever its roots in past history, is no longer relevant to the conditions in which Europe finds itself in the closing decade of the twentieth century.

NATIONS, REGIONS AND EUROPE

DAVID MARQUAND*

EVER since the nation-state first appeared on the stage of European history, its nature, worth and destiny have been the subjects of fierce controversy. The controversy has, of course, taken different forms at different times; many schools of thought have contributed to it. In Britain, however, three have been particularly influential. Even today, preconceptions derived from their accounts of the matter provide the intellectual framework for the burgeoning debate on the territorial dimensions of the British state and of the evolving European Union of which Britain is part. Yet, as so often in similar circumstances, the protagonists in the debate are apt to forget the provenance and logic of their own assumptions. If we are to make sense of their arguments, and come to terms with the complex and contested place of nationhood, nation-states and sub-national territorial entities in present-day Europe and, *a fortiori* in present-day Britain, we should look at the accounts which these schools of thought have offered.

The simplest and most dramatic of them is the Marxist. Its central premise is that the proletariat—by definition, the carrier of the future—is also by definition internationalist. The workers have, and can have, no fatherland. If they think they have one, they are either the victims of false consciousness or the prisoners of a pre-proletarian past or both. For nationalism, however defined, is the reactionary, petit-bourgeois, above all *irrational* refuge of doomed social forces, whose only possible future lies in the dustbin of history. The future is international, not national—first internationally capitalist, then internationally socialist. Indeed, it is internationally socialist in the long run only because it is internationally capitalist in the short or medium run. For capitalism is, in a crucial sense, 'progressive': the 'unconscious tool of history' as the British were in India.[1] It sweeps away the divisions between the petty, introverted communities of the past and drags them, willy-nilly, into a world market governed by world-wide imperatives. In the exhilarating phrases of *The Communist Manifesto*:

> In place of the old wants, satisfied by the production of the country, we find new wants, requiring for their satisfaction the products of distant lands and climes. In place of the old local and national seclusion and self-sufficiency, we have

* The author is Professor of Politics at the University of Sheffield, former MP and chief adviser in the Secretariat General of the European Commission, member of the Liberal Democrats' Policy Committee, and author *inter alia* of *The Unprincipled Society* (1988). He is also joint editor of *The Political Quarterly*.

[1] Karl Marx, *New York Daily Tribune*, 25 June 1853, quoted in Leszek Kolakowski, *Main Currents of Marxism*, vol. 1, *The Founders*, Clarendon Press, Oxford, 1978, p. 348.

intercourse in every direction, universal inter-dependence of nations. And as in material, so also in intellectual production. The intellectual creations of individual nations become common property. National one-sidedness and narrow-mindedness become more and more impossible, and from the numerous national and local literatures there arises a world-literature.

The bourgeoisie, by the rapid improvement of all instruments of production, by the immensely facilitated means of communication, draws all, even the most barbarian, nations into civilisation. The cheap prices of its commodities are the heavy artillery with which it batters down all Chinese walls ... It compels all nations, on pain of extinction, to adopt the bourgeois mode of production; it compels them to introduce what it calls civilisation into their midst, *i.e.* to become bourgeois themselves. In one word, it creates a world after its own image.[2]

Nationalism was thus an attempt to spit into the wind of history, a refuge for sociological detritus. And this was, above all, true of the 'barbarian', pre-modern, provincial nationalisms of small and backward peasant communities trying to resist assimilation by the advanced, modern, cosmopolitan nationalities whose languages and cultures have become the vehicles of the highest forms of bourgeois civilisation. The advanced, 'historic' nationalisms of the Germans, the English, the French and, in the New World, the Americans may serve, however unwittingly, as the agents of modernity. The nationalisms of the small, historyless slavic peoples of central and eastern Europe belong to essentially the same historical category as African or Red Indian tribalism. The motive force behind them is a blatant wish to cling to a pre-capitalist, pre-scientific past, from which capitalism offers a kind of liberation. Insofar as they represent anything more than straightforward sentimentality, they are camouflage for social interests and formations which are becoming steadily more obsolete.

Not only is nationalism reactionary and irrational, it is a diversion from the battle that really matters. The only social conflict in which the proletariat has real interests at stake, the only social conflict that holds out the promise of ultimate human emancipation, is the conflict between classes. If national conflicts cut across the primordial conflict between classes, distracting the proletariat from its historic mission to prepare itself for the destruction of capitalism, only the bourgeoisie will benefit. Sometimes, it is true, a national cause may serve the proletariat's cause; the Irish struggle for national liberation, Marx thought, deserved the support of the English working class, since it was directed against the common enemy of both. More often, nationalism is a tool of the bourgeoisie, which uses it to further its own ends.

The Leninist derivative of the Marxist account adds a further twist. Before the Revolution, the Bolsheviks were for national self-determination, but only when it served the interests of the proletariat. As

[2] Karl Marx and Friedrich Engels, *Selected Works*, volume 1, Foreign Languages Publishing House, Moscow, 1951, pp. 36–7.

Lenin put it, they were concerned with 'the self-determination of the *proletariat* in each nationality rather than the self-determination of peoples or nations'.[3] After the Revolution, Communists did not see the Soviet Union as a nation state or even, in essence, as a multi-national state. Its very name asserted an internationalist ideology rather than a national identity or even a set of national identities; as that name implied, it was the multinational embodiment of the principle of proletarian internationalism, claiming the allegiance of the working class throughout the world. Though Stalin used Russian national sentiment to buttress his position, particularly during the second world war, when he needed all the support he could get, it is a mistake to see him as a Russian or, for that matter, as any other kind of nationalist. His regime trampled on Russian traditions at least as savagely as on other national traditions; the Russian people suffered at least as much from the terror it unleashed in the name of proletarian internationalism as did any other Soviet nationality.

Liberal versions

The second account is that offered by what are best termed liberal internationalists. Its parentage is not as obvious as that of the Marxist account, but possible authors include Adam Smith, Richard Cobden and John Stuart Mill. There are some intriguing similarities between liberal internationalism and Marxism. For it too nationalism of any sort is suspect, and the nationalism of small and 'backward' peoples, not merely suspect but reactionary, irrational and harmful to the peoples concerned as well as to the progress of civilisation. To John Stuart Mill, the champion of tolerance and minority rights, it seemed beyond dispute that it would be better for a Breton or a Basque to be a Frenchman, with all the privileges of French citizenship, than 'to sulk on his own rocks, the half-savage relic of past times, revolving in his own little mental orbit, without participation or interest in the general movement of the world'.[4] As that implies, another similarity between liberal internationalism and Marxism is that both are, in an important sense, teleological doctrines. For both, history is moving inexorably and inevitably towards a knowable goal—in one case, towards the goal of world-wide socialism and in the other towards the goal of world-wide capitalism.

But there is a difference as well. Marxism is a doctrine of conflict, though not of national conflict. Liberal internationalism is a doctrine of *harmony*. Individual and social interests are naturally harmonious. Provided the free, competitive market is not distorted by private monopolists or by a foolish and power-hungry state, and provided all

[3] Quoted in Kolakowski, *op. cit.*, vol. 2, p. 400.
[4] Quoted in Anthony H. Birch, *Nationalism and National Integration*, Unwin Hyman, London, 1989, p. 39.

recognise that the free competitive market allocates resources more efficiently than any other mechanism, the laws of political economy will work to the benefit of all. And what is true of societies is also true of the world. The pursuit of prosperity is not a zero-sum game. 'As a rich man is likely to be a better customer to the industrious people in his neighbourhood than a poor', Adam Smith pointed out, 'so likewise a rich nation'.[5] Given the chance, world-wide free trade, also operating according to the laws of political economy, will spread wealth from rich nations to poor ones. And, as all nations realise that they all benefit from the free working of the world market and from the international division of labour which the world market makes possible, national conflicts will become things of the past. As the Anti-Corn Law League put it, the greatest result of free trade would be 'to draw men together, to thrust aside the antagonism of race, creed and language, and unite us in the bonds of eternal peace'.[6]

The third account—that of what might be called liberal nationalists—is the most difficult to describe. Its adherents often overlap with the liberal internationalists; often, liberal internationalists slip into liberal nationalism without realising it. However, it is best understood as a third account, not as a sub-theme of the second. Its champions include Mazzini, Thomas Jefferson, Gladstone, in some of his multifarious manifestations Lloyd George, and above all Woodrow Wilson. According to it, nationalism is neither reactionary nor irrational. On the contrary, it reflects an important—in some versions, a supremely important—part of the human psyche. Liberal nationalism agrees with liberal internationalism in holding that national interests are naturally harmonious. It adds, however, that this natural harmony will become manifest in practice only if all nations enjoy their natural right to self-determination. National conflicts result from the oppression of one nation by another: from denying to some nations their right to self-determination and from thwarting thereby the natural, proper, laudable wish of national groups to live in freedom according to their own laws and customs. Statehood, in short, is essential to full nationhood. But once all nations enjoy statehood, the reign of world-wide harmony will dawn as in the account given by the liberal internationalists.

This leads on to the most obvious and, in some respects, the most important practical difference between liberal nationalism and liberal internationalism. Where liberal internationalists disdain small and 'backward' peoples, and applaud their assimilation by 'advanced' and metropolitan cultures as a form of progress, liberal nationalists display a special sensitivity to their claims. Gladstone championing the Bulgarians and Montenegrins; Lloyd George leading the 'pro-Boers'; Woodrow Wilson insisting that the small slavic nations of central and eastern Europe must enjoy the right to self-determination—these are characteristic expressions of one of the central themes of liberal nationalism. It is quite alien to the

[5] Adam Smith, *An Inquiry into the Nature and Causes of The Wealth of Nations*, University of Chicago Press, Chicago, 1976, vol. 1, p. 520.
[6] Quoted in Asa Briggs, *Victorian People*, Odhams Press, London, 1954, p. 225.

instinctive, if often only half-conscious, metropolitanism of the liberal internationalists. It follows that there is a certain tension within liberal nationalism which is missing from liberal internationalism. Suppose a small people, having rightly struggled to be free, and having thereby achieved self determination, does not wish to join the harmonious world order which liberal nationalists join with liberal internationalists in seeing as the ultimate expression of their ideal? Suppose, indeed, that a small people is struggling for the freedom to stick to an illiberal culture, with illiberal values? What should the conscientious liberal nationalist do then? In the golden age of liberal nationalism, in the late-nineteenth and early-twentieth centuries, these questions were rarely addressed. As the rest of the twentieth century has amply demonstrated, they were always implicit in the liberal nationalist project.

The accounts in practice

The complex and paradoxical history of the twentieth-century European nation-state must be seen against this background. Few would deny that it has made nonsense of the first account. Except on rare occasions, working-class parties have succeeded in conditions of pluralist party competition only when they have abandoned proletarian internationalism and to the extent that they have abandoned it. The reason is only too obvious. The workers *have* had fatherlands; they have been much more willing to die for their fatherlands than for the dream of proletarian internationalism; even in time of peace, nationalism has been a far more potent agent of mobilisation than internationalism. Even more obviously, the system built on the Leninist version of the Marxist account has collapsed, in large part because nationalism has inspired the masses whom that system was supposed to represent to revolt against the political elites which derived their legitimacy from the memory of the October Revolution and from the vision of proletarian internationalism which lay behind it. Now even the Soviet Union is unravelling, in large measure because the nationalities of which it is composed, including the supposedly dominant Russians, are re-asserting national loyalties, national identities and national interests against the increasingly bewildered custodians of Bolshevik internationalism.

The fate of the liberal internationalist account is more mixed. Two terrible European wars, which eventually became world wars, not to speak of a multiplicity of national conflicts in the Third World, hardly conform to the prognosis it implied. Its champions could, however, explain some of these unfortunate experiences away. After all, the founding fathers of liberal internationalism did not say that the world was bound to become conflict-free; they only said that it would be conflict-free if governments had the sense to follow liberal internationalist teachings. The two world wars and, for that matter, the disheartening national

29

conflicts of the Third World, can be accounted for, within the liberal internationalist paradigm, as the predictable results of irrational attempts to
achieve national economic self sufficiency by deliberately avoiding the
disciplines and eschewing the benefits of the international division of
labour. Governments were too stupid or too wicked to see that the reign of
international harmony would dawn if only the principles of *The Wealth of
Nations* were universally applied. They put their faith in national autarchy
instead of in international free trade; the resulting trade wars led inexorably to real wars.

At first sight, moreover, the history of post-war Western Europe gives
great comfort to the liberal internationalist camp. The European Community, which has been one of the greatest success stories of post-war
history, can be depicted, without much violence to the facts, as a triumph
for the liberal-internationalist ideal. The creation of a vast European
market in place of narrow national markets; an attempt to maximise
prosperity all round by removing barriers to trade and facilitating cross-
border competition; the pursuit of these goals through the pooling of
national sovereignties and the transfer of competence from national states
to supranational institutions—if Cobden were alive today, he could be
forgiven for seeing all this as a logical extension of the principles underlying his famous free-trade treaty with Napolean III's France.

Beneath the surface, however, the picture is more complex and prob-
lematical. Upward transfers of competence from national capitals to
Brussels, Luxembourg and Strasbourg have been accompanied by
growing turbulence below the level of the state. The story of Community
Europe has been one of supranational integration, but of sub-national
differentiation. The pressures behind the latter have varied a good deal
from place to place; no single explanation will do justice to them all. That
said, they all have one crucial feature in common. In the German Federal
Republic, in which sub-national territorial identities have been constitutionally embodied from the start, such pressures have been virtually
absent. In the other large member-states of the European Community
(and in at least one of the smaller member-states) territorial groupings
which do not feel that their identities, aspirations and interests are fully
satisfied by the nation-states concerned have demanded recognition for
these identities, aspirations and interests. An incomplete, but impressive
roll-call of the groupings concerned includes the Scots, the Welsh, the
Bretons, the Basques, the Alsatians, the Occitans, the Corsicans, the
Frieslanders, the Flemings, the Catalans and the Sardinians. In all the large
Community member-states apart from Britain, moreover, governments
have embarked on policies of regionalisation, downward devolution or
even federalism or quasi-federalism to accommodate the identities and
aspirations in question.[7] The liberal internationalist model, in short, has

---

[7] For a fuller discussion of the contrast between British and continental European experience in this field see Colin Crouch and David Marquand (eds.), *The New Centralism: Britain
out of step in Europe?*, Basil Blackwell, Oxford, 1989.

applied only to the relationships *between* Community members; *within* them, forces for which that model has no place, and with which it cannot easily come to terms, have become increasingly significant.

Then does the third account provide a satisfactory guide to Europe's post-war experience? At first sight, the answer appears to be 'yes'. The challenge to the collapsing citadel of Bolshevik internationalism—particularly in the Baltic States and the Caucasus and even, to some extent, in the Russian Republic itself—has been phrased in language which might have come straight from Woodrow Wilson. As Scotland, Flanders and the Basque country all show, the same is true of some (though by no means of all) the territorial challenges which the established nation-states of Western Europe have faced from within their own borders. On closer inspection, however, the experience of post-war Europe has dealt a severe blow to the liberal nationalist account as well as to the other two. It is simply not true that national conflicts are everywhere the fruit of the oppression of nations rightly struggling to be free by unjust alien intruders. As such names as Belfast, Brussels, Estonia, Transylvania, Kossovo and Nagorno-Karabakh bear anguished and sometimes bloody witness, the suppressed major premise of the liberal nationalist account—the assumption that all nations occupy clearly demarcated territories to which no other nation can have a legitimate claim—has turned out to be dangerous nonsense. The fact is that ethnic groups do not come in neat territorial parcels, easily separated from each other. They overlap—obviously in space; less obviously in time and in the myths and counter-myths which encapsulate memories of past time. That, of course, is why attempts to settle complex territorial disputes in accordance with liberal nationalist doctrine, as by the Allies in 1919 and by innumerable Third-World regimes since 1945, have so often come to grief.

Nations and regions

For different reasons, then, none of the classical accounts I have tried to describe can encompass the experience of post-war Europe. The proletariat has not proved more internationalist than the bourgeoisie; if anything it has been less so. Though the member-states of the European Community have, in some respects, conformed to the precepts of liberal internationalism, smaller territorial groupings have pulled in the opposite direction. Though territorial aspirations have often been articulated in the language of liberal nationalism, the central premise from which that language derives its persuasive force has turned out to be false. So where do we turn instead? How *should* Europe's post-war experience be interpreted?

I cannot hope to offer a complete answer to these questions. The most I can do is to sketch out a possible approach. It begins with another look at the strange and, at first sight, paradoxical coincidence between supra-national integration and sub-national differentiation. The first is fairly easy to understand. As I suggested a moment ago, it can be assimilated without much difficulty to the models of liberal internationalism. The nation-states of western Europe, devastated by the second of the two terrible wars, decided to knit their economies together and to integrate some of the most important economic functions of their respective governments in order to do so. The result was that their economies became more and more interdependent, with the further result that their governments became less and less able to exercise sovereignty in the economic sphere. Little by little, they were impelled to the conclusion that their polities would have to follow where their economies had led: that sovereignty which could no longer be exercised on the national level would have to be exercised on the supra-national level instead.

The second process—the process of sub-national differentiation—has been far more complicated. It is clear that the historic nation-states of western Europe have faced pressures from below as well as from above: pressures to devolve as well as pressures to integrate. It is clear too that, if these two sets of pressures continue to operate in the future as they have in the recent past, the end product will be a Europe at once enormously more united and enormously more variegated than the Europe of the last 200 or 300 years—a Europe in some ways more reminiscent of medieval Christendom than of the nation-state-dominated Europe of the late-nineteenth and early-twentieth centuries. Pre-modern Europe was, after all, a patchwork of kingdoms, principalities, duchies, counties, provinces, bishoprics and city states, all of them subject to the authority of a pan-European Church. The first task of the emergent nation-state—or rather of its rulers—was to obliterate the ancient boundaries which were the legacy of that patchwork, to impose the language and culture of the capital upon the whole of the territory over which they had jurisdiction and, in the process, to build a 'nation' out of disparate, localised communities to which the notion of nationality meant nothing. But the 'national' identities thus procured were the products of contestable (and contested) political programmes, not of objective cultural or even economic realities, while the geographical boundaries of those identities owed more to the accidents of battle and the vagaries of dynastic marriage than to some inexorable fate. No iron law of history decreed that the peasants of Franche Comte would one day be turned into Frenchmen rather than into Burgundians or even Germans,[8] that Madrid was to be the capital of a Spanish nation-state and Lisbon of a Portuguese one but that Barcelona was not to be the capital of an independent Catalonia, or that the low German dialect which the English call 'Dutch' was to become the official language of a nation-state known as The Netherlands.

Pace the rival teleologies of Marxism, liberal internationalism and

[8] Eugen Weber, *Peasants into Frenchmen: The Modernization of Rural France 1870–1914*, Chatto and Windus, London, 1977 contains the best account I know of the way in which the French state tried systematically to obliterate older territorial identities in order to create a French 'nation'.

32

liberal nationalism, history is now turning back on its tracks. Ancient boundaries, ancient identities, even, in some cases, ancient languages are coming in from the cold. So far from accepting cultural euthanasia, the submerged, historyless peoples whom Marx and Mill consigned to oblivion, and many of whom even Gladstone and Woodrow Wilson forgot, have been on the march. In doing so they have called into question the single most important of the ideological premises of the European state-system—the double proposition that people and nation are one, and that the nation is, or should be, embodied in the state. The result is that the nation-state, for so long the supreme focus for European political loyalties, is now caught in a nutcracker embrace between Brussels, Strasbourg and Luxembourg on the one hand and a host of local, regional and provincial centres on the other. For if people and nation are not necessarily one; if territorial identities cannot always be subsumed in an over-arching national identity; if there are stateless peoples and multi-peopled states; then the claim of the sovereign nation-state to be the supreme political embodiment of the sovereign people is hard to sustain. And if the nation-state is no longer seen as its embodiment, why should it not be embodied, at least in part, in a European union? Scots may not be English or Basques Frenchmen, but they are all Europeans.

At this point in the argument, it is only fair to add, the teleologists are likely to object that many—perhaps most—of the non-state territorial pressures I have mentioned are not really 'national' in character, but only 'regional'; and that, since 'regional' identities and 'regional' claims are obviously less deserving of respect than 'national' ones, they cannot have the effects I have attributed to them. This may appear to be a narrow semantic point, but an important political question is concealed within it. What is to count as a nation? Plainly, there is no objective test. For what it is worth, my own view is that there is and can be no generally acceptable definition, according to which some territorial entities can be classified as regions and others as nations. Nations are regions which made it, which succeeded in establishing a claim to nationhood, sometimes conquering other regions in the process. National cultures are regional cultures which were successfully imposed on other regional cultures. One man's nation rightly struggling to be free is another man's potential alien oppressor: one man's trivial and rightly subordinate region is another's nation rightly struggling to be free. When territorial aspirations are described as 'regional', particularly when they are then contrasted with other aspirations described as 'national', it is usually with bad faith, the intention being to suggest that the first set of aspirations are somehow less serious, and therefore deserve less consideration, than the second.

A few examples will help to pin down the point. One possible criterion of nationhood as opposed to regionhood—a criterion much favoured by the Scots—is that the territory in question should once have been a state. But Bavaria, Hanover, Tuscany and Piedmont, which are not normally classified as nations, were states of sorts much more recently than Scotland;

Wales, which is normally so classified, at any rate when Welshmen are present, was never a state at all. Another possible criterion is the existence of a separate language. Unfortunately, that criterion gives the Flemings and perhaps the Basques and the Catalans a better claim to nationhood than that of the Irish, who now possess an indubitably separate, sovereign nation-state of their own. A third possible criterion is the possession of a historic identity, giving rise to common loyalties and shared memories which endure through time. But virtually all the territorial groupings whose aspirations I have mentioned can and do point to a historic identity of some kind. That is one of the reasons why they have the aspirations. The truth is that these groupings are no less 'organic', or 'natural', or 'historic' than the nation-states within whose boundaries they lie, and that the identities they embody are no less real. Sometimes, those identities are proclaimed under a national banner and sometimes under a regional one, but the distinction between the two is artificial. What matters is that the proclamations are becoming louder and more resonant.

The cultural economy of regional rebirth

The question is, why? Two answers, or sets of answers, stand out. The first has to do with the technological and structural changes which have transformed the economies of the industrial world in the last twenty years. Notoriously, the information revolution, the growth of small-scale 'flexible specialisation' in industry, the shift of mass-production manufacturing from Europe to the so-called Pacific rim and the possible emergence of a new kind of 'disorganised capitalism' in place of the organised capitalism of the post-war period[9] have made it increasingly difficult for nation-states to promote economic development from the centre—either through indirect macro-economic manipulation or through direct intervention. But there is no warrant for the recently fashionable conclusion that public power *as such* no longer has a worthwhile economic role, and that the market should therefore be left to its own devices. On the contrary, there is plenty of evidence that, in this new world of disorganised capitalism as much as in its organised predecessor, economic development depends upon a complex symbiosis between public and private power. The central-state is not, however, the only agency capable of bringing public power to bear on economic activity; and in the new era of disorganised capitalism, sub-national institutions are in a better position than national ones to cope with the problems and to seize the opportunities which technological change is bringing in its train.

[9] For flexible specialisation and disorganised capitalism see, in particular, Michael J. Piore and Charles Sabel, *The Second Industrial Divide: Possibilities for Prosperity*, Basic Books, New York, 1984 and Scott Lash and John Urry, *The End of Organized Capitalism*, Polity Press, Oxford, 1987.

One reason is that the technological and economic upheavals of the 1970s and 1980s exacerbated the familiar problem of territorially uneven economic development. Inevitably, the old industrial regions, where traditional mass-production manufacturing was concentrated, bore the brunt of the Schumpeterian 'gale of destruction' which accompanied the technological and economic transformation of the period. As so often in history, the shift of resources from old activities to new was also a shift from certain regions to others—from the English North-East to the Thames Valley, from North Germany to South, from Wallonia to Flanders, and so on. At the same time, the central-state found it more difficult to shield weaker regions from the consequences of uneven economic development—or, at any rate, to do so by and through the instruments on which they had relied in the boom years of the 1950s and 1960s. In that period, regional policy focused on the provision of incentives to attract footloose mass-production, multi-branch industry into depressed regions. But one of the chief consequences of the current economic transformation is that footloose industry of this sort is no longer available to be attracted on the necessary scale. Meanwhile, it became increasingly clear that the factors which cause depressed regions to fall behind are more complex than was realised twenty years ago and that locating the branch plants of multi-branch firms in such areas is unlikely, by itself, to enrich their indigenous resources—particularly the human resources on which economic development increasingly depends.

Yet the issues of territorial justice, which traditional regional policy was designed to address, have not been—cannot be—banished from the political agenda. The social and economic arguments against allowing economic development to be disproportionately concentrated in favoured regions, while the less favoured sink into a vicious spiral of depression, emigration and deteriorating social capital, are as powerful and as resonant today as they were in the 1960s or, for that matter, in the 1920s. The obvious implication is that these issues will have to be addressed with different policies, implemented with different instruments. In the knowledge- and skill-intensive economies of the late-twentieth century the crucial resources for regional economic development are, by definition, knowledge and skill. Sub-national agencies, closer than central government can possibly be to the entrepreneurs and information flows of the region for which they are responsible, are much better placed to strengthen local networks of skill and knowledge than is central government, and therefore much more likely to develop the indigenous capacities of the region. The Land Government of Baden-Würtemburg is one classic case in point; the Scottish Development Agency another. As both these examples suggest, moreover, one way to disperse knowledge and skill is to disperse political power. Centralised polities, with dominant capital cities, which act as magnets for the head offices of firms and the associated research and development activities, inevitably foster centralised economies. Political decentralisation, as in Federal Germany or the United States, encourages economic decentralisation.[10]

Powerful though they may be, however, 'hard' economic arguments of this sort would not have cut much political ice if attitude and sentiment had been adverse to them. The reason they have carried conviction is that they have increasingly chimed with the mood of the times. In this respect, at any rate, cultural change and economic change have run together. The age of flexible specialisation and disorganised capitalism is also the age of Samuel Beer's 'romantic revolt'[11] and of Ronald Inglehart's 'post-materialism'[12]—an age which, in almost all western countries, has seen a new stress on the values of authenticity, autonomy and personal fulfilment and a new revulsion against externally imposed identities of any kind. Associated with these values are a growing belief in the need for popular participation in decision making, a growing suspicion of bureaucracy and particularly of remote, large-scale bureaucracy, a growing unwillingness to take traditional authority on trust and a growing yearning for the familiar, the small-scale and the face-to-face in a world which seems ever more rootless, more homogenised and more impersonal. The result is challenge to established authority in the name of a new populism, a challenge to class and group loyalties in the name of a new individualism and a challenge to the central state in the name of a new provincialism. Most Europeans want supranational institutions to make public policy in certain limited areas where the nation-state can no longer make its will effective, but few want an American-style melting pot. And, for an increasing number, 'national' identities, constructed in and imposed from the capital cities of the Community's member-states, do as much violence to this yearning for authenticity as would a pan-European melting pot constructed in Brussels, Luxembourg and Strasbourg.

A Europe of the regions?

The logic points to a Europe of the regions in place of the present Europe of the states—to a Europe in which the macro-economic functions of government are mostly discharged by Community authorities, while micro-economic intervention is mostly left to regional or provincial ones; in which sovereignty is shared out between different supranational, national and sub-national tiers of government, according to the principle of subsidiarity; and in which political identities are multiple rather than

[10] For a fuller discussion of this point, see Judith Marquand, *Autonomy & Change, The Sources of Economic Growth*, Harvester Wheatsheaf, Hemel Hempstead, 1989, pp. 154–172.
[11] Samuel H. Beer, *Britain Against Itself: the Contradictions of Collectivism*, Faber & Faber, London, 1982, pp. 107–208.
[12] Ronald Inglehart, *The Silent Revolution: Changing Values and Political Styles Among Western Publics*, Princeton University Press, New Jersey, 1977.

singular, with both a European and a regional or provincial dimension as well as a national one. Whether such a Europe will in fact come into existence it is impossible to tell. As the pace of supranational integration speeds up, and the Community's 1992 project makes it still more difficult for the national tier of government to exercise its imagined sovereignty in the economic sphere, the economic role of the sub-national tier is likely to become even more important. As regions and provinces become more powerful, they are likely to loom larger in the consciousness of their peoples. They are also likely to form more cross-national alliances on issues of common concern, and to develop more direct links with the Community's supranational institutions, over-leaping national governments and administrations. But there is a big gap between evolutionary, *de facto* regionalisation on these lines and a *de jure* regional structure, with clearly demarcated functions and lines of accountability, and that gap will not be crossed without a decisive act of political will. Because of this, there is not much point in speculating about the precise form which the constitution of a Europe of the regions might take. The only certainty is that it would run with the grain of the times and that the elements out of which it might be constructed lie around us.

SCOTTISH IDENTITY AND THE CONSTITUTION

ROBERT McCREADIE*

TEN years ago the distinguished Scottish historian, Professor Geoffrey Barrow, delivered an inaugural lecture at the University of Edinburgh on 'The Extinction of Scotland'.[1] It was a lecture of extraordinary pessimism, a lament for a small and distinctive European nation which had allowed itself to be so completely dominated by its more powerful neighbour, England, that it had largely ceased to exist. In the course of four centuries, beginning with the union of the Scottish and English Crowns in 1603, Scotland had been swiftly deserted by its nobility, and its educated classes had become so completely anglicised that they regarded purely Scottish concerns as parochial and expressed outright scepticism about their ability to govern themselves. 'If Scotland survives', Barrow concluded, 'it survives in the largely unconscious habit of the vast majority of ordinary people, to whom it has not yet occurred to be anything but Scots or to be living anywhere but in Scotland.' The immediate cause of Barrow's pessimism is easy to discern: his lecture was prepared in the aftermath of the disastrous devolution referendum of 1979, which had delivered a small but insufficient majority in favour of the Labour government's proposals for a Scottish Assembly. If Scottish electors could not agree wholeheartedly on something so basic to national self-expression as a legislature—even a subordinate one—what future could there possibly be for any meaningful Scottish identity?

To the average English observer the picture of Scotland painted by Barrow in his lecture will probably seem as accurate today as it did a decade ago. Scotland's identity is considered to be largely geographical and its cultural and political differences are thought of as regional variations on a British theme whose dynamic is essentially English. It is generally supposed that Scotland, in the sense of a separate nation, disappeared some three centuries ago, and most sensible Scots have no serious desire to resurrect it. Even this level of awareness is probably an exaggeration, for the real (as opposed to mythical) Scotland has always received so little attention from the London-based media that many English people—including members of the intelligentsia—lack even the

---

* The author lectures in law at Edinburgh University. A former Labour parliamentary candidate, he has been Vice-Chairman of the Scottish Liberal Democrats since 1988, and is their main negotiator in the Scottish Constitutional Convention. He also chairs the Convention's Constitutional Working Group.

[1] G. W. S. Barrow, *The Extinction of Scotland*, Scots Independent (Newspapers) Ltd., Stirling, 1981.

most superficial knowledge of the true nature of its differences. Consequently the intelligent English visitor who spends some time in Scotland today may be completely unprepared for, and indeed somewhat disoriented by, what he finds. For, far from being extinguished, he will encounter a nation whose population has probably never before shown such an intense awareness of, and interest in, its own history, culture and development—including its political development.

If one accepts Barrow's gloomy conclusion that Scotland only exists in the unconscious minds of ordinary people, this intensity of interest becomes almost impossible to explain. However, on this occasion, in allowing his normally acute historical sense to be clouded by pessimism, he has failed to acknowledge the existence amongst Scots of all classes, and particularly the educated classes, of a quite *conscious* awareness of Scotland's status as a nation—in other words, the existence of a specifically Scottish consciousness. He has also failed to recognise that this consciousness had been very gradually heightened in the post-war period as a result of a quiet revolution whose origins can be traced back to the latter part of the nineteenth century.[2] The key features of this revolution have been the regeneration of a distinctively Scottish political culture, an expansion of Scottish historical research, a reassessment of Scotland's intellectual and artistic traditions, a revival of interest in its language and traditional cultures (Gaelic as well as Scottish) and a conviction that there is nothing provincial or inferior about addressing universal human concerns through literature, drama, art and song rooted in historical or contemporaneous Scottish experience. The failure of devolution certainly dented that confidence initially (as Barrow's lecture graphically illustrates), but the debate raised Scottish consciousness to a new pitch and, for all its rivalries and frustrations, ultimately served to consolidate and strengthen it.

Aping the English

Few Scots therefore doubt that their national identity is both contemporaneous and historical, or that it has a political as well as a cultural aspect. On their travels abroad they often assert both aspects of that identity in the expectation of being taken seriously, and with the purpose (it must be admitted) of avoiding the adverse consequences of being labelled as English! However the marginalisation of Scotland within the United Kingdom as a result of three centuries of English hegemony has inevitably affected its status abroad, and the nationalist-minded Scot soon discovers that although the romantic image of Scotland—the land of tartan and whisky, of heather and sea-girt mountains—is almost universally recognised, his assertion of its political and cultural distinctiveness often causes genuine puzzlement. Is Scotland not simply a part of England? Does it

[2] See Lindsay Paterson, 'Are the Scottish Middle Class Going Native?' in *Radical Scotland*, No. 45, June/July 1990.

really have a culture which is in any significant sense different from England's? How can it lay claim to any meaningful political identity when it gave up its own parliament almost 300 years ago and recently rejected one when it was offered?

Foreigners, of course, can be chided, enlightened and then happily forgiven for their tactless lack of awareness, but it is an entirely different matter when our nationalist-minded Scot meets with the self-same reaction on his more frequent trips south of the Border. Unfortunately for him, there are few nations in the world with less awareness of their own national identity than the English—probably because that identity has never been seriously challenged—and he should therefore not be surprised to find them impervious to arguments about the political and cultural status of a people whom, from their point of view, they effectively absorbed long ago. The Scots, it will be argued, are well-educated, entrepreneurial souls, dour and canny in their personal relationships, and with a penchant for argument—qualities which, in Mrs Thatcher's opinion, made them natural Thatcherites.[3] But there is really nothing more to their distinctiveness than that. And how can they possibly want a parliament of their own when they have obtained so much benefit from being part of the United Kingdom? After all, is it not the case that England subsidises Scotland to a considerable degree? Indeed, is that not why Scottish voters consistently support Labour?

Scots are usually reluctant to admit that they are themselves partly to blame for these sorts of attitudes. Until recently they seemed happy to adorn themselves with many of the symbolic trappings of national identity whilst allowing much of its substance to fade into obscurity. They maintained a plethora of national institutions—banks, newspapers, sports teams, a library, orchestras, art galleries and museums, to name but a few—and carefully nurtured the romantic, sentimental image of Scotland and its people so skilfully manufactured by Sir Walter Scott and his second-rate, 'kailyard' successors. Yet at the same time they allowed an anglocentric and 'inferiorist' perception of their nation to flourish in the classrooms of their own schools—the very forcing-houses of national identity. Scottish history, except for its romantic (and often fictional) aspects, was largely ignored in favour of an English-oriented, 'British' history which portrayed Scotland—if indeed it was portrayed at all—as a poor, undeveloped country whose achievements since the Union of 1707 were in large measure due to English influences. With the exception of Burns, Scott and perhaps R. L. Stevenson, all recognised in England as writers of international stature, the bulk of Scottish literature went unread and unremarked. The names of Robert Henryson, William Dunbar and Gavin Douglas, three of the major poets of late medieval Europe, were unknown to children who studied in detail the works of Chaucer,

---

[3] James Mitchell, *Conservatives and the Union*, Edinburgh University Press, Edinburgh, 1990, p. 120.

Shakespeare and Milton. Nineteenth-century writers such as James Hogg, John Galt and William Alexander, whose novels are so vital to an understanding of their times, were passed over in silence in favour of eminent English writers such as Austen, Trollope and Dickens. Hugh MacDiarmid's name, if it was mentioned at all, was declared to be synonymous with dark and troublesome thoughts about which it was really better not to know.

A particular problem with many of these writers was (and is) that they wrote in Scots, a language which, from the eighteenth century onwards, under the influence of English attitudes, was increasingly frowned upon by the Scottish middle class as a medium for first written and then verbal communication. Ignoring its separate origins and development, they viewed it as a vulgar and ungrammatical form of 'proper' English, and over the generations many a Scottish child whose most intimate thoughts and feelings were shaped by its expressive vocabulary was made to feel shame at continuing to use it when he entered the school classroom. An even worse attitude was displayed towards Gaelic, Scotland's other national tongue, to such an extent that it was almost completely destroyed. Given the importance of language in maintaining national identity, it is hardly surprising that when linguistic antipathy combined with historical neglect, it caused generations of Scottish people to believe that their culture was, and indeed always had been, a provincial and somewhat inferior version of English culture.

The democratic myth

In politics too, similar forces were at work. Scots often claim to be more democratic in their politics than the English and are usually more than willing to provide a justification for such heresy. They tend to begin by referring to the democratic structures and beliefs of the Church of Scotland—the dominant influence in Scottish life from the Reformation until the Disruption of 1843—and then continue with the assertion that popular as opposed to parliamentary sovereignty was the basis of government in pre-Union Scotland, and remains a fundamental principle of the Scottish constitution. An enquirer who, understandably, wants some evidence for this assertion will probably find himself referred to writings as varied as the Declaration of Arbroath (1320), the works of George Buchanan (an influential, sixteenth-century humanist whose book, *De Iure Regni Apud Scotos*, was written to justify the deposition of Queen Mary) and the *Claim of Right* of 1689 (which condemned James VII for trampling on the Scottish constitution). However, although it is certainly true that a genuine concern for popular government has permeated the Church and the writings of scholars and poets down the centuries, it has amounted to no more than that. Until the creation of the Scottish Constitutional Convention—which, as we shall see, has adopted popular sovereignty as its guiding principle—there was in fact very little in Scottish political life, either before or after the Union, to suggest any great love for democracy.

From 1707 until 1885, when the office of Scottish Secretary was revived (it had been abolished after the 1745 rebellion), the Scots tolerated, albeit without any great enthusiasm, an aristocratic, *laissez-faire* system of government which put political power into the hands of a few anglicised Scots with influence in London. At first the system suited them reasonably well because it gave them considerable freedom to manage their own local affairs—undemocratically, of course—without significant interference from London. However, as the nineteenth century progressed it became more and more apparent that Westminster was neglecting Scottish needs, and, in 1885, through the combined influence of Irish Home Rule and a period of intensive lobbying by Scottish MPs and interest groups, a Scottish Secretary was appointed to handle Scottish business. Pressure to establish a Scottish Parliament, however, was restricted to only a handful of people. Although the Scottish Secretary slowly gained in power and influence after 1885, becoming a full Secretary of State in 1926 and obtaining direct responsibility through the Scottish Office (created in 1939 out of a number of independent Boards) for an increasing range of functions previously exercised by Whitehall departments, the lack of time at Westminster for purely Scottish affairs became more and more apparent. Yet until the 1960s the pressure for a Scottish legislature to remedy this democratic deficit was fitful and, with the notable exception of the signing of the Scottish Covenant by two million Scots in 1949–50, largely restricted to enthusiasts in the political parties (particularly the small Liberal and Nationalist parties).

There were many reasons for this state of affairs, the chief ones being Scotland's relative economic prosperity, the opportunities for advancement provided by the British state and empire, a sense of solidarity born out of the traumas of two World Wars and—perhaps most important of all—the political dominance of a UK labour movement which put class above national identity and firmly suppressed the enthusiasm for Home Rule amongst some of its Scottish members.[4] Yet it is unlikely that any of these factors would have prevented the creation of a Scottish parliament had the Scottish public been sufficiently enthusiastic about democracy to insist on it. The fact is that they had no particular concern for democratic self-government as long as the Union offered the best prospect of continuing economic advance. Other multi-national states might have evolved satisfactory systems of government based on federalist principles, but the Scots, who prided themselves on their internationalism, remained so parochial in their thinking that until recently they stubbornly refused to look beyond their own shores.

---

[4] Ian Donnachie, Christopher Harvie and Ian S. Wood (eds), *Forward—Labour Politics in Scotland 1888–1988*, Polygon, Edinburgh, 1989, pp. 35–38 and 72–75.

The great awakening

Nevertheless, although the Scots' awareness of their national identity was greatly weakened by their acquiescence in an anglocentric conception of themselves, it was not, as Barrow implies, destroyed. Ordinary people remained very conscious of their own separate history—even if, for most of them, it amounted to only a few dramatic peaks glimpsed through a tartan veil—and they were particularly sensitive about their diminished status in the world. At war and on the football field they were invariably Scottish first and British second—a reflection of what the late John Macintosh astutely termed their 'dual nationality'[5]—and any Englishman who dared to slight their nation could be fairly certain that he would regret his incautious remark! Furthermore, and perhaps more importantly, a significant number of educated Scots kept in touch with the details of their history and culture and transmitted their knowledge, insights and enthusiasms to succeeding generations. To that extent Scotland was no different from any other nation which found itself dominated by a larger neighbour. What did distinguish it from most of these nations was that it was apparently prepared to swallow its pride, even if it hurt, and accept its diminished status as an appendage of England.

However, by the mid-1960s, as the full extent of Britain's economic decline gradually became apparent, and Labour was found to be no more successful than the Conservatives in checking it, the argument that the Union still benefited Scotland began to seem rather threadbare. The SNP was the main beneficiary of the resulting disenchantment; between 1966 and 1974 its vote increased from 5 per cent to 30 per cent and it captured 11 of the 72 parliamentary seats. The party undoubtedly received a significant boost from the discovery of North Sea oil and the adroit campaign which it launched in 1973 under the famous slogan, 'It's Scotland's Oil'.[6] Labour responded to the SNP threat by drawing up plans to devolve power to a Scottish Assembly. Although the long battle over devolution was finally lost in 1979, mainly because of the enmity between these two parties and the deep split in Labour's own ranks, the consequences proved to be less devastating than had originally been feared.[7] The idea of a Scottish parliament had lodged itself firmly in the minds of many people who had previously given no thought to it, and the debate about Scotland's political future had helped to focus critical attention on many other aspects of Scottish life and thought.

[5] Henry Drucker (ed), *John P. Mackintosh on Scotland*, Longman, London, 1982, p. 141.
[6] Christopher Harvie, *No Gods and Precious Few Heroes: Scotland 1914–1980*, Edward Arnold, London, 1981, pp. 159–160; Roger Levy, *Scottish Nationalism at the Crossroads*, Scottish Academic Press, Edinburgh, 1990, pp. 26–27.
[7] Ray Perman, 'The Devolution Referendum Campaign of 1979', in N. Drucker and H. M. Drucker (eds), *The Scottish Government Yearbook 1980*, Paul Harris, Edinburgh, 1979, p. 53.

In the ensuing years, through books, magazines and exhibitions, and the increased attention paid to Scottish affairs by the media (particularly television), many educated Scots became more familiar with aspects of their history and culture which had been denied to them. They realised that Scotland was not, as so many English (and Scottish) historians had claimed, a completely undeveloped nation before the Union of 1707. Geology and geography had certainly conspired to make it poor economically (although no more so than other parts of Europe) but it had not been poor intellectually. They discovered, for example, that the Renaissance had been well established in Scotland by the beginning of the sixteenth century and that the broad philosophical tradition of its universities, rather than, as had so often been claimed, the Union of 1707, was a principal cause not only of the Scottish Enlightenment, that extraordinary flowering of intellectual and artistic life which took place in the eighteenth century, but also of the nation's strength in the natural sciences in the nineteenth- century.[8]

The long-standing belief that Scottish literature had consisted of only a few meteoric figures such as Burns and Scott gradually began to be dispelled. Henryson, Dunbar and Douglas were rescued from their inferior categorisation as 'Scottish Chaucerians'. The extraordinary wealth of folk literature, in Gaelic as well as Scots, became increasingly recognised.[9] An investigation of nineteenth-century literature revealed that the sentimental fiction of the 'Kailyard School' of writers, produced mainly for an Anglo-American audience, which had created such a misleading impression of Scotland at home and abroad, ran counter to the mass of robustly realistic fiction written for Scottish audiences, most of it completely unexplored.[10] Nineteenth- and twentieth-century novels which had long been out of print were republished to critical acclaim by a reinvigorated Scottish publishing industry. A Scots dictionary and thesaurus were produced in response to the renewed interest in the Scots language, and instantly became best-sellers.

On the artistic front too, important changes took place. In an un-precedented deluge of publications, art historians produced convincing evidence of a Scottish artistic tradition which was not derivative, but firmly rooted in the interests and character of the Scottish people themselves. The art of the eighteenth century, for instance, long considered merely provincial, was explained for the first time in the context of the preoccupations of Scottish Enlightenment philosophers, and the links between nineteenth-century painters and vernacular literature were at

[8] George Davie, *The Democratic Intellect*, 2nd edn., Edinburgh University Press, Edinburgh, 1964.
[9] For example, David Buchan (ed), *Scottish Tradition—A Collection of Scottish Folk Literature*, Routledge & Kegan Paul, London, 1984.
[10] William Donaldson, *Popular Literature in Victorian Scotland*, Aberdeen University Press, Aberdeen, 1986, ch. 5.

long last made explicit.[11] Artists such as the 'Glasgow Boys' (and 'Girls' too), Charles Rennie Mackintosh and the 'Scottish Colourists', many of whom had made a considerable impression on Europe in the late nineteenth and early twentieth centuries, but had failed to be appreciated in their own land, were reassessed and their distinctively Scottish qualities of colour, realism and drawing recognised. The strength of Scottish architecture—not only the classicism of such as the Adam family, but also the vernacular tradition that contributed to the castellated architecture of the fifteenth and sixteenth centuries, the 'Scottish Baronial' style of the nineteenth century and the innovative constructions of Mackintosh himself—began to be properly appreciated.

As a result of these developments, members of the Scottish intelligentsia now talk quite unselfconsciously about a third 'Scottish Renaissance'. However, it is important for an understanding of the political mood of present-day Scotland to be aware that this renaissance, like the first one, has involved not only a rediscovery and celebration of the past, but also an explosion of intellectual and artistic activity based on contemporary Scottish themes. A considerable amount of new fiction and poetry has been published in the past decade, much of it imbued with the realism that is such a distinctive characteristic of the Scottish intellect, and young artists have received international acclaim for their imaginative development of the Scottish figurative tradition. Through drama produced for the theatre, and increasingly for television and films, the unvarnished realities of Scottish working-class life have been presented to British audiences in language which makes no concession to the linguistic demands of English people. The Scottish philosophical tradition (which largely died out in the universities in the latter half of the nineteenth century), is attracting renewed attention, partly because it is seen as a suitable intellectual vehicle for justifying, and preventing further erosion of, Scottish educational principles.

But perhaps most important of all for an understanding of Scotland's present political mood is the fact that this renaissance has not been confined to 'highbrow' culture. In the past two decades popular culture has thrown off its imposed, 'White Heather Club' image, with its emphasis on kilts, haggis and bagpipes, and firmly rooted itself in the urban lifestyle of most Scottish people, tapping amongst other things a rich vein of working-class humour, Scotland's extraordinary wealth of folk music and a fascination for Scottish sport that borders on the fanatical. This renaissance of popular culture has been particularly evident amongst young people, who are showing themselves to be far more nationalistic than either their parents or their grandparents. Their strong sense of Scottish identity is now expressing itself in a preference for pop music produced by Scottish-based bands, who draw some of their inspiration from Scottish and Gaelic

[11] Duncan Macmillan, *Scottish Art: 1460–1990*, Mainstream Publishing, Edinburgh, 1990.

45

music. Anyone who regularly attends Scottish pop concerts will be left in no doubt, from the remarks made by musicians on stage and from audiences' reactions to them, of a very direct link between musical nationalism and political nationalism, a link which nationalists and Home Rulers alike have naturally been extremely keen to exploit.[12]

Thatcher's English Nationalism

On its own, this heightening of Scottish consciousness, which is partly a consequence of the devolution referendum, and partly spontaneous, might have had no great political significance. However, in the decade since that event it has combined with a number of important political developments to produce a heady political brew which now threatens as never before to destabilise the Union. The first of these developments was the election in 1979 of a Conservative administration headed by a Prime Minister who dismissed any suggestion that legislative authority should be devolved from Westminster to Edinburgh—although she had implied before the referendum that devolution would remain a live issue in the Conservative Party even if there was a 'No' vote—and who was perceived as indifferent to, indeed ignorant of, Scotland's distinctiveness. As the years of Margaret Thatcher's régime passed, the coal, steel and ship-building industries—the symbols of Scotland's former industrial grandeur—finally disintegrated, new industries faltered and failed, unemployment climbed steeply, social security policy became more restrictive, local authorities were stripped of their financial autonomy and Scots found themselves unwilling guinea-pigs in an experiment to determine whether a poll tax might be suitable for their English brethren (unfortunately for Mrs Thatcher, and to the delight of most Scots, her failure to heed the disastrous results eventually contributed to her downfall).

Although the Conservatives continued the century-old practice of transferring functions from Whitehall to the Scottish Office, and, from 1982 onwards, as a sop to devolutionists, allowed occasional meetings of the Scottish Grand Committee to be held in Edinburgh, none of this caused the slightest flicker of interest. Mrs Thatcher's abrasive personality—considered by many Scots to exhibit the worst traits of southern English nationalism—combined with adverse economic circumstances to overshadow everything else. The number of Conservative MPs in Scotland fell from 22 in 1979 to only 10 in 1987. Thereafter the Select Committee on Scottish Affairs, which had been established as an afterthought in 1979 to provide a much-needed forum for investigation and criticism of Scottish Office policy-making, ceased to meet because of the

[12] See commentary in *Radical Scotland*, No. 46, Aug/Sept 1990, p. 14; also Pat Kane, 'Who do we really think we are?', *The Scotsman*, 29 September 1990.

lack of Scottish Conservative backbenchers able and willing to serve on it. For the first time the party of government in the UK found itself under siege, accused of governing Scotland badly against the clearly expressed wishes of its people. Paradoxically, in obstinately upholding the Union settlement of 1707, Mrs Thatcher had managed to undermine the consent on which it was based.

Independence in Europe

The second political development appeared to have no great significance at the time, but could have the most profound consequences for Scotland's future. To put it simply, the Scots—or rather the Scottish National Party— found Europe. Between 1984 and 1989, influential members of the SNP, including its chairman, Gordon Wilson, its sole MEP, Winnie Ewing, and the former Labour MP, Jim Sillars, were instrumental in forging a coalition which resulted in the party dropping its long-standing opposition to the European Community.[13] In 1988 the party formally adopted yet another brilliant, three-word slogan—'Independence in Europe'—and instantly transformed the Scottish debate by removing it from its parochial UK setting. If Scotland became independent, it would not be a small, isolated country on the European periphery, as the SNP's opponents derisively claimed, but an active member of the community of European nations, participating in European decision-making on an equal footing with England.

In making this change, which was fiercely opposed by some fundamentalists, the SNP hoped to refute the charge of separatism and counter allegations that independence would threaten Scotland's trade links with England.[14] There is little doubt that the strategy succeeded to an extent that probably surprised even its most ardent supporters. Although the SNP's opponents argued that Scotland's membership of the Community was a matter solely for the Member States, including the UK (or what was left of it), and there were many reasons why at least some of them might wish to oppose or delay it, the introduction of a European dimension into Scottish politics caught the imagination of many people who had previously been indifferent to the Community but who were gradually becoming aware of its revolutionary potential.[15] The increasing awareness of Scotland's cultural links with Europe also played a role, albeit a subsidiary one. As a result it soon became virtually impossible for

[13] Allan Macartney, 'Independence in Europe', Alice Brown and Richard Parry (eds), *Scottish Government Yearbook 1990*, Unit for the Study of Government in Scotland, Edinburgh University, 1990, p. 35; James Mitchell, 'Factions, Tendencies and Consensus in the SNP', ibid., p. 49.

[14] Jim Sillars, *Scotland—The Case for Optimism*, Polygon, Edinburgh, 1986, ch. 10.

[15] See Dr Robert Lane, 'Scotland in Europe: An Independent Scotland in the European Community', in Wilson Finnie, C. M. G. Himsworth and Neil Walker (eds), *Edinburgh Essays in Public Law*, Edinburgh University Press, Edinburgh, 1991.

politicians and commentators to discuss Scottish independence except in the context of full Community membership.

The SNP's emphasis on Europe proved far more influential than has so far been acknowledged. After the European referendum of 1975 the Labour Party in Scotland had moved with elephantine slowness towards a grudging acceptance of Community membership. However the interest generated by the SNP's volte-face helped its pro-European faction to argue successfully for a much more positive approach, and for some consideration of how Scotland might be represented within the Community whilst remaining part of the UK. This had important consequences for the discussions that subsequently took place within the Scottish Constitutional Convention (see below). The vision of an independent Scotland in Europe also presented a challenge to Liberal Democrats and others who favoured a Scottish Parliament in a federal UK as the comprehensive solution to Scotland's political problems. If the main responsibilities of a UK federal government—essentially defence, foreign affairs and macro-economic policy—were to be gradually transferred to the European Community, as had begun to seem increasingly likely, what was the point of creating a UK federation in the first place? And if a Scottish Parliament were established, whether or not within a federal UK, was it not equally likely that some of *its* important responsibilities would also drain away to the Community, where they would be exercised on Scotland's behalf by an English-dominated UK government? Perhaps the best solution was a two-stage process in which Scotland achieved control of its domestic affairs through a Scottish Parliament and then, via a transformed 'Europe of the Regions', obtained a direct say in European decision-making. Thereafter, assuming that Europe increasingly took over the UK's responsibilities, Scotland's links with London would be rendered redundant.

A new claim of right

The third political development was undoubtedly the one which, until 1988, seemed to have the least potential. In March 1980, exactly one year after the abortive 1979 referendum, a number of committed devolvers formed the Campaign for a Scottish Assembly, an organisation of individuals and affiliated bodies whose sole aim was the creation of a directly elected legislative Assembly for Scotland. The CSA attracted support from across the political spectrum, and, in 1981, following discussions at its National Convention, it published a 'Blueprint for Scotland'. This emphasised the need to achieve a broad consensus of opinion behind an Assembly scheme and, significantly, made reference to the United Nations Charter in proclaiming the right of Scotland, as a nation, to determine its own political future. For the next few years the CSA continued its policy of quiet lobbying, drawing praise for its persistence but apparently achieving very little. Then, in 1985, it reverted to a well-established Scottish tradition, and called for the establishment of a Constitutional Convention, composed of elected or delegated members (but including all Scottish MPs), to draw up an Assembly scheme, turn it into a Bill and present it to Parliament as the democratically expressed wishes of the Scottish people. This ambitious proposal had a mixed response, particularly from the Labour Party in Scotland, which had always carefully distanced itself from the CSA. Labour's official position, articulated in the summer of 1986, was that a Convention was unnecessary because a Labour government would be formed after the next election with a firm commitment to establish a Scottish Assembly.[16]

Unfortunately for Labour, that was not to be. After the return of the Conservatives in 1987 the CSA decided to establish a Constitutional Steering Committee chaired by Professor Sir Robert Grieve, a distinguished former chairman of the Highlands and Islands Development Board, and composed of a number of well-known people representing a wide range of Scottish interests. Its secretary, Jim Ross, who prepared the Committee's report, had an impeccable pedigree, for he had been the Under-Secretary in charge of devolution at the Scottish Office between 1975 and 1979. The Committee's report—provocatively entitled *A Claim of Right for Scotland*[17]—was published in July 1988 and its impact was immediate. In restrained and elegant prose the Committee referred to the two previous Claims of Right which the Scots had issued against misgovernment (in 1689 and 1842 respectively) and proceeded to register a third: that Scotland had the right to insist on articulating its own demands and grievances rather than have them articulated for it by a government utterly unrepresentative of Scots.

The report was uncompromising in its assertion of Scotland's status as a nation and in its condemnation of successive UK governments for breaching both the letter and the spirit of the Treaty of Union—which many Scottish authorities consider to have the force of fundamental law.[18] The so-called 'British' Constitution came in for particularly scathing criticism: it was in fact an English Constitution which, far from protecting parliamentary democracy, had concentrated political power in the hands of one person, the Prime Minister, to a degree that was unequalled in any other western society, and failed to provide any clear or binding constitutional limitations on the exercise of that power. In these circumstances the Scots could not expect to be given any constitutional opportunity for self-determination and they would therefore have to take matters into their

[16] Susan Deacon, 'Adopting Conventional Wisdom—Labour's Response to the National Question', *Scottish Government Yearbook 1990*, p. 68.

[17] *A Claim of Right for Scotland*, Campaign for a Scottish Assembly, Edinburgh, July 1988; see also Owen Dudley Edwards (ed), *A Claim of Right for Scotland*, Polygon, Edinburgh, 1989.

[18] See, for example, the opinion of Sir Thomas Smith in *The Laws of Scotland, Stair Memorial Encyclopedia*, Law Society of Scotland/Butterworths, Edinburgh, 1987, Vol. 5, paras. 338–360.

own hands. The Committee recommended the establishment of a Constitutional Convention to act as a focus of resistance to Westminster government and as a forum for drawing up a new constitution for Scotland.

The Scottish Constitutional Convention

This time the recommendation that there should be a Constitutional Convention struck a responsive chord. The Scottish National Party, already committed to setting up a directly-elected Convention in the event of winning an outright majority, agreed to support it.[19] So too did influential bodies such as the Scottish Trade Union Congress, the Convention of Scottish Local Authorities and all the Scottish churches.[20] The Scottish Conservatives, not surprisingly, refused to have anything to do with the recommendation, but the Labour Party in Scotland, mindful of its leading role in Scottish political life and acutely aware that a Constitutional Convention might be exploited by the SNP, swallowed its doubts and also agreed to participate.

Then came the Govan by-election: in a sensational result the SNP candidate, Jim Sillars, overturned a Labour majority of more than 19,000 and gave a completely unexpected boost to the Committee's recommendation. A cross-party meeting to discuss the membership and remit of a Convention was quickly arranged for the end of January 1989, and it seemed at long last that the desire for a consensus might stop the bitter feuding between Labour and the SNP. Unfortunately that proved to be wishful thinking; within a few days of what had been a surprisingly amicable and successful meeting, the SNP leadership decided to withdraw. It complained that its Convention representation was too low, and that Labour had refused to adjust it in the light of the results of the European elections later that year or to agree to a referendum to allow the Scottish electorate to choose between the status quo, independence in Europe and the scheme drawn up by the Convention. However, few doubted that, on this occasion, personal and political enmities had proved too strong.

If the SNP hoped that its withdrawal would deal a fatal blow to the Convention, it was mistaken. Indeed, if any damage was done, it was to the SNP itself, for its decision was heavily criticised by the Scottish media and proved controversial amongst its own members, many of whom had no objection to independence through a two-stage process, with a Scottish parliament as the crucial first stage. Labour, on the other hand, although

[19] Isobel Lindsay, *The Scotsman*, 2 February 1989.
[20] See Jock Stein (ed), *Scottish Self-government: Some Christian Viewpoints*, The Handsel Press, Edinburgh, 1989 and William Storrar, *Scottish Identity: A Christian Vision*, The Handsel Press, Edinburgh, 1990.

divided about the Convention, found its freedom restricted by the pressure of public opinion; it therefore decided to remain, partly to gain at the SNP's expense and partly to ensure that it controlled what went on. At the end of March 1989, the Convention held its first meeting in the Assembly Hall in Edinburgh, a venue deliberately chosen for its historic significance as the meeting-place of the General Assembly of the Church of Scotland. At the close of that meeting virtually all the Scottish members of the Westminster and European parliaments, and representatives of the Labour Party in Scotland, Scottish Liberal Democrats, Social Democratic Party, Co-operative Party, Communist Party, Scottish Green Party and the Orkney and Shetland Movement (but not the SNP and the Conservatives) joined with representatives of the trades unions, the churches, the local authorities and the Gaelic and ethnic communities in adopting a founding Declaration which acknowledged 'the sovereign right of the Scottish people to determine the form of government best suited to their needs'. The Declaration committed the Convention to agreeing a scheme for an Assembly or Parliament, obtaining the approval of the Scottish people for it and thereafter asserting their right to secure its implementation.

Many commentators and Convention participants (particularly Labour ones) saw no great significance in this declaration of Scottish popular sovereignty. However the Scottish Liberal Democrats, who drafted most of the Declaration after the first cross-party meeting, deliberately included it for two reasons: to help focus attention on the constitutional aspects of a new Scottish settlement and on the right to self-determination granted under the United Nations Charter (which they knew Labour wanted to ignore); and to persuade the SNP to rejoin the Convention. The SNP had made it clear at the cross-party meeting, and in subsequent private negotiations between SNP and Liberal Democratic leaders, that a declaration of Scottish as opposed to Westminster sovereignty was a precondition of any return. Unfortunately, although Labour accepted the reference to Scottish sovereignty—having opposed it when Jim Sillars raised it at the cross-party meeting—its refusal to discuss a multi-option referendum ended the remote possibility that the SNP could be persuaded to return. However the focus on popular sovereignty, and thus on how best to exercise and safeguard it, proved a far more successful strategy than the Liberal Democrats had ever imagined. During 1989 and 1990, as the Convention, assisted by small Working Groups, inched towards a consensus on a new Scottish settlement, it became clear that much of the controversy was being generated by detailed constitutional proposals put forward by the Liberal Democrats, and that Labour, which was ill-equipped to discuss such matters, was consistently giving ground.

First of all the Liberal Democrats sought a commitment to an eventual federal structure for the UK and this was agreed after initial Labour hostility. They then sought, and eventually obtained, agreement that the powers of a Scottish parliament and executive, and its relations with the

United Kingdom and the European Community, should be entrenched to prevent them being easily altered by a UK government. Their proposal that the Scottish government should open a European office in Brussels to facilitate relations between itself and Community institutions (already suggested by David Martin, an influential Labour MEP) and that it should have an entrenched right to representation in UK delegations to the Council of Ministers and other bodies, was also accepted after initial opposition. Their suggestion that fundamental rights and freedoms should be guaranteed by an entrenched Scottish Charter of Rights incorporating and improving upon the European Convention on Human Rights was rejected by Labour at first, but the support of other Convention participants and of a public consultation exercise ensured that it too was eventually agreed. So too was a recommendation that Orkney, Shetland and the Western Isles, with their separate history and cultures, should have devolved legislative powers over matters directly affecting them, such as fishing and housing. (Orkney and Shetland had voted 'No' overwhelmingly in the 1979 referendum.)

It was hardly surprising that the most contentious of all the constitutional issues raised by the Liberal Democrats proved to be electoral reform. They had made it clear at the outset that their continuing participation in the Convention depended upon agreement being reached on a system of proportional representation (PR) for elections to a Scottish parliament. They had long preferred the Single Transferable Vote, the system used for European and local government elections in Northern Ireland (and to elect Scottish education authorities between 1918 and 1929). The Labour Party in Scotland, on the other hand, was firmly opposed to this, for the simple reason that the first-past-the-post (FPTP) system continued to work in its favour; with just 42 per cent of the popular vote it controlled 50 of the 72 Westminster seats, 7 of the 8 European seats and most of urban Scotland's regional and district councils. Nevertheless there was a mood within the Convention in favour of change and there were also influential activists within the Labour Party in Scotland and the trades unions who argued that FPTP should be abandoned in favour of PR because it worked to Labour's disadvantage in UK parliamentary elections. In addition there was a strong women's lobby within the Convention which wanted serious consideration to be given to a proposal by the STUC Women's Committee (the so-called '50–50' proposal) that a Scottish parliament should contain equal numbers of male and female representatives.

Labour was eventually persuaded to consult its membership and in March 1990, after much lobbying, its annual conference passed a resolution which rejected FPTP, approved equal representation for women and instructed the Executive Committee to bring forward proposals which would ensure that the representation of parties in a Scottish parliament was 'broadly equal' to the number of votes cast. The resolution did not explicitly approve PR (an indication of how sensitive it was) but Convention colleagues quite understandably concluded that it could mean nothing else. They were, however, mistaken; Labour immediately stated that it had only rejected FPTP and needed another year to decide whether to choose a system based on PR! Fortunately the Liberal Democrats felt that they had achieved a great deal and decided not to withdraw. Thus the Convention's final report[21] simply noted the rejection of FPTP and added that the electoral system chosen had to ensure that the number of seats was 'broadly related' (the word 'equal' had somehow disappeared!) to the number of votes cast. Liberal Democrat opposition to the '50–50' scheme—largely because it limited electors' freedom to select the candidate of their choice—caused it to be shelved, but the report did finally endorse equal representation for men and women. A compromise scheme for political parties to select a female quota was rejected, but may yet prove the most likely solution.

Powers of a Scottish Parliament

Given the central importance of the powers of a Scottish Parliament, it is at first sight surprising that they caused so little controversy. The reason, however, was simple: the Convention representatives had no difficulty in agreeing that the existing powers of the Scottish Office (most of them conveniently listed in the Scotland Act 1978) should be transferred to a Scottish parliament, and they held very similar views on a radical extension of these powers to include such important matters as strategic economic planning, the Scottish universities, social security administration, the environment and all aspects of transport. The proposals in the Convention's final report in fact leave very little to Westminster except defence, foreign affairs and macro-economic policy—all responsibilities which representatives with nationalist leanings (of which there are many) believe are likely to be exercised increasingly by European institutions. The expansion of powers that received the greatest attention—and indeed the only one that caused any difficulty—concerned economic and industrial policy. Labour's centralist tendencies made it cautious about transferring too much authority to Edinburgh, and its concern to appear moderate even made it hesitate about including a reference to public ownership. However Campbell Christie, the much-respected General Secretary of the STUC, played a central role in overcoming these doubts and achieving a consensus that Scotland should have strategic economic planning powers in respect of key Scottish industries—such as whisky, food processing, textiles and steel (a sore point because of British Steel's brusque refusal to retain the Ravenscraig steel plant). It would also have powers to co-ordinate the Scottish components of certain UK industries (essentially the financial, oil, gas and petrochemical sectors), control of

---

[21] Scottish Constitutional Convention, *Towards Scotland's Parliament* . . . , Edinburgh, November 1990.

industrial research and development and responsibility for monopolies and mergers.

The Convention made surprising headway on a radically different approach to the financing of Scottish government. Under Labour's 1979 devolution proposals a Scottish Assembly would have had no powers of taxation, a defect rectified in 1987 when the party introduced a Bill giving its Assembly power to vary the rate of income tax. However it continued to insist that the bulk of Scottish expenditure should derive from a block grant calculated by the Treasury under the so-called 'Barnett Formula'.[22] Others, including the Liberal Democrats, favoured a much more radical approach entitling a Scottish Treasury to retain all taxes and duties paid by Scottish taxpayers and to make a contribution to the UK Treasury to cover Scotland's share of UK services. The difference of opinion stimulated a wide-ranging debate which roamed over such controversial matters as whether Scotland could actually support itself (Labour thought not, but others disagreed), why no information was available about total Scottish revenues, and whether the south-east of England, some of whose right-wing inhabitants regularly accused the Scots of being 'subsidy junkies', was not itself the biggest 'junkie' of all.[23]

Eventually a variant of the German system was proposed under which Scotland was assigned a proportion of certain specified taxes in lieu of a block grant. Labour felt these should be UK taxes, but others argued that they should be income tax and VAT paid by Scottish taxpayers, to enable a Scottish government to benefit from any buoyancy resulting from its economic policies. At first Labour demurred, arguing that Scottish taxpayers would have to be identified and this would be administratively difficult. Unfortunately it immediately found itself hoist with its own petard, for its own tax-variation proposals required just such an exercise to be carried out! Agreement was therefore reached that a Scottish government should be entitled to all income tax and VAT collected in Scotland, and the arrangements should be reviewed regularly with a view to assigning other taxes and duties. The Convention also agreed that equalisation—based on an accurate needs assessment—should continue because of Scotland's geographical and economic disadvantages, and that the Parliament should have power to vary the rate of income tax—but only within a margin of two or three pence in the pound, to counter Conservative allegations that it would increase taxes by as much as 20 per cent.

---

[22] On Scottish public finances and their reform see James G. Kellas, *The Scottish Political System*, 4th edn., Cambridge University Press, Cambridge, 1989, Ch. 12; David McCrone (ed), *Financing Home Rule*, Unit for the Study of Government, Edinburgh University, 1990; David Heald, *Financing a Scottish Parliament*, Scottish Foundation for Economic Research, Glasgow, Discussion Paper No. 1, Glasgow, 1990.

[23] On the latest figures, Scots get 23 per cent more per head of *identifiable* public spending than the UK population as a whole; see Heald, op. cit., Table 5. For a spirited account of the hidden subsidies which go to the south-east of England, see George Rosie, 'Scotching The Myth', *Scotland on Sunday*, 25 November 1990.

The UK and Europe

Visitors to the Convention were particularly struck by the lack of attention given to Scotland's representation at Westminster and in the UK Cabinet. There were in fact two quite separate reasons for this. On the one hand, Labour was reluctant to raise the spectre of Tam Dalyell's famous 'West Lothian Question'—why should Scottish MPs at Westminster vote on English domestic affairs if English MPs cannot vote on Scottish domestic affairs?—or contemplate any reduction in the 72 Scottish seats because of the consequences for its ability to govern the UK (or rather England) effectively, or indeed to govern it at all. It also felt (as did others) that it was wise to retain the Scottish Secretary in the UK Cabinet, although it conceded that it was difficult to see what he would do, particularly if the Scottish and UK governments were of different political persuasions. On the other hand, there were Convention representatives whose interest lay in reforming Scotland and whose attention had shifted from the UK to the European Community. They envisaged that under the Convention's proposals Scotland would largely govern itself and the Community would eventually assume the key responsibilities retained at Westminster (see above). Their prime interest lay in establishing a Scottish Parliament which would join with other parts of Europe in pressing for a direct say in European decision-making through a 'Europe of the Regions'. If English politicians objected to Scotland's UK representation—indeed if they wanted it reduced before agreeing to a Scottish parliament—it was for them to say so.

So what does the future hold for Scotland and for its Convention? The answer undoubtedly depends on the outcome of the next General Election. If Labour wins, it will be expected to keep its promise to legislate for a Scottish Parliament during its first year in office. Whether or not it chooses to implement the Convention's scheme is of course another matter, but the success of the Convention has now made that a little more likely. In a little-noticed speech delivered in Paisley in November 1990, a few days before the launch of the Convention's final report, Labour's Deputy Leader, Roy Hattersley, committed the UK Labour Party for the first time to implementing the *Convention's* proposals. 'Our scheme', he declared at Paisley Town Hall on 13 November 1990, 'will be firmly based on the framework established by the Convention.' For those who had laboured long and hard to persuade Labour to take the Convention seriously, it was a moment to savour. However, if, as many people expect, the Conservatives win the election with only a handful of Scottish seats— the so-called 'Domesday Scenario'—the future becomes extremely difficult to predict.

Support for independence has been rising steadily, and by the end of 1990 it had reached 39 per cent (double the level of support for the SNP), with 44 per cent favouring Home Rule. If the Conservatives remain intransigent, it is very probable that support for independence will continue to rise and the SNP will be the main beneficiary. However it is almost certain that a majority, or at least a very large minority, of Scots will continue to support Home Rule. That may be enough to persuade the SNP and the Convention to co-operate in organising a multi-option referendum to determine once and for all which of the three options—the status quo, independence in Europe or the Convention scheme—commands the greatest support. If it is the Convention scheme—and at present most people think it would be—then Scottish MPs may have to give serious consideration to withdrawing from Westminster to force the Conservatives to concede a Scottish parliament.[24] It would be a very unwise administration which allowed such a situation to develop, but the Conservatives know well how to be ruthlessly pragmatic when the chips are down. They are most likely to respond by offering a parliament which is far weaker than most Scots would like. If they do, the Scots would be well advised to accept it, for, like the Scottish Office, it will almost certainly gain in power and authority after it is established.

On the other hand, of course, nothing may happen at all! Many shrewd observers believe that Scotland's political leaders are incapable of acting decisively, or, to be more specific, that Labour's Scottish leadership are not prepared to risk damaging their relations with their English colleagues. However, as far as this particular observer is concerned, the increasingly confident mood of the Scottish people makes it likely that Labour *will* have to act decisively if the Conservatives win the next election. One way or the other, therefore, it is not unreasonable to predict that Scotland will have a parliament within the next decade. And within a decade or so of that it is not unreasonable to envisage Scotland as a country which governs its own affairs and participates directly in European decision-making in a transformed 'Europe of the Regions'. The UK may still exist, but, with the loss of power to Brussels, London government will have simply withered away as far as Scotland is concerned. We will then see whether *The Economist*'s brand-new vision of an independent Scotland,[25]—a confident nation, full of innovative businesses and bright people, with entrepreneurs buzzing around its ancient universities, a financial centre drawing venture capitalists from all over Europe, and low taxes and cheap land sucking in manufacturing and service companies—becomes a reality, or whether the geographical and economic problems which have dogged Scotland throughout its history will simply be transferred from the British to the European stage.

[24] In a BBC poll in March 1990, 60 per cent approved of Scottish Labour MPs withdrawing if the Conservatives won the General Election.
[25] *The Economist*, 25 May 1990.

THE CONSTITUTION OF WALES

DAFYDD ELIS THOMAS*

IT would be giving in to temptation to write down that there isn't one. In the sense of having a written document, like the American one, the UK doesn't have one either. So both countries[1] are in the same position. But since the one, United Kingdom, encompasses Wales, then it could perhaps be argued that Wales suffers from a double absence of a constitution. But another argument can be made that whereas the United Kingdom does not have a written constitution, Wales has. For the absence of a constitution for Wales, indeed the absence of Wales itself, was specifically legislated for in acts of the English (*sic*) parliament in the early sixteenth century. This was followed up by the *Encyclopaedia Britannica* in the nineteenth century, 'For Wales see England'. Historians of earlier periods can point to a body of texts of mediaeval Welsh law, apparently coexisting alongside English law, and might this then be called a constitution?[2]

There are the might-have-been constitutions of imagined polities: the principalities of the early mediaeval period, ending with the Glyndŵr uprising; the claims for a national university, church, and parliament: all of them revived by nineteenth century Liberals. But to argue this way is to go for a much too literal understanding of the word constitution. Figuratively, Wales is constituted, is made up.[3]

Of what then is this Wales made up? This is the question which this essay tries to answer. Is it a nation or a region or both, should it be viewed as part of Britain, of the United Kingdom, or Western Europe, in a trans-Atlantic mode or in a pan-Celtic twilight, or all of these, or none? What

---

* The author is MP for Meirionnyd Nant Conwy and President of Plaid Cymru, broadcaster and formerly tutor in Welsh Studies at Coleg Harlech.

[1] 'Nation is intended in its meaning as a territorial division containing a body of people of one or more nationalities and usually characterised by relatively large size and independent status. Because a standard definition of national state . . . is too restrictive for my purposes I prefer instead the term "nation state". Country of course refers to "a political state or nation or its territory". Despite these differences in meaning the referent is essentially the same entity, and therefore I use the three terms interchangably.' I agree with this statement of Robert Dahl in his *Democracy and its Critics*, Yale University Press, 1989.

[2] For the latest discussion see Rees Davies, *Domination & Conquest 1100–1300*, Cambridge University Press, 1990.

[3] Constance Perin argues: 'In its several senses, then, "constitution" bridges the semantic, biological and social dimensions these essays explore: the constitution of meaning—the ideas by which we construe our world to make it more intelligible, less uncertain; the human constitution—our species' biological dispositions; and our American Constitution—its principles enabling the negotiation and renegotiation of meaning we live by', *Belonging in America*, Wisconsin University Press, 1988.

kind of body politic does it have? Should it be given a health check, as a living organism, or a post mortem? I will now cheekily assume the conclusion. It is idle to be too exercised about definitions, Wales just plain is. Here it is. But since I am now writing in London what was first spoken of in west coast Wales, let's say 'there it is'. It is a place, but not a thing; well it is partly a thing as it has a material landscape, spaces, places, but also peoples. So it is therefore a social process, a cultural figure, it exists first and foremost and probably finally in language. Or in two languages. Dylan Thomas authored the phrase 'The two-tongued sea'.[4]

But its fact of two languages only appears odd when set against the myopic, monochrome monolingualism of Englandness

> To me monolingualism, both individual and societal, is not so much a linguistic phenomenon (even if it has to do with language), but rather a question of a psychological state, backed up by political power. Monolingualism is a psychological island. It is an ideological cramp. It is an illness, a disease which should be eradicated as soon as possible, because it is dangerous for world peace. It is a reflection of '*linguicism*'[5].

There are, in sociolinguistic facts, more multilinguals in the world than there are monolinguals. Though the monolinguals apparently always seem to think that when multilinguals exhibit their multiness they are in fact 'talking about us', as if we had nothing better to do.

Two names

So in line with two-tongued sea, the land has two names. Cymru. Wales. These are quite obviously two different places. Linguistically, literally, and certainly figuratively, this can be demonstrated to be the case. This should not be seen as too serious a problem, except from the point of view of those who try to construct a simplistically coherent identity. Cymru in Welsh obviously figures as a land where Welsh-speakers live, though the first and only written Welsh constitution in the Welsh language was drafted in Patagonia in the middle of the nineteenth century. But as with most minority groups, peoples, nationalities, the sense of a relationship between language and territory would seem to be part of the constitution of the group or nationality. The absence of such a link, in various periods of time, for the Palestinian and Jewish peoples, are exceptions to the rule. Welsh-language place names are the signs that make meanings in that landscape. Such place names defy translation. As the two-tongued sea, so too is the mountain which has two names. Snowdonia with its three or four month snow line at a thousand metres is also Eryri, the eagle's place. The difference between the two namings, the two words, the two languages jostling to stand on the same peak, or peaks, make for a diversity and

---

[4] 'A Child's Christmas in Wales', Dylan Thomas *Collected Stories*, Dent, 1981.
[5] Tove Skutnabb-Kangas, *Minority Education: From Shame to Struggle*, Clevedon and Philadelphia, 1988.

liveliness, set against which the one-named landscape looks stilted and still.

To try to say that Wales, or its then population, was mainly monolingual once and that in the Welsh language, is to try to remember what cannot be brought to mind in any meaningful way. Like Brythonic residues and traces on worn ogam-stones, that culture has gone too. The English language cannot be painted out or switched off. For it is not the language of England but one of the two languages of Wales. Indeed the English people in England can hardly lay claim to the English language, when there are now not only far more speakers of English outside England, but in socio-linguistic fact, more second-language speakers of English as learners, than native speakers even beyond the shores of England herself.[6]

Wales figures then, in the English Welsh language, in a very different way from the way in which Cymru figures in the Welsh. Identity, what is similar or in common, appears through comparing and contrasting. In the Welsh language the very definition of Welsh people as non-Welsh-speaking Welsh persons (*Cymry di-Gymraeg*) is negative. Yet although these identities do not coincide, or identify with one another necessarily or always, both languages figure in the landscape. By survey and census the ebb and flow of the numbers of speakers of these languages register on graphs and maps. Disappearing Welsh speakers from rural parishes are replaced by urban nursery school children. But as the domain of the older Welsh language (as if that meant something) extends, so its register continues to drop, and the demands which have generated response from public agencies for the one leads to a jealously guarded demand for space for the other.

'How come you get so much money for your language from a foreign government?' asked a visiting American professor of socio-linguistics. That can only be explained by pointing out that the government is not foreign. There is a whole structure, a whole constitution of Wales, which can be seen as being particularly responsive to demands for language concessions and policies. The late 1980s saw not only new broadcasting legislation taking the Welsh language broadcasting model of the Wales Fourth Channel Authority (*Sianel Pedwar Cymru*) and applying it to Gaelic in Scotland, but also the placing of the Welsh language alongside English in the national curriculum. According to the Minister, the phrase national curriculum when used in England refers to England, but when in Wales refers to Wales.[7]

A whole system

Within and across both languages a whole system which is part administrative, part policy-making, part accountable, part bureaucratic, very

---

[6] Sidney Greenbaum, 'Whose English?' in *The State of The Language*, Christopher Rix, ed., University of California, 1990.

[7] *Official Report*, Standing Committee Education Reform Act 1988.

quasi democratic, constitutes the government of Wales. It is easy to point to the Welsh Office, a territorial department of state, with its 3,000-odd officials mainly based in Cardiff, and its £4 billion budget, with its 1,500 appointed places on nominated bodies. The latest trend is to name public bodies with a Welsh language name, *Cadw, Tai Cymru*, avoiding the ambiguity of the adjective Welsh, whether applying to language or to nation (*sic*). But drawing attention to the specific way in which Wales and its political system is written in legislation is very often the least helpful way of writing the events which have changed its politics since the Second World War. It has been a study of incremental institutional change. Metaphors of growth and organic extension have to be eschewed. More appropriate was the statement of a not yet retired quango person who therefore must remain anonymous when he referred to 'the long march westwards'. It is precisely that talking up of Wales as a nation and a people and a country which has made it more and more become that. The very contradictariness of the events and outcomes only make it move in a more lively fashion.

Talking of devolution leads to a rejection of the idea, or concept, of a democratically elected assembly. But the very rejection of the concept by popular vote in the 1979 referendum did not stop the talking. The talking and the writing in the institutional process of Whitehall/Cathays Park, Cardiff government circles continued as if nothing had happened. Indeed the very 'failure' of meeting a democratic deficit, itself seemed to push more in the direction of non-elected governmental activity. This should not surprise me. For a representative democracy is only a relatively small, and largely theatrical part of government. And politics, as sites of the language of power, is almost everywhere. So by not being realised, by being rejected, but by being a reference point for continuing argument, the idea of not having an elected assembly or parliament actually leads to having more powers. So Welsh counties call themselves the Assembly of Welsh Counties, and affiliate to the assembly of European regions, directly being part of a European network. The Welsh Office itself responds to become one of the partners of the high-technology confederation of European regions and smaller nations. Continually talking the national 'language' actually continues to make Wales, event by event, more 'national'.

Ideological nationalists object to it being called a region, even a European region, but the BBC as always finds a compromise by calling Scotland, Wales and Northern Ireland 'national regions'. The language of national regions calls up someone somewhere to 'speak for England'. And so it goes on. Meanwhile, down and across in Cardiff, Newtown, and other centres of 'Welsh power', actually existing nationalism (*sic*) is talking itself up. The existence of the Welsh Office, itself brought about by a Welsh political discourse, then calls into being a whole series of semi-autonomous pressure groups and national lobbying organisations in the voluntary sector to lobby itself. A Wales CBI makes necessary a Wales

TUC, a Shelter Wales, a CND Cymru, a Wales Anti-Apartheid, not to mention the already existing cultural institutions of the Welsh Rugby Union, the vaguely co-operating religious denominations, with the quangocracy itself containing and delimiting a whole cast of thousands of lead persons who constitute the running of the system.

As appropriate to such a talked up society, communication and media are themselves part of the talking and making of, and the result. *Weekday Wales, Wales This Week, Wales on Sunday*, are all a mediated talking of and remaking of Wales. The Welsh Development Agency together with the Welsh Office press office and the *Western Mail* newspaper have been regular generators of 'good news about the principality'. This is nation building, the role so often described by mass communication studies of emerging states in the so-called Third World. Importing, or reimporting, a cultural decolonisation model would not be apposite. Yet it is in this area of the media that institutions based in Wales have something like international relations. '*Jeux sans Frontières*' on S4C.

Inadequate frameworks

Writing in this way of the constitution of Wales deliberately works to avoid a series of inadequate frameworks: frameworks which are themselves designed to trap Wales as a place, or places, with its peoples, a singular and specific set of events, and non-events, making up its 'history', within other frameworks (that of a United Kingdom, or of 'Europe'). Such writing fits in neatly with a particular discourse of politics and political science. Within that approach, intellectuals, theorists, media persons and other politicos can be let loose among peoples or places looking for 'a sense of identity'. Such a notion of a 'sense of identity' is then related in a reified way to the absence of a 'constitution'. By such cyclical reasoning then peoples and places can be written of as such a history, at least from the point of view of the writers of that history. Happily, for the peoples and places themselves, in themselves, this is not a problem. For whether or not they are written in a particular kind of history viewed from outside themselves, or partially from within themselves, does not present them with a problem in themselves. This is not to say that specific and particular histories cannot be written by different peoples from outside what is often called 'contexts'. But what the concepts of theory so often fail to do is touch the particularity, the spaces, the places, the events that are here and there but not everywhere. Conventional political science, then, as a slightly more reflective older cousin of conventional representative politics sets out with a concept of political systems, and takes this theoretical baggage on a journey into other spaces and places, time zones and time warps. There it seeks to apply these criteria in what used to be known as an objective fashion to the happenings of places, and therefore to come away with a judgment. An analytical statement which describes and prescribes, and even proscribes, what it imagines to be real or true, for that place.

Doing this from the inside, from within a group, playing through the internally perceived inadequacy of concepts and belief systems, is more difficult, and lays one open to charges of betrayal. Yet if the argument is that all that nationalist rhetoric does is translate into Welsh or into Wales, and sometimes not very adequately, the running and ruling concepts of British state or other nationalisms, then who is representing what to whom and with what purpose? Bill Readings puts it particularly aptly:

> Politics, then, is not simply a question of who is represented, since the exercise of domination is the effect of the representational apparati that have governed the understanding of cultural experience. For example, under capitalism the function of commodification is to submit all events to the rule of capital by reducing them to representations of value within a system of exchange. Existence is thus determined as an effect of representation.[8]

What I am arguing for here is that the politics of and for change requires a rewriting, and a rereading, of the dominant and dominating concepts of political and social science discourse, including that very idea of representation itself. The issue is not the representation of a more or less already existent 'Welsh identity', to the institutions of the United Kingdom state and by extension those of western Europe. Existing statehood, or the lack of it, or the partial nature of it, does not represent the only way of talking about places and events in relation to 'the political'. A constructed notion of a 'sense of identity' can be read as the obverse for 'minority groups' of the notion of citizenship; a conceptual construction of minoritiness which simultaneously maintains marginality.

Writing this another way, we (me in the writing and you in the reading), should ask each other where the real problems lie? A supposed or constituted or constructed English or British identity would seem to me to be inherently much more problematic, and more threatening in terms of fire power, than any Welsh identity, should we care so to construct one. What I am saying is that the very notion of an identity, of a conceptual or even felt sameness of experience, is no longer, if it ever was, a useful category for writing about political and ethical issues, whether in the area of culture or anywhere else. What is Welsh identity? I am uncertain, though I know there are a lot of them. What is the Welsh experience? Again there are many of them, and they are still going on. The idea that we need to try to reconstitute a variety of events and places into some kind of coherent whole seems to me itself to be a rather futile exercise. Indeed it is an exercise which is designed to fit the smaller diversities, differences and specificities into some greater whole. It seems to me that refusing this greater whole or even refusing to reconstruct and reconstitute a smaller whole, is no longer, is the one remaining useful practice. Why should we try, or even desire or need, to fit ourselves into such superimposed structures?

---

[8] Bill Readings, *Introducing Lyotard: Art and Politics*, New York, 1991.

Within the existing structures of the United Kingdom state, Wales is fundamentally unrepresentable. Yet it continues to present itself, to be present to the networks of powers in which it is inscribed. To the extent that peoples from various Waleses refuse to be so inscribed tightly and conveniently, there can be kept open the continual possibilities of other ways of talking and doing. The idea of a British nation state is obviously itself deeply fissured. But the idea of a coming nation state for Wales seems to me to be equally undesired, and undesirable. It might be argued that it should be seen as desirable from the point of view of an expression of identity. But what is this identity that seems to require expression? Rather should we see it as various groups, places, peoples, wanting to be in their place in the small rain, and occasionally in weak sunshine. There is no rule or law that requires that these peoples should have any particular kind of representation. What they want, now, and probably then is to be able to continue to be present, to present themselves, or ourselves, in a way that they can work at, for themselves. They do not need to be constructed or constituted as a minority in relation to an alleged majoritarian democratic state. Neither is their existing access, or future access, to these spaces predetermined by their relations with the state, or the market. What people do in relation to specific events in times and places is to ask for and feel a need to make certain things happen. More often than not these are not articulated within coherent meta-language frameworks. Those frame-works are usually only useful for structures that wish to deny, rather than facilitate making things happen. State-speak uses the language of unity and identity to impose uniformity. State-speak also seeks to put back into itself the idea of political power, as residing in spaces which it itself already controls, or pretends to control.

Most theories of the nation state and their attendant discourses together with versions of democracy and representing politics, need increasingly to be seen as part of the problem, not as anything approximating a solution. Indeed the imposed and constructed solutions are precisely what are here being rejected, against which we would want to set down specificities. Not some grand narrative of a United Kingdom, or a United States of Europe, albeit constituted on the basis of regions, but specific and particular events and places, not even needing to be identified in a series, and certainly without needing to be wrapped up in a concept, or categorised as an experience.

For the purpose of this argument, which is not the putting forward of a thesis, I will take the Welsh language as that which is most unrepre-sentative, and yet continually insists on being present. The Welsh language is legally absent from representation to the institutions of the British state, in particular its Parliament. The speaking of Welsh in the place of speaking, the Parliament of the United Kingdom, is actually not permitted. Yet it was that same parliament which, having banned the language from the courts and administration, also legislated even in the sixteenth century compelling its use in state religion. The same parliament which cannot

63

allow the language to be spoken within itself, legislates for it to have a space and place within education and the media, as I have written about above. One of the reasons why the campaigns to extend the domain of the Welsh language have been more 'successful' than any campaign for an elective representational political apparatus, is this very specificity of its presentness. To speak what is formally not to be spoken, to make signs which are not to be signified, let alone to be regarded as significant, is to make a direct challenge within particular events. And for the peoples who makes those challenges, their presentations cannot be simply erased.

Language and discourse

It is clearly mistaken, following the phraseology I have used, that such specific sites of linguistic disputation and shift should themselves be turned into a series of purporting to defend or announce a 'Welsh identity'. It is at once much simpler and denser than that. Language presents a site of sharp difference, but it is only one. Topography, geography, and the interaction between market mechanisms and territoriality, themselves also mark out differences. So too does the very sharp difference between a production process, the work which it is, and what it produces, particularly as waste, in relation to the environment, or what I still think is better called nature. In the land of Wales, in the cultural reverberations and very greenness of spaces and places, the deep conflicts of environmental policy are seen.

The discourse about the environment is another vocabulary which has entered the language of politics.[9] But this speaking of the environment brings the spatial and the temporal more sharply into political talk. Actual spaces whether inner city, valley or countryside together with the effects of processes on actual environments, waste disposal, pollution, allegedly harmless level of radioactivity, bring the talk around to a new sense of fragility. Environmental talk questions in a critical fashion the production and consumption talk. Significantly that talk also can be partly reintegrated into previous or other discourses as in 'green consumerism'. But green talk, as attention to the spatial effects of production processes, leads to a questioning of centralisation and of systemic bigness. This questioning and attendant lifestyle changes exemplified by a new wave of moves to the countryside to try to find a green space and place, in its turn contributes to different kinds of politics in the formerly perceived peripheral places.

This in its turn lights up the institutional stage-set written about earlier. As issues of nuclear decommissioning, chemical waste reprocessing, open cast coal mining, hill farming practices, and national park access, coastal pollution and derelict land clearance, become dramatised on the terrain of Wales, this shows the Welsh Office system in its light and shadow. At once

[9] See Necdet Tymor, *Environmental Discourse*, London, 1982.

64

a territorial department with statutory powers in environmental matters, it could just about write up to ten pages of text in the government's recent green paper.

The most striking feature of the Welsh Office for Welsh media watchers is that it has become the most prominent place in Wales in which to protest. Demonstrations about everything from the government's policy in the Middle East and the Gulf war across to the closure of the smallest one-class primary school, not to mention health services, farming, chemical pollution, the poll tax, higher education cuts, all these conflicts about powers and resources in and against the political system are acted out in front of that building. This is the actually existing government of Wales. It is the state of Wales. Secretaries of state, particularly the previous incumbent, acted as if they were prime ministers of Wales. Flanked by motorcycle outriders speeding out of Stuttgart airport, on yet another European high tech trail. And what were those outriders there to protect him against?

To read representative politics as if it were a piece of rather expensive street theatre may not suit conventional political science. But as a way of describing the political debate in and around Wales, I think it is more than a metaphor. The incremental development of a system of power, at once demanded and devolved, has developed its own dynamic. But I do not want to replace the language of nation statism, with its notions of metro-politan departments administering regions, by the language of super-statism whereby European regions fit together as some kind of building blocks for a greater European unity. We have chased notions of homogeneity and unity, and common citizenship, within the nation state. With what net effect is a matter of argument. Hetrogeneity, diversity, and a localism which by letting go and letting be implies a non-dominant non-universalist globalism, represents an alternative order. Nations and regions which culturally and politically did *not* become their own nation states, or dominating over other nations or groupings by being partially included, and thus were partly excluded from 'nation state building', these are in a better position to understand and work for a different form of international disorder.

Obsession with statehood

Statehood, or the lack of it, has been the central obsession of all nationalists, those who had it and those who didn't have it. It is no less an obsession for Brits and Anglos, because it is unspoken. Indeed the more central the issue, the less spoken it is. So the national questions of Wales and Scotland, in the way that they are posed at the end of the twentieth century, together with the questions on the island of Ireland, and on mainland Europe, west and centre and east, perhaps bring us towards starting to ask, if not to answer, the question of England, Britain and the Queendom.

Wales and Scotland, in their internal diversity, together with England and its regions, have always figured in that dominant discourse which is called United Kingdom politics. All attempts to tippex them out have failed. Equally unsuccessful, in my view, have been those attempts to create a Scottish and Welsh nationalist discourse taking its model from West European nation state ideology. Not having been part of its own nation state appears as a weakness for some who would argue for Wales to be differently constituted. But from the perspective of a now and a possible future such an apparent weakness or lack may be a strength. The lack of an over-developed Wales-based nation state system perhaps necessitated the stronger development of sections of Welsh civil society. Community, locality and internal differences can function for the groups and individual life stories as a bonding rather than a passport-defined nationality. Confusion about being British, Welsh, European, male, or being a bit of all four and more, should not be seen as specifying a lack of identity. Why should identity itself be seen as singular, when it can be much more comfortably felt as relaxed and plural?

Always, however, with that niggling need to define against England. Not the actual England beyond those black and white comforting border towns, fenlands, broadlands, peaks or post-industrial moors, or London, Birmingham, Manchester, Liverpool, Leeds and Sheffield, which bear signs of a possible international England, but the constructed England of the Englishness of English literature, itself in turn the dominant discourse of somewhere else called Britain but one somehow devoid of most traces of Celticism, and of black culture and politics. These other figures will not go away, and will continually and joyfully refuse to be assimilated. Making assimilation a goal was wounding and oppressive, and it still is. From the petty incidents of racism, linguism and sexism it is but a short step to the xenophobic construction of a variety of aliens, together with the totally unverifiable assertion that 'our institutions are the best in the world'.[10]

From a view centred in Ukanian statehood, Scotland, Wales and Northern Ireland are anomalous, to be controlled by territorial departments. From the point of view located in those countries, coupled with the view from the European mainland, British state institutions themselves appear archaic, populated by nationalistic residivists, left, right and centre. Such a deconstructive view from another place reads the institutions differently from an inside view, whether on the stage or in the auditorium.

I began by rejecting the temptation to write down that Wales didn't have

[10] I cannot compete with Edward Pearce's sharp piece of Brit self-analysis 'What suppressed sense of inferiority about trade deficits, institutionalised and rising unemployment, and an over-valued currency make war so attractive to them? Why are they such swaggering bullies; why are they emotionally dependent on American smiles; why do they want so badly to re-live their past? Britain, with its mixture of laziness and pack mentality, its power worship and ache for violence, its habit of sucking up and spitting down, is not these days a country you can like much, still less respect. War, I fear, is all the British are good for'. (*Guardian*, 6 February 1991.)

a constitution. It is probably more appropriate to point out that it doesn't have a national theatre. This however does not mean that it doesn't have regional or community theatres, or that the drama of politics or any other form of social life does not continue as street or pub or club or parlour or TV studio theatre. The nation, however we may think of it, cannot avoid being presented, if not represented, in all aspects of its social and cultural life. But achieving or not achieving greater powers of decision taking at the national level is a matter of judgement. Constitutions are paradoxically possibly the least important ways of constituting a national or an international community.

NORTHERN IRELAND: ALLEGIANCES AND IDENTITIES

KEVIN BOYLE*

It is not difficult to express the Northern Ireland problem in terms of identity and allegiance. There have been and remain two national identities and two sets of allegiances, one British and one Irish. There has been and there continue to be a struggle between these identities, over which is to dominate, a conflict which has intensified since the onset of the Troubles over two decades ago. Let me explore this contest of national identity and allegiance. But I will also discuss the intimately linked issue of constitutions. The central question for Northern Ireland, as ever, is its constitutional status: what that status is and how it might evolve. If, as seems likely, we are entering on a decade of constitutional reassessment and reform in both states on these islands, then the implications for Northern Ireland can be positive and far reaching.

The Province has been written out of the on-going debate on constitutional change in Britain. There is an implicit agreement among those discussing the future shape of relations between the Crown, and between the dominant nation of England and the nations in Scotland and Wales, that for these purposes the United Kingdom means the larger island. Which is of course understandable but nevertheless ironic since Northern Ireland is all about the failure of the constitutional union of the four nations on these islands under the same dominant nation and the same English Crown. It is too late to question Northern Ireland's exclusion from the debate; but any concern with what is the most serious of Britain's present territorial crises must at least raise issues which should be considered by all who are seeking to change what must now be called the internal constitution of Britain.

In the other state on these islands, Ireland, there are also, following the election of President Mary Robinson, stirrings of constitutional discussion and proposals for reform. In December 1990 for the first time since the Irish constitution was adopted in 1937, a debate took place in the Dail on the constitutional claim to Northern Ireland. Unlike the case of Britain, the movement for constitutional reassessment in Ireland is directly influenced by the challenge of Northern Ireland. The new president, the

* The author is Professor of Law and director of the Human Rights Centre, Essex University, and has written widely on Northern Ireland and on human rights internationally. He is co-author with Tom Hadden of *inter alia*, *Ireland a Positive Proposal* (1985) and *The Anglo-Irish Agreement, a Commentary* (1989).

occupant of an institution modelled on the British sovereign, has the distinction of being the first public figure in the history of the Irish state whose proclaimed hand of friendship and love for all the people of Northern Ireland was not shrugged off in predictable ways in those circles which delight in the description of diehard Unionist.

But the possibilities of peace in Northern Ireland cannot, despite the heartfelt wish of the larger island, be left to the Irish. It must involve both countries because Northern Ireland and its divided people, Catholic and Protestant, Unionist and Nationalist, have identities linked to both countries and its constitutional arrangements; now in rubble are the outcome of political decisions for which both Britain and Ireland bear responsibility. The one element of hope in decades of despair about Northern Ireland is that this message can be said to have been accepted, at least in principle, as a result of the Anglo-Irish Agreement.

If domestic constitutional change in both countries can create new possibilities for Northern Ireland, external constitutional developments can equally contribute. The Europeanisation of both islands, particularly through their shared external constitution in the European Community, will force a reassessment of all relationships on these islands and in particular on the two principal influences on the present tragedy of Northern Ireland: 'Britishness' as an historical integrating force and the reactive tradition of Irish separatism. Seventy years on, the effort to maintain the conflicting identities and allegiances of Unionist and Nationalist communities within the narrow ground of the Six Counties without a transformation of the relations between the Irish state and the British state is fruitless. The possibilities exist to achieve this transformation over the next decade within a new European constitutional framework and a new European citizenship.

The elements of identity and allegiance

One and a half million people are intermixed on one fifth of the land mass in the North East of the island of Ireland. One million are descendants of Scottish and English settlers in the seventeenth century, Anglican and Dissenters by religion and a half million are descendants of those the settlers ejected, the indigenous Gaelic speaking and Catholic Irish. From the first census in the nineteenth century the religious proportions of the population have broadly remained constant. In Antrim and Down, Protestants outnumber Catholics by five to one. In Belfast, following Catholic inward migration during the industrial growth of the city in the nineteenth century the proportion has remained stable at four to one. In the counties of Londonderry and Armagh there has been a small continuing majority of Protestants while in the remaining two counties Tyrone and Fermanagh there has persisted a small majority of Catholics.

Centuries of conflict between the two populations and between the two

KEVIN BOYLE

islands have left a deeply divided society. But a deeply divided society is
not a totally divided one, as the late John Whyte pointed out.[1] Beyond
issues of constitutions and religion the people of Northern Ireland are
remarkably similar to each other and, by and large, to the people who live
anywhere on these islands. But for that reality two decades of appalling
conflict would have been much worse. But this is not to underestimate the
intense alienation and bitterness which now exists between the communities and which shows no sign of reversal.

An anthropologist working in Northern Ireland, quoted by Whyte,
notes:

> With only very limited and specific exceptions the cultural heritage for the
> Catholic is likely to be much the same as that of a Protestant of the same social
> class living in the same geographical area. There are no distinctively Protestant
> or Catholic dialects, nor agricultural practices nor housetypes nor pottery
> techniques nor styles of cooking. Family life is much the same on both sides as
> indeed is the broader social morality.[2]

The British Social Attitudes survey published in 1990, which for the
first time included Northern Ireland, adds to this picture of cultural
homogeneity.[3] Thus social class as a factor of identity has the same
significance in the perceptions of people in Northern Ireland of both communities as it has throughout Britain. People in Northern Ireland indeed
feel closer to those of the same background than in Britain. On attitudes
towards economic equality and the role of the state, both British and
Northern Ireland society emerge as identical in terms of the correlation
between social class and attitudes to equalitarianism.

There is a difference in attitudes between Catholic and Protestant alike
and other parts of the UK over morality: such issues as premarital sex,
homosexuality, artificial insemination and measures against pornography.
On all such questions the Northern Ireland people of both communities
were significantly more conservative than respondents in Britain, even
when compared with church-goers in Britain. The only difference of
opinion between the two communities was over abortion with the
Catholics expressing greater disapproval. It might be added that on such
issues North and South of Ireland are at one in reflecting a greater faithful-
ness to traditional Christian precepts and the strength of the Churches.

These shared attitudes and aspects of identity of the Northern Ireland
communities were reasonably well known before the 1990 Social
Attitudes Survey. But this confirmation is important if the issues which do
divide the people of Northern Ireland are to be understood properly.
These are matters of Church and State, religion and politics.

[1] John Whyte, *Interpreting Northern Ireland*, Clarendon Press, Oxford, 1990, p. 17.
[2] Buckley, quoted in *ibid* p. 15.
[3] J. Curtis and T. Gallagher, 'The Northern Ireland Dimension' in R. Jowell, S. Wither-
spoon and L. Brook (eds), *British Social Attitudes, the Seventh Report*, 1990/91 Edition,
Gower, Chapter 9.

70

The facts of religion and politics

First the facts about religious practice. The 1990 Report on British Social Attitudes confirms that religion matters to a far greater extent than in Britain or the rest of Europe. Northern Ireland is the most religious part of the United Kingdom and is comparable to the rest of the island of Ireland in religious observance. In the survey only 12 per cent of the population describe themselves as having no religion compared with 34 per cent in Britain. The Presbyterians are the largest Protestant denomination (23 per cent) with Anglicans next (18 per cent) and other Protestants 8 per cent. Catholics constitute 36 per cent of the population. Over 50 per cent of the population claim to attend church once a week compared with just 12 per cent in Britain. In denominational terms the weekly church attendance figures represent 44 per cent of Protestants and 86 per cent of Catholics.

The 1990 Social Attitudes survey confirms the consistent pattern of several decades of polling political attitudes in the province. There is a fundamental divide between the majority and the minority community and a high correlation between perceived national identity and attitude towards the constitutional position of Northern Ireland.

When asked about their preferred political future for Northern Ireland, only 3 per cent of Protestants supported reunification as against 56 per cent of Catholics. As has been found in earlier surveys, the Protestant population is much more adamant about rejecting a united Ireland than are Catholics in support of it. Thus a bare majority of Catholics support unification and overall two-thirds of the population prefer to remain in the United Kingdom.

Party identification mirrors these preferences. The 1990 survey did not reveal a single Protestant respondent who supported the SDLP, not to mention Sinn Fein. Only a handful of Catholic respondents supported the Unionist parties. Apart from the small cross-sectarian Alliance Party voting is within two blocs, Nationalist and Unionist and competition for votes between the parties occurs within those blocs not between them.

When asked, to describe national identity, 66 per cent of Protestants described themselves as 'British', a further 27 per cent described themselves as 'Ulster' or 'Northern Irish'. Four per cent only described themselves as 'Irish'. In 1968 Richard Rose found 20 per cent of Protestants describing themselves as Irish.[4] The 1990 survey confirms the evidence of studies in the 1970s and 1980s, that as the Troubles have persisted more and more Protestants claim British identity.

The evidence is clear that the Unionist population, however alienated at present from Westminster, retains a fundamental belief in the Union—the

[4] Richard Rose, *Governing Without Consensus: An Irish Perspective*, Faber and Faber, 1971, p. 208.

1688 Settlement of a Protestant Crown in Parliament (that very formula that so enrages Scottish and Welsh nationalists). Their political commitment is to an indefinite link with the British state. Their political leadership in the two unionist political parties, the Ulster Unionist Party and the Democratic Unionist Party, is divided over the best way to ensure that, whether through a restoration of devolved government at Stormont or through integration with Britain. In the 1987 Westminster elections the UUP took 37.8 per cent of the vote and the DUP 11.7 per cent.

The British Social Attitudes study also confirms the identity of the majority of Catholics as Irish—60 per cent so described themselves, only 2 per cent described themselves as 'Ulster'; 25 per cent termed themselves 'Northern Irish', and 10 per cent described themselves as 'British'. The Nationalist population is more complex because while its identity is not in doubt in terms of being Irish, it is divided over the issue of allegiance. Consistent polling over the years has demonstrated that the majority do not now consider the present Irish state as their state. The Social Attitudes survey shows that a significant percentage accept the present status of Northern Ireland as part of the United Kingdom. Not surprisingly there is no support for a return to a Unionist dominated Stormont government. But the majority and an increasing percentage as expressed in voting behaviour offer support for a united Ireland.[5] What divides the Nationalist community and their main political parties, the SDLP and Sinn Fein, is how the ideal of a united Ireland is to be achieved. Provisional Sinn Fein and its military counterpart the IRA belief that it must be forced through armed struggle and consider themselves as the successors to the revolutionaries who declared an independent republic in 1916. Support for Sinn Fein comes from the Catholic working-class constituencies of Belfast and Derry and from the small farmers West of the Bann. The SDLP stands for constitutional nationalism, the achievement of a united Ireland by consent. SDLP support is from broadly the middle-class voters west of the Bann and the over thirties. In the 1987 Westminster elections the SDLP won 21.1 per cent of the votes compared with 11.4 for Sinn Fein.

Religious or political conflict?

What is to be made of these consistent facets of identity and political allegiance is the subject of the considerable scholarly literature of the Troubles so admirably summarised in John Whyte's *Interpreting Northern Ireland*. It should come as no surprise that there is no consensus, particularly over whether the causes of conflict are religious or political. This writer's position is that it remains at heart a political conflict with a religious dimension. Religious denominations, Protestant and Catholic, are found throughout the United Kingdom and there are significant

---

[5] Brendan O'Leary provides a detailed survey of trends in voting in Northern Ireland over the decades 1969 to 1989 in *Fortnight*, Nos. 281, 298, February, March 1990.

differences between them in social and other attitudes. They are not now divided, however, by the question of national identity. Religion everywhere on these islands has influenced and shaped the different national identities. In Northern Ireland the two identities reflect the influences of different churches but are not a product of the doctrinal differences between the churches.

Yet religious differences do contribute to communal division. They exacerbate the underlying political conflict. Militant Protestantism, such as expressed through the tenets of the Reverend Ian Paisley's Free Presbyterian Church and the insistence of the Roman Catholic Church on maintaining separate schooling create social distance and radically, reduces opportunity for cross-community contact and dialogue. One of the most positive policies emanating from the Northern Ireland Office in recent years has been direct support and encouragement for integrated schooling. But significant change in educating young people together will take a long time. The 1990 Social survey found that 71 per cent of schools in the Province are either wholly Catholic or Protestant in ethos. There are many governmental and non-governmental forces working to advance mutual understanding and awareness of each community's cultural traditions. The churches, with the significant exception of the Free Presbyterians, constantly promote interfaith dialogue. But this important work North and South of the border cannot dissolve a conflict which is structural rather than personal.

The Northern Ireland situation therefore is not the fault of religion. There are for all practical purposes two national communities and the problem is how they are to be reconciled. On the argument advanced here the primary responsibility for finding a new accommodation lies with the two governments and states, Irish and British. The tensions and division that have wracked Northern Ireland since its creation have come about because of the failure of the British state to integrate these islands and as a result of the struggle of the Irish nationalist movement to secure its identity through the separation of the islands. Northern Ireland is the constitutional fault line left by the history of English efforts to dominate the islands and the choice made by Irish nationalism to pursue separatism before unity.

A second point is that a solution cannot be constructed with the building materials of the past, within the outmoded structures of the nation state with its exclusive claims to allegiance and to territory. Neither community in Northern Ireland can be coerced or cajoled into abandoning identity in the interest of obsolete theories of national sovereignty and independence. That is the lesson of Northern Ireland's past.

The creation of Northern Ireland

Northern Ireland is constantly introduced as an integral part of the United Kingdom. In fact it never has been, but whether from guilt or indifference the constitutional myth is rarely challenged. Northern Ireland came into existence as the residual part of a Home Rule deal for Ireland forced from a reluctant British state still defined as the heart of an empire. The struggle for Home Rule for Ireland in the 1880s and into this century was marked by fulminations and division over the threat to the integrity of Empire, the Union under the Crown and the challenge to parliamentary sovereignty of a self-governing Ireland.

The frustration of Home Rule demands over decades for the Irish majority fuelled the Easter Rising of 1916 and the military struggle that led to the negotiation of a dominion-style separatism for the Twenty-Six Counties. Ireland then by the 1920s was a combination of two constitutional structures: a dominion in the South and a 'Home Rule' parliament in the North which was in theory subordinate to Westminster.

The truth is that once the internal battle in Britain over Irish separation was won, Ireland moved off the constitutional agenda. Little distinction was drawn between the dominion, the Irish Free State and Northern Ireland. Northern Ireland disappeared from parliamentary and public concern and was left to its own devices until the events that led to re-involvement in 1969. The majority community and its Unionist government predictably set about securing itself in power and suppressing the minority community and its identity. The story of exclusion and discrimination against the minority needs no repetition. The important point to emphasise is that Britain acquiesced in the peculiar form of Protestant Ascendancy to which the minority community was subjected until it revolted in 1968. The Civil Rights Movement was essentially about the rejection of that subordination by the Catholic community. Britain's initial and reluctant reentry into the province with troops in 1969 quickly took a disastrous turn when the imperative of restoring order was pursued to the point that the Nationalist community became convinced that the soldiers were there to restore Unionist hegemony. The resistance turned to violence and saw the reemergence of the moribund IRA with the consequences with which we all now live.

Statehood in the South

If London had for over half a century ignored the minority identity in Northern Ireland, it is equally true that governments and people in the South consistently failed to come to terms with the authenticity of the Unionist's position. While in the Anglo-Irish Agreement of 1925 the Irish Free State had recognised the boundary between North and South, it was a reluctant acceptance. But successive governments failed to pursue policies that might have led to new possibilities of reconciling the two parts of the country. While the desire to assert a separate identity for the state after centuries of English domination was understandable, the effects of policies of Gaelicisation and rejection of British symbols reinforced the gulf between North and South. The assertion of the Catholic Church's power over public affairs, in particular education, equally served to reaffirm for Northern Protestants the foreigness of the Southern state. Seen through Northern Unionist eyes the Irish state has failed to achieve a separation of church and state despite the constitutional pledge to that effect. The adoption in 1937 of a constitution which incorporated a territorial claim to the counties of Northern Ireland was particularly damaging. Over the years the Republic's claim to the North was, in the eyes of the Protestant majority, interpreted as an assertion of the illegitimacy of its institutions and a justification of the IRA's campaign to overthrow those institutions, whatever denials to the contrary came from Dublin. At a minimum the combination of an explicitly Catholic ethos of the state with an assertion of jurisdiction over the North heightened tension within Northern Ireland; and it also reinforced the extreme Protestant character of many of those who exercised power in Northern Ireland, especially power over the life of the Catholic community.

The decision finally to leave the Commonwealth and declare a Republic in 1948 were legitimate exercises of sovereignty; but the costs in terms of the state's objective of Irish unity were ignored. Britain's response to the decision to declare a republic was to ignore equally the true nature of Northern Ireland. The Ireland Act of 1949 declared that Northern Ireland would remain part of His Majesty's Dominions until a majority wished otherwise. But the majority meant the Unionist community; there was no comfort for the minority in that claim to sovereignty.

The Anglo-Irish Agreement

The recognition that the Northern Ireland problem had these external dimensions dates from the 1980 Thatcher–Haughey Dublin summit which gave birth to the concept of 'the totality of relations on these islands', a concept which continues to have potential. The explorations of those relations by officials from both countries led to the signing of the Anglo-Irish Agreement on November 15, 1985. Regrettably misnamed (it ought to have been the British-Irish Agreement), it nevertheless was a watershed in the complex and bitter 800 years of entanglement of the cultures and political systems on these islands.

Its principal achievement has been to recognise the Northern Ireland problem as a problem for both islands and their mutual history, not simply an internal religious conflict. The Agreement expresses the central fact that the province is composed of two communities, one British and one Irish. The objective of the policy of both governments is to lay to rest the conflicting claims of the two countries to Northern Ireland by recognising both the British and Irish traditions in Northern Ireland and thus in Ireland as a whole. In the role created for the Irish government within Northern Ireland on behalf of the Nationalist minority the accord breaks with the constraints of exclusive sovereignty in favour of the first steps

75

towards the recognition of the reality of interdependence that results from the interwoven historical fabric of these islands.

There is a formal acceptance by Ireland that Northern Ireland's status is to be determined by the wishes of a majority within Northern Ireland and that a majority wish its current status as a part of the United Kingdom to be maintained. The agreement eschews radical constitutional change. By making express provision for Irish unification only by consent of the majority of people in Northern Ireland the agreement effectively rules out any form of unification as an immediate option. By providing expressly for devolution on a basis acceptable to both communities in Northern Ireland and for consultation with the Irish government pending agreement on devolution, it effectively rules out the integration of Northern Ireland with the rest of the United Kingdom. By restricting self-determination for the people of Northern Ireland to a choice between remaining part of the United Kingdom or joining a united Ireland, it effectively rules out any form of independence; and by making no provision for any revision of the existing boundaries of Northern Ireland it effectively rules out repartition.

The agreement's critics can and do point to its failure to make an impact on the political violence and to the massive scale of Unionist rejection it engendered, which has to date paralysed political movement within the province. At the time of writing there is still a prospect that the protracted efforts of the Secretary of State to open talks between the Northern Ireland political parties and the two governments may prove successful. The search for a new accommodation between the two populations has been and continues to be frustrated by the resistance of the Unionist community to change and the virulence of the IRA campaign. But even should these talks fail, the premises of the agreement will continue. It is a long-term document and will have long-term effects.

Deepening relationships

What needs to happen now outside of the theatre of Northern Ireland is the consideration of how the further deepening of relationships between these islands as a whole can proceed. Nothing could be more important if the tensions within Northern Ireland are to be reduced. As suggested at the outset, constitutional reform in both Britain and Ireland can prove to be part of that process.

The agenda of such as Charter 88, a written constitution and a Bill of Rights, with new relationships between the traditionally dominant nation or culture, England, and the hitherto subordinate entities of Wales and Scotland, has significance for Northern Ireland. For its challenge to English dominance has deep symbolic significance in both parts of the Irish island. A subject not on the agenda of Charter 88, but which could figure in constitutional discussion, is the ending of the particular forms of links between Church and State in England. That has also a resonance in Northern Irleand if not on the whole island.

On the other great end of constitutional renewal, the recovery of individual rights and freedoms, Northern Ireland both stands to gain and provides a salutary lesson of the consequences of their neglect. The greatest indictment of the complacency of British theory towards the substance of democracy and the protection of human rights is to be found today on the streets of Belfast. There is little to commend a system that was transplanted to Stormont from Westminster, that put all faith in a sovereign parliamentary institution in the province, when only one party, that of the majority population, ever had a chance of winning control of it; and a system, moreover, where no entrenched safeguards were left in law or the courts for the excluded minority community.

As has been stressed, however, Northern Ireland is a place of divided identities. Change south of the border therefore is as important to prospects of a peaceful future as change across the water. Internal debate now under way on constitutional reform in the Irish state, the agenda of such as the New Consensus Group, which seeks to abandon the territorial claim on Northern Ireland and to construct a more pluralist society, specifically the full separation of church and state, equally hold promise for Northern Ireland. There is increasing understanding in the South that a united country can take many forms, primarily as expressed in the actual relations of its people; and that as an objective any form of unity has to be consciously worked for, not asserted as a claim of right to be somehow restored. It is the latter concept of a united Ireland that the Provisionals insist on and it is bankrupt.

A new integration

The undoubted reality of this era, the interdependence of the countries, needs to be looked at again through its current and rapidly evolving European expression. This could lead us to envisage new institutional relationships which could provide further bonds to the common cultural heritage of all who live on this Atlantic boundary of Europe. Such structures can evolve from the foundation of the Anglo-Irish Accord. An example is the recently created Parliamentary Assembly, linking Westminster and the Oireachtas. This is also perversely misnamed as the Anglo-Irish Assembly. If devolved or national parliaments are established in Scotland and Wales and hopefully Northern Ireland, then such bodies should equally participate. But in any event the different cultures in Britain should explore ways of establishing independent relationships with the two parts of the island of Ireland, as equally should both parts of Ireland with them. The purpose is not to restore the British Isles as a state or to recreate relationships which reflected English hegemony, but to find a new formula which clearly reflects the historic common sources of identity. The new developments in Europe should prove to be a catalyst for integration on new terms of equality.

KEVIN BOYLE

The European opportunity

An impact of the European Community on the Northern Ireland situation has been long expected, ever since joint membership of Ireland and Britain in 1973. But it has hardly been obvious to date even with the imminence of the single market in 1992. Yet the pace has suddenly quickened. The extraordinary developments across the wider Europe and the Soviet Union since 1989 have intensified the integrating forces within the EC. In December 1990 in Rome, Mr Major and Mr Haughey approved on behalf of both countries the outline framework of the Conference on European Political Union. The emergence over the 1990s of a supra-national political structure in the Community, however unclear its final shape and powers at this point may be, is now certain. Earlier in the same December, Mrs Thatcher and the Irish Taoiseach signed the historic affirmation of the fundamental change resulting from the end of the Cold War, the Paris Charter for a New Europe. This enshrines the concept of Europe as a continent to which the security and prosperity of both islands is linked in notions of solidarity rather than independence.

A new concept of the integration of the peoples and states on these offshore European islands on conditions of equality, impelled by these wider radical developments, augers well for a less destructive future for Northern Ireland and therefore for these islands as a whole. Separatism, as expressed in the Unionism and the Nationalism which partitioned Ireland and created a gulf between the state of Ireland and Britain, is obsolete. Dominance and the subordination of the cultures of these islands by England is equally obsolete. What can replace them is the concept of a European citizenship with allegiance distributed between region, country and Europe. Such developments, for example, could allow for the development of a more inclusive sense of Irishness to embrace the Northern Unionist.[6] The emancipation of the four nations and cultures of the islands from the strait jacket of national sovereignty and exclusive national identities, expressed in exclusive and hostile territorial arrangements, should be the goal for the decade of the 1990s.

The objection may be made that nothing has been said about the violence. But the continued pursuit of political goals by violence will be finally brought to an end by people and people are mobilised by ideas. The ideas for constitutional renewal in Britain and Ireland and the ideas being exchanged in the Europe of the Community and the wider Europe offer real stimulus for radical change within and between these islands. We should grasp the opportunity.

---

[6] Roy F. Foster, 'Varieties of Irishness' in M. Crozier (ed), *Cultural Traditions in Northern Ireland*, Institute of Irish Studies, Queens University, Belfast, 1989, p. 20.

78

IRELAND: IDENTITY AND RELATIONSHIPS

JOHN A. MURPHY*

THE Republic represents that part of Ireland which has long since forsaken the bosom of the Ukanian family to set up house on its own. It has an obvious interest in any future political change affecting Northern Ireland but otherwise its immediate contribution to the general discussion about the constitutional future of 'these islands' can be only that of a friendly (for the most part) neighbour. 'These islands' is an ingenious Irishism intended to avoid the supposedly objectionable imperial connotations of 'British Isles'. Yet much of Irish heritage and identity *is* British, however unpalatable this may be to doctrinaire Irish-Irelanders. That being said, 'Irishness' today has been largely shaped by the experience of independence over seventy years, by the State itself and its institutions.

The ceaseless debate about the nature of Irish identity keeps numerous summer schools in business. A great deal of social diversion characterises these schools—the wags say that at the Yeats School students drink between lectures whereas at the Merriman School they lecture between drinks—and given the requisite stamina and finance, one need not walk on dry land from May to October. The schools reflect, nevertheless, a genuine intellectual and cultural preoccupation with identity. This is, I suppose, chiefly an intelligentsia exercise and the plain people of Ireland have more mundane things to worry about.

Independent Ireland is in many ways a state in pursuit of a nation—which is the opposite of, say, nationalist Scotland's case. For one thing, the Northern Ireland conflict makes the Republic's citizens feel that Ireland as a whole is unfinished business. The North is a tragic catalyst of discussion and slow change. Apart from that, the identity debate seems necessary because the identity kits bequeathed to us by nationalist ancestors—and to a large extent reflected in our Constitution—have never really worked and are now seen to be inadequate. Modern Ireland has not realised any of the historic scenarios. The Enlightenment radicals of the 1790s and the romantic nationalists of the 1840s hoped for a union of Irishmen transcending sectarian animosities. Vibrant popular nationalism of the late nineteenth century looked forward to a prosperous and Catholic nation. Gaelic ideologues of a century ago, and the revolutionary generation they inspired, believed that an independent Ireland would undo the

* The author is Emeritus Professor of Irish History, University College, Cork. He is an Independent member of the Irish Senate, representing National University of Ireland graduates. He writes extensively on Irish history and politics with particular reference to Northern Ireland and Anglo-Irish affairs.

cultural conquest and restore not only the Gaelic language but what was often described, with enthusiastic vagueness, as 'the Gaelic order'. Another, if minority, tradition was that of the 'Workers Republic', with its millenial aspirations. Yet a further variation on a theme was Eamon de Valera's invocation of a frugal, rural and Gaelic utopia. In some cases, all these different visions were incongruously combined into one. Modern Ireland, though rather uneasily aware of the grand destinies planned for it, has become something different from all the scenarios, while trailing various remnants and aspirations.

Gaelic and Catholic

The concept of 'Gaelic Ireland', in particular, calls for some comment. Patrick Pearse, the martyred revolutionary of the 1916 Rising and a cult figure down to the 1960s, had urged the creation of an Ireland 'not only free but Gaelic as well'. The Civil War factions (1922–23) professed a common cultural ideology. The primacy of Irish remains a constitutional aspiration and one of the two great national aims of the dominant Fianna Fáil party; some areas of public life retain a cosmetic bilingual gloss; and the Gaelic dimension gives colour and flavour to the lives of many individuals and families. Yet the indigenous Gaelic-speaking communities of the western seaboard have been decimated by emigration and anglicising pressures, and there is not any longer a *natural* Irish-speaking community which might sustain, for example, a living creative literature in Irish. In a word, the revival policy has failed, because of mistaken strategies, political hypocrisy and public apathy—or more fundamentally because it was an impossible project from the start. The failure to attain a national objective, the gap between profession and performance, the element of self-deception and pretence—all this is one explanation of a sense of national malaise, lying behind the endless identity debate.

Perhaps the commonest outside perception of the Republic is that of a strongly Catholic country. In the early decades of the State, when religious belief and practice were remarkably strong, the Catholic aspect of identity was self-consciously proclaimed as the chief distinguishing mark of a country which clearly had not achieved any of its utopias, neither a 'Gaelic order' nor a 'workers republic'. Catholic Ireland, intensifying pre-independence patterns, reached its faith-and-fatherland apotheosis in the Eucharistic Congress of 1932, with the State participating as fervently as the Church.

But Catholic Ireland ain't what it used to be. The monolith of solid belief and practice has fragmented. By continental European standards, church-going still seems extraordinarily active but *à la carte* Catholicism has replaced the former take-it-or-leave-it doctrinal menu. The 96 per cent Roman Catholic population of the Republic now comprises a wide spectrum ranging from the orthodox and devout through the casual half-believers to those who in increasing numbers return themselves in the censuses as having no religion. What bishops have to say still makes news in Ireland but their pronouncements nowadays have more to do with social justice than sexual morality. The heavy-handed authoritarianism of the 1940s and 1950s has disappeared. Links between church and state are loose and discreet. Nineteenth-century European observers were struck by the similarities between Ireland and Poland, two devoutly Catholic countries for whom faith and fatherland were interchangeable. Today, Poland seems unaltered in that respect but time has moved on in Ireland.

It may be asserted that the constitutional referenda of 1983 and 1986 (with large majorities against abortion and divorce, respectively) reveal Ireland to be as conservatively Catholic as ever it was. In fact, much of the objection to abortion was not specifically Catholic, and the proposal to introduce divorce perished on the rocks of taxation and inheritance proposals, not because of any opposition to the principle of divorce, for which there persists surprising (50 per cent +) popular support. That being said, many Irish people combine a liberal approach to individual behaviour with a reluctance to forsake what they believe to be the ancestral ethos.

All in all, it may not be too extreme to describe the Republic as post-Catholic and post-nationalist. It certainly has shed the xenophobic aversion to 'alien' influences.

Modern Ireland

What has replaced the discarded cultural furniture of the 1920–1960 period? What are the identity features of the Republic of the 1990s and how does it relate to Northern Ireland, Great Britain, the EC, and the world beyond? Before discussing this question, I should note the recent presidential campaign resulting in the election of Mary Robinson. It is too early yet to say whether this has been a catalyst for widespread change in popular attitudes. However, it is instructive to contrast the vision of Ireland ('open, tolerant, inclusive', vibrant, reconciliatory) evoked by President Robinson on her inauguration day, 3 December 1990, with the picture Eamon de Valera sketched of 'the Ireland which we dreamed of' (rural, frugal, Gaelic) in his oft-quoted St Patrick's Day 1943 broadcast. Both speeches are aspirational and visionary, but they reflect certain realities of their respective periods. They give definitions of Ireland which are worlds apart.

What, then, is the personality of modern Ireland which Mary Robinson hopes to mould to her heart's desire? Part of the answer is bleak, since emigration seems to be an integral part of the Irish experience, and poverty and unemployment mar the lives of perhaps one-third of the citizens. Social and family legislation leave much to be desired. Yet the country is experiencing a remarkable renaissance of letters. The Irish continue to make the English language creatively their own. Music, drama and poetry are resurgent. Something of this cultural vitality was evoked in Mary Robinson's presidential campaign, and in her acceptance and inauguration speeches. At a popular level, there are many opportunities for social enjoyment—that distinctive combination of lively conversation, warm companionship and musical expression described as 'crack', a straightforward English word apparently, popular misconceptions notwithstanding! The 'crack' is often good today in small-town Ireland: in terms of a relatively good environment and low population density, Ireland is still a rural country, although its culture and preoccupations are increasingly urban. The personality of the country is also the beauty of the landscape, something made much of by the Irish Tourist Board, though there are those who believe that absolute tourism corrupts absolutely. There are marvellous regional variations, just as there are miraculously preserved local differences of speech and accent in the face of admass pressures, though the colourful and idiomatic Kiltartanese or Hiberno-English of my boyhood has given way to relatively standard English.

The state itself, with its institutions, has been a formative influence on the identity of modern Ireland. In the first place, this means the experience of statehood itself. Only the very old have any significant memories of the days before independence. Independence has meant some achievements and many disappointments, but as with the process of growing up itself there is no going back. The citizens of the Republic are adults, so to speak, flawed perhaps but mature, and they have paid for their independence in more ways than one. In contrast, the people of Northern Ireland, through no fault of their own, have not yet come of age, and the Welsh appear to enjoy identity without responsibility. The Irish experience of managing, or mismanaging, its own finances should cool the ardour of the Scots for fiscal independence, or at least indicate to them the pitfalls to be avoided.

Some surprise was expressed in the course of the recent presidential campaign that the Fine Gael candidate, Mr Austin Currie, TD, Co. Tyrone-born *quondam* Stormont MP and NICRA veteran, should have encountered in the electorate a marked partitionist attitude. On the canvass, the Fine Gael party was often asked why it couldn't have chosen an 'Irishman' as candidate! In fact, the assumed common identity of the Republic's citizens and the North's Catholics is at odds with the divergent histories of the two partitioned areas over seventy years. We should note as well a distinctive Northern identity in the first place, as well as the South's increasing distancing of itself from the Northern conflict.

As Bernard Crick has observed of the British, the Southern Irish have no agreed name for their state. Does a nebulous nomenclature reflect uneasy identity? 'Eire', paradoxically, is seen as a rather patronising Englishism, though constitutionally correct, and is never used by Irish people except when they're speaking Irish. 'The Republic' is coming only slowly into popular speech, being too formal, too controversial or too sacred! The 'Free State' is constitutionally outmoded by fifty years but is used widely by Northerners, most out of colloquial habit, but in the mouths of Provo supports out of contempt. The 'Twenty-Six Counties', geographically correct and politically neutral, is in diminishing use. 'The country' and 'the nation' are popular and journalistic synonyms for the state, though the use of 'the nation' in this sense is deplored by those who regard the nation as co-terminous with the un-united island.

While continuous constitutional debate may reflect a society uneasy with its present state, Irish absorption in political and electoral processes is a central and indispensable mark of our identity, evolving over two centuries. In 1990, as is well-known by now, the Presidency of Ireland unexpectedly became the focus of various aspirations of a society in the process of change. But the real meat of Irish democracy is party politics. Our legal and parliamentary structures are, of course, a British legacy, but we have pioneered the party system and public involvement in elections. The development of popular and populist politics in the United States and Australia, for good *and* ill, was largely an Irish phenomenon. Irish politics at home is given its distinctive character by the intimacy and informality of a small country with a strong rural background. The voters are on familiar terms with their representatives and (unlike the UK and the US, for the most part) can accost them in the flesh as well as watch them on television. Television, of course, has supplanted the chapel gate as the politician's forum and has added immeasurably to the appeal of Irish politics as a great spectator sport.

Popular culture is in large part shared with the rest of the world, particularly the English-speaking world, but there is some considerable distinctiveness in the areas of music and sport. The great and joyous 1960s revival of traditional music shows no sign of slackening off. Despite the rival attractions of other sporting codes, Gaelic football and the ancient and heroic game of hurling maintain their popular appeal. The organisation of these Gaelic Athletic Association games over the last century has heightened the sense of *county* identity and thus nativised a British-imposed administrative division. Fierce county loyalty and fervour were in particular evidence in my native Co. Cork in September 1990, as a unique hurling-football double was achieved in the knock-out All-Ireland (island-wide) championships. Red and white flags proudly fluttered on business and public buildings alongside, or more often instead of, the national tricolour.

The four provinces of Ireland—Munster, Leinster, Connaught and Ulster—are very ancient, if indeed not prehistoric, divisions but (with the obvious exception of those six Ulster counties which comprise Northern Ireland) they have little 'identity' or administrative significance today. They survive mainly as divisions in various sporting codes, as convenient regions in weather forecasting and, curiously, as constituencies of the European Parliament. In early and medieval Ireland there were sub-provincial regions of political significance, and today there survive rich regional sub-cultures but, apart from administrative groupings in areas such as tourism and health boards, the country has no real regional policy. There is half-hearted discussion of badly-needed reform in local government but a marked absence of political will to replace the county-based set-up of 1898. Local government is sickly, incompetent and ill-funded and there is an unhealthy degree of centralised government, the outcome of various administrative developments in pre-independence Ireland. There is a contradiction between the centralised State's hostility to any meaningful regional policy within its own jurisdiction and its insistence that the EC should apply regional policies to the Republic as a peripheral region of the Community. It should also be noted that there is little popular demand for any new departure in the direction of regional devolution.

It has already been emphasised that the personality of modern Ireland has been very much shaped by the state and its institutions. This is particularly true of attitudes to the outside world. History and geography make a worldview imperative, and the state is in a sense defined by its worldview. While the citizens are extremely interested in, and very well informed about, foreign affairs, the public view oscillates between the extremes of perceiving Ireland as having an inordinate global influence and self-deprecatingly regarding it as having no importance whatsoever.

Foreign policy has grown out of, and away from, the earlier preoccupation with Anglo-Irish relations and the isolationist neutrality of World War II. From the 1960s, a positive if modest role in the United Nations combined a certain independent stance with peace-keeping duties in various trouble spots. There was opposition to nuclear proliferation as well as an ex-colonial sense of affinity with the oppressed of Latin-America and the Third World generally. Sitting rather uneasily with this global internationalist stance was the self-enlightened regard and affection for the United States, as well as the new commitments entailed by EC membership and the quickening moves towards European union. By the end of 1990, it remained to be seen whether that certain independence in viewing the world could co-exist much longer with the common foreign policy-making process of the Community, or how Irish 'traditional neutrality' could survive at all under increasing European pressure for a defence union. A nice illustration of these tensions was provided by the Gulf crisis, when relatives of trapped hostages demanded that the government should realise the rhetoric of 'traditional neutrality' and negotiate unilaterally with Saddam Hussein. The government's rather embarrassed response was to stress the need to maintain solidarity with the member states of the Community. However, in the overall perspective, there is a virtual consensus in Irish politics that EC membership has raised the country's profile and enhanced the national identity, especially in the pomp-and-circumstance context of Ireland's tenure of the EC presidency, in the first half of 1990.

Northern Ireland

Nearer home, the Republic's attitude towards Northern Ireland is complex and changing. The basic nationalist assumption in the twenty-six county area used to be that Irish identity was flawed by Partition and would not be made whole until the British-occupied fourth green field, the 'fairest province' (a de Valera phrase) was restored to the motherland. This irredentist position was supported by a strong map-image of an undivided island, a deeply-entrenched historical sense of the right to insular integrity, a plethora of extra-political all-Ireland institutions based on common interests and the presence of a large southward-looking nationalist minority in Northern Ireland, the Republic's Sudetenland, as it were. All this is reflected in the opening articles of the Irish Constitution, adopted in 1937 when nationalist passions were running strong, and resentment over partition intense. The now much-debated Articles 2 and 3 express an unambiguous territorial claim to Northern Ireland.

Irredentist attitudes persisted (no matter how weakly and inter-mittently) up to the 1960s when a new self-confidence took hold in the Republic, resulting in a more relaxed and tolerant attitude towards the North. An all-party constitutional committee recommended that an expression of fraternal aspiration to unity should replace the arrogant territorial demand but the suggestion was not acted upon. With the outbreak of conflict in Northern Ireland in 1969, there was a regression for a time to the old nationalist feelings, and public opinion strongly identified with the beleaguered Catholic kith-and-kin in Derry and Belfast. But from the mid-1970s, an increasingly sober assessment led to a fundamental questioning of the old irredentism. The Republic's citizens were baffled by the deadly sectarian animosities of the North and revolted by terrorist atrocities committed in their name. They were very conscious of the heavy costs of security, declining tourism and lost investment, and they became aware above all of the awesome problem of incorporating a million 'intransigent' Unionists and an ailing Ulster economy into a united Ireland. While some still cherished a lingering unity aspiration they were not prepared to press it in practice, and by the end of 1990 they regarded a peaceful settlement in the North as the imperative rather than all-Ireland territorial unity. Also, this development further confirmed an acceptance that the seventy-year-old state, rather than a notional united Ireland, was the real matrix of identity. Northerners of both persuasions were increas-ingly seen as 'different', if not ungovernable.

The British connection

If South–North relations are much more complex than Irish-American simplicities allow for, so too are West–East or Irish-British attitudes. Here also there is a new script but the old one has not been cast entirely aside. A presumably apocryphal story has it that a former president of Ireland, accepting the credentials of the British Ambassador, referred impishly to the 'chains' that had historically bound Ireland to England. 'Links, sir, links' hissed an alarmed aide. The links at the level of state relationships are firmer and more positive than they have ever been, in spite of, or indeed very much because of, the Northern Ireland troubles. The 1985 Anglo-Irish Agreement may have infuriated some sections of Northern Ireland opinion and disappointed others but it has proved to be the mechanism for a remarkable rapprochement between the two sovereign governments in the British Isles. The establishing of an Anglo-Irish parliamentary tier has also been a great success. Matters are likely to improve further with the departure of Margaret Thatcher who, like a London lady unhappily married a century ago to an Irish aristocrat, 'never quite saw the point of Ireland, really'. One of the difficulties of the relationship is the imbalance in mutual awareness. Britain looms large in the Irish consciousness while the reverse is not the case. This is as much a function of geography as of anything else. Irish people are very familiar with London, and not only *en route* elsewhere, while Prime Minister John Major has not yet, significantly, set foot in Dublin.

Even when peace finally breaks out in Northern Ireland, and Community member-states move ever closer towards union, the Anglo-Irish relationship is likely to remain characterized by tensions arising from history, disparate economies, unequal strengths, cultural and temperamental divergences, and different worldviews. All will never be sweetness and light. We still exhibit the prickly sensitivity of the scarred ex-colonial, and suspect that the British, even our hibernophile friends among them, have a lingering post-imperial tendency to patronise us. I have spoken of two scripts, one not yet quite discarded. Since 1985 in particular, the two sovereign governments are partners in resolutely opposing terrorism and in seeking a political accommodation in the North. Anglophobia in Ireland is now a fitful and intermittent flicker, and only with great difficulty and skilful orchestration can it be made to burn brighter at times of crisis. A trivial incident—a British patrol boat in Irish territorial waters—will suddenly became a violation of Irish sovereignty, or British insensitivity about Irish constitutional procedures will cause Irish editorial writers to affirm vehemently the independence of our courts. (Sovereignty is as much a neurotic preoccupation for Ireland as defence is for Britain, both concepts being equally outdated and illusory.) In such moments, the old script is reached for (Articles 2 and 3 will do), and for a brief while our friendly partner becomes once again our erstwhile enemy and the occupier of our national territory.

Of course, Britain also has two scripts, though one of them may have been Mrs Thatcher's personal possession, and now hopefully forms part of her private papers. (Incidentally, the Iron Lady's English nationalism was extolled by Irish sovereignty enthusiasts who detested her in other respects.) When things are going reasonably well especially in the area of security, the Irish are jolly good chaps, after all, and socially charming, of course. When there are difficulties about extradition, or nationalist lapses at Dublin government level, the image of the feckless, irresponsible if not downright treacherous Irish (as during World War II and the Falklands adventure) is dusted down and suggested rather than made explicit. But mercifully this script, too, enjoys only a brief lease of life. Another interesting inconsistency is that while Britain's role in Northern Ireland is presented as that of honest broker between the warring tribes, royal and government visiting firemen and women invariably give aid and comfort to *their* people, and never to beleaguered nationalists. Many Tories regard Northern Ireland as rightful British territory and vital to British defence requirements. Such people are the mirror image of our nationalist fundamentalists.

Away from government and politics, the Irish public's relations with Britain are obviously close and interlocking at all levels. The anti-British feelings of a fanatical core are certainly not shared by the public at large which is appalled by IRA terrorist atrocities on the 'mainland'. The only negative feelings have to do, not surprisingly, with British security reactions to the Northern conflict. Dormant instincts are aroused by the inconvenience and unpleasantness of the Prevention of Terrorism Act, by the fears that extraditees will be ill-treated, by the anti-Irish nastiness of the British tabloids and above all by the formidable evidence of 'British injustice' where Irish suspects and prisoners are concerned. What is required in all this is not only the reconciliatory redress of injustice but historic statements of goodwill towards Ireland from major British politicians reflecting truly Gladstonian magnanimity.

But let us dwell here on those positive links which enable Irish-British relations to transcend yesterday's difficult history and today's remaining problems. Ireland is in so many ways the beneficiary of British culture, and in turn Irish studies are at last beginning to lift off in Britain. We have inherited the British politico-legal system, though we may work it with an Irish difference. In some respects, Ireland is a regional variant of British linguistic and literary identity. At an everyday level of mixing, Irish people get on extremely well with their neighbours across the Irish Sea, as they must do in their vast emigrant numbers. Compared to the vicious anti-Irish stereotypes of the past, the Irish jokes retailed today by British comedians are benign and innocuous, though the sensitive reaction of the Irish in Britain is understandable, delicately positioned as they often are.

A common popular culture extends to an avid interest in British royal doings (is an exchange of state visits between two women heads all that outlandish an idea?) and in cross-channel soccer. An intriguing and symbolic illustration of the neighbourly relationship was the Republic of Ireland's performance in the World Cup in the summer of 1990. A largely English-born and English-resident team, qualifying as 'Irish' through family and emigrant connections, became the focus of nation-alistic hero-worship extending to the elementally English manager and expressing itself at its most intense when the opposing team was the ancient enemy!

Just as the Protestant—Catholic tension in Northern Ireland needs to be eased in a larger context away from the 'narrow ground', so the Anglo-Irish relationship in turn would greatly benefit from a wider setting. At one time, that might have been provided by the British Commonwealth, but Ireland never really accepted an imposed Commonwealth as an extended family and, understandably but shortsightedly, rejected its potential for friendship and reconciliation. Today the larger family to which we both belong, and which may help to bring us closer and develop further common interests, is the European Community.

Also through the Community, Ireland may discover a land of which she is at present singularly ignorant—Britain of the regions. Throughout this paper, I have used, as Irish people tend to do, the terms English, Anglo and British as interchangeable. There is a large confusion here. Should not the Anglo-Irish Agreement properly be termed the British-Irish Agreement, or perhaps that would have its objectors as well? 'Anglo' may have represented the realities of power more accurately, and by the same reasoning, the Irish should complain about 'English' rather than 'British' injustice.

A concluding reflection

This leads me to a concluding reflection of some relevance to the main-stream concern of the 1990 Coleg Harlech conference. Within the outer circle of the developing Community, the Republic and the North, in whatever constitutional relationship, may rediscover a more geographic-ally natural inner circle—'these islands', the British archipelago. At the moment, the Republic's business with the neighbouring island is almost exclusively transacted with London and the metropolitan south-east. This applies to political developments, financial dealings, news coverage and even, to a large extent, emigration. Apart from some Celtic fringe contacts, the Republic is largely unaware of regional aspirations in Britain, partly because of the continuing preoccupation with the London—Belfast—Dublin triangle. It is commonplace to remark that too many British people have no contact with Ireland, but it is less often noted that nationalist obsessions and the Northern question have prevented the Irish from exploring Britain in all its varieties of nation and region. Some years ago the interesting concept of IONA (Islands of the North Atlantic) was mooted. Despite the alluring association of the acronym with Colmcille, the Irish evinced little enthusiasm for the idea, because it came from a Unionist source and was therefore suspect, and also because of chronic sovereignty neurosis. All may be soon changed utterly with the diminution of national sovereignties, the rapid pace of EC integration, the corresponding emphasis on regional development, and the simmering constitutional debate in the United Kingdom. In future Coleg Harlech conferences on national identities, the Republic's 'friendly neighbour' role may be replaced by that of vitally involved participant.

THE ENGLISH AND THE BRITISH

BERNARD CRICK*

As I HAVE said before, I am a citizen of a country with no agreed colloquial name.[1] Its official name is the most rarely used. The Central Office of Information publishes a useful annual with a big overseas circulation amazingly called (if one ever thinks about it) '*Britain*' – a province of the late Roman Empire. And the Preface admits a difficulty:

> Care should be taken when studying British statistics to note whether they refer to England, to England and Wales ..., to Great Britain, which comprises England, Wales and Scotland, or to the United Kingdom (which is the same as Britain, that is Great Britain and Northern Ireland) as a whole.

But is 'Britain' usually used as 'the same as' the United Kingdom as a whole? When I say 'Britain' I mean the mainland and deliberately say 'Great Britain' to include Northern Ireland. In the OED early usages of 'Britain' refer to the island. Its summary of early modern usage is unusually confused: 'The proper name of the whole island, containing England, Wales and Scotland, with their dependencies; more fully called Great Britain; now used for the British state or Empire as a whole' – perhaps they simply forgot (as is so helpful to do) about Northern Ireland; or is it one of the 'dependencies'? The CIO is surely wrong and the OED confused or evasive. And so, most of the time, are most of the English.

The term 'Britain' only became used for the Kingdom of England in Tudor times, partly to cement the Arthurian myth of the new dynasty and partly, as the great Queen grew old, to build a bridge to her heir. He was proclaimed as James VI of Scotland and 'James I, King of Great Britain', king of two realms, not one, although one had changed its name.[2] The same formula was used in the text of the Act of Union of 1707; and throughout the eighteenth century ministerial writers made unsuccessful attempts to establish as colloquial useage 'North British' and 'South British', as if the English and Scottish nations had gone out of business. There was a brief attempt, amid facetious derision, to call all kinds of Irish 'West Britons'.

English statesmen finally hit on a better tactic to close the old back door,

---

* The author is Emeritus Professor of Politics, Birbeck College, London, Honorary Fellow, University of Edinburgh, and author of *In Defence of Politics*, *George Orwell: a Life*, and *Essays on Politics and Literature* etc. He is also a past editor and current chairman of the editorial board of *The Political Quarterly*.

[1] 'An Englishman Considers his Passport', *The Irish Review*, Autumn 1988.
[2] Brian P. Levack, *The Formation of the British State: England, Scotland and the Union 1603–1707*, Clarendon, Oxford: 1987, pp. 1–8.

THE ENGLISH AND THE BRITISH

not political and cultural integration but a state-fostered cult of a depoliticized Scottish identity: the 1822 state visit of George IV to Edinburgh, commissioned by the cabinet, orchestrated by Sir Walter Scott himself (the clans were reborn – or invented – as Unionists).[3] And Melbourne encouraged the young Queen to visit Scotland, not at all for her health. Luckily she liked it. Her children wore plaid just as children of Viceroys of Ireland were to wear the green. Many of the old English Tories had a clear and politic sense of the diversity of the United Kingdom. In India too they came to practise a politics of cultural tolerance, not assimilation; indirect rule, not administrative centralism as in the Spanish and French empires. Unlike the new breed of self-made men and women, they had some sense of history; and, unlike most socialists, a sense that discontinuities between sociology and government were possible, given political will and skill. They took for granted that the main business of domestic politics was the conciliation of Scotland and Ireland (the idea that Wales was any threat to the unity of the United Kingdom came much later), was holding the United Kingdom or 'Britain' together. They were ruthless in maintaining English political dominance; but, on the whole, let numbers, wealth and territorial advantage take care of that. They had little desire for cultural hegemony, and they viewed Scottish and Irish culture either with a cynical tolerance or with a romantic attraction. It was Tory administrators on the ground who defended native customs against the rationalizing, liberal zeal of the Benthamites in the East India Company's offices.[4] Also the English aristocracy were acceptive of Scots and Irish with talent and manners getting a share of the patronage. The empire was useful in that respect, and the reformed civil service.

Englishness

The sense of identity of the English is almost as difficult to specify as the name of the state. Perhaps the minimum definition of a nation is a group who think they have the same general characteristics. The difficulties begin when one looks for actual characteristics. It is actually easier for the other nations in the British Isles. There are objective differentiators: in Ireland and Wales religion and language; in Scotland a national history. But there is also, to varying degrees, a helpfully integrative anti-Englishness; or at least a pleasing consciousness of being different from the English.

In all this symposium, the most elusive thing is Englishness itself. Other contributors hint (elsewhere shout) that it is all bad, shouldn't exist or at

[3] Hugh Trevor-Roper, 'The Highland Tradition of Scotland', in Eric Hobsbawm and Terence Ranger, eds., *The Invention of Tradition*, Cambridge University Press: 1983; and John Prebble, *The King's Jaunt*, Collins, London: 1988.

[4] E. T. Stokes, *The English Utilitarians and India*, Oxford University Press, 1959.

BERNARD CRICK

best that the English are imperceptive of the finest qualities of the others. I think the modern English are often imperceptive. But non-abusive discussions of Englishness are rare. And what is even more odd, they are hard to find among the English. The test is bibliographic. Look at the subject catalogue in any major library under 'nationalism'. One will discover references to shelves of books on nationalism, whether analytical, polemical and celebratory, under American, French, German, Italian, etc., and certainly Irish, Welsh and Scottish, but often none, or astoundingly few, under 'English'. Perhaps a handful of right rubbish written for the Public School prize-giving market of a generation ago.[5] Every year some books of merit appear on what it is to be Scottish and Irish (dozens still on de Crevecoeur's vintage question, 'what then is this American?'), but only a handful of serious reflections on Englishness by Englishmen. Admittedly many novels explore variants of Englishness; but serious studies under 'non-fiction' are few.

Why this dearth? One can pluck from the air conservatively English traits of understatement, taking things for granted, distrust of theory and explicitness, once-upon-a-time a calm contentment that needed no words, and euphemism and suppression; and all those characters in V. S. Pritchett's short stories who never finish sentences, the cult of the social hanging participle. But such explanations are circular. A better one may be political, as I have already hinted: that the old governing class knew that the main business of politics was holding the United Kingdom together. And once, for whatever reasons, the tactic was adopted of tolerating, even stimulating, national cultural identities (so long as state power was not challenged), then it would follow that any deliberate cultivation by the English (as happened everywhere else in nineteenth century Europe) of a cult of nationalism would be disruptive.

As Burke had argued over the American question, the preservation of power most often involves restraint of power: sovereignty must be tempered by prudence and magnanimity. What even a Boston Anglophile (A. L. Lowell) was to call 'a certain condescension in the English' often caused offence, but historians, statesmen and publicists by and large tried not to make matters worse. Of course, there were notorious exceptions – the Victorian cartoon character, Ally Sloper, loathed, like Alf Garnett, all foreigners including Scots and Irish; but the evidence of bibliography is clear. And there is another and a related explanation: imperialism became the substitute English nationalism, and the cult of service (and spoils) in Empire was something that could be shared and was shared among the other nations; not merely shared but celebrated in song and story. The Empire was not simply Cobbett's 'system of outdoor-relief for the indigent sons of English aristocracy'. Think how so many of Kipling's imperial tales include figures from each of the four nations (however hierarchically at times). It was the *British* Empire.

[5] Please enter your own references to taste.

THE ENGLISH AND THE BRITISH

This political explanation fits a common stereotype of Englishness: *tolerance*. It is not an attribution at all common before the eighteenth century, but then seemed part and parcel of a consciously sought new era of political stability. 'Fundamentals are dangerous: there are some issues in life which are better left sleeping', said George Savile in *The Character of a Trimmer*, 'we will raise only the issues on which we may disagree without imperilling our country; and even on them we will disagree with buttons on the foils'. Toleration is to be taken seriously, warts and all. After all, it was pursued as policy of state after 1688 and as an Anglican theology of latitudinarianism, trimming between Romanism and Calvinism (the Aristotelian *via media*, I mean, as advocated long before by the judicious Hooker). Protestant toleration still involved discrimination against Roman Catholics, but the motives were mainly political; all things in history are relative and all toleration has limits. Voltaire's image of the tolerant English had another side to the coin, *Albion perfide*. That could almost be a summary of the mental attributes needed to hold the new United Kingdom together: on the one hand, toleration; but on the other Machiavellian guile or force against any threat to the unity of the kingdom, perceived as order itself. Hence there was not merely the defeat of a bold, lucky but hopeless foray in 1745, but the savage destruction of the clan system that had made it possible.

Certainly Englishness is to be found more in the specific circumstances of her history, like the reaction to the fear of renewed civil war in both England and Scotland in the 1688 to 1707 generation, than in the 'this sceptred isle' school of thought. Lord Blake's *English World* is a coffee-table book, but a superior one with real matter in it. Yet he says in his Introduction:

> England's coastline has helped to shape both the history of the English nation and psychology of the English character . . . The long centuries during which the land was free from invaders meant that there could be a continuity of tradition impossible on the war-torn continent. . . . Some characteristics on which both natives and visitors have tended to agree have to do with national psychology; egoism, self-confidence, intolerance of outsiders, ostentatious wealth, social mobility, love of comfort and a strong belief in private property. . . . We come back to the cliché that Britain is an island, a fact that has been subtly decisive in so many aspects of her history.[6]

Notice that he suddenly becomes aware that 'England's coastline' has the slight hiatus of Wales and Scotland, so while the sense of his argument cries out for John of Gaunt's 'England, bound in with the triumphant sea', yet even though he is an English historian and not a geographer he has to

---

[6] Robert Blake, ed., *The English World: History, Character and People*, Thames and Hudson, London: 1982, p. 25. Sir Ernest Barker's symposium, *The Character of England*, Clarendon, Oxford: 1947 is interesting, but no contributor discusses the 'British' dimension or sees any interaction with 'the others', also the flaw of Gerald Newman's otherwise excellent *The Rise of English Nationalism: A Cultural History*, 1740–1830, Weidenfeld, London: 1987.

say, on sad point of fact, '*Britain* is an island'. Having gone so far he might
have noted that before 1688, and spasmodically afterwards, the Celtic
periphery was often as 'war-torn' as the continent (some connection with
English history?). And more 'subtly' (if he were as subtle as Hugh
Kearney), he would see that the land was not always free of invaders (don't
Scottish, Welsh and royal armies recruited in Ireland count?); and that 'the
continuity of tradition' began in times when neither modern borders
nor modern configurations of nationality were applicable; and that at all
times then and since the intermingling of the people of these islands, their
interaction with each other, culturally, socially, economically and
militarily, is far, far greater than his (I dare to say) somewhat Little
Englander account allows.

Any deep exploration of Englishness must begin by seeing it as a
relationship.[7] There is the familiar protest literature of English intrusion,
oppression or 'the Englishing of Scotland'. But there is very little that
acknowledges frankly the benign effect of the common English language;
just as from English thinkers and writers there is little reflection on how
much that we call English is a product of dealings with the other peoples.

Nonetheless, and here I agree with Lord Blake, a 'strong sense of
individualism' is remarkable. Alan Macfarlane in his important *The
Origins of English Individualism* (1978) sees its roots far earlier than the
capitalist market, as Weber, Tawney or C. P. Macpherson had all argued.
He sees it in the absence, compared to continental Europe, of a peasant
class in the early middle ages, so that even rural society from at least the
thirteenth century was remarkably more of a money than a service
economy, more mobile and more individualistic, less tied to family and
clan. His account of the relative mobility of social class ties in with
Namier's famous perception that England at the accession of George III
was a highly class conscious country, indeed, but one with a quite unusual
and almost infinite gradation of social classes, through which people could
rise or fall almost imperceptibly. And Tocqueville saw in the English
concept of 'the gentleman' a bridge between bourgeois and aristocrat
lacking in France.

The cult of 'the gentleman' would repay serious study. It was an English
product and much emulated. It encapsulated many clichés about the
English character: love of property but respect for persons; a certain
savoir faire going with no great intellectuality; wanting to know what's
going on but distrust of ideas and of aesthetic (as much as of religious)
enthusiasm; a love of style but a dislike of ostentation; a refusal to let
experts decide but willingness to take advice; a certain respect for
amateurishness; a love of leisure and sport and thus a limited capacity for

---

[7] As Philip Dodd put it: 'the definition of the English is inseparable from that of the non-English; Englishness is not so much a category as a relationship', in Robert Colls and Philip Dodd, eds, *Englishness: Politics and Culture 1880–1920* Croom Helm, Beckenham: 1986, p. 12.

sustained work; a cult of good manners – which, after all, has implications for the parliament house not simply the private house; a social tolerance of the upwardly mobile from trade or industry, but aversion to any obsessive commitment to making money; not to forget, something genuinely and oddly English, a belief that a good life moves back and forth from town to country, country to town;' and from all this a conscious cultivation of a somewhat conformist code of behaviour, but resulting in a self-satisfied inner-security that allows for a great deal of cynical toleration of eccentricity or even of verbally threatening behaviour. However odd this seems to nationalists today, the cult of the English gentleman had a great integrative or restraining effect (depending on one's viewpoint) on the actual and potential leadership elites of the other three nations. But it had a profoundly negative effect on both entrepreneurial spirit and on positive citizenship – it marginalized any putative republican tradition of citizenship in England in marked contrast to Scotland and Ireland.

Orwell's bold attempt to characterise Englishness in *The Lion and the Unicorn* and in *The English People* deserves attention. He sees not the gentry but the lower-middle class as the backbone of an England which, if he sentimentalises it at times, he asserts that he has every right to care for and love as much as Welsh, Scottish and Irish celebrate their countries. And he has no easy answers for what he dislikes in it. He blames these on the English themselves: their snobbishness, the conceit and constraint of class, the greed of the rich – the famous image, 'a family with the wrong members in control'. He cannot take the easy path out of the other nations' intellectuals; to amend Yeats, 'whatever wrongs this country's got the English brought to pass'.

Some of Orwell's insights are eroded by time: 'the gentleness of English civilisation is perhaps its most marked characteristic. You notice it the instant you set foot on English soil. It is a land where the bus-conductors are good-tempered and the policemen carry no revolvers'. And some were truer of the masses than of the classes: 'the English hatred of war and militarism . . . the songs the soldiers made up and sang of their own accord were not vengeful but humorous and mock-defeatist. The only enemy they ever named was the sergeant major'. Orwell assumed a communal fellow-feeling or an habitual fraternal morality, 'common decency', in the lower-middle class and the working class (his 'common man' was close to Kant's and Jefferson's); whereas he thought that the morality of the upper-classes had become degraded by a purely competitive individualism. But his common man's morality may well have been attrited by ten year's of Thatcherite bombardment in the popular press. Yet his picture of the '*privateness* of English life' still rings true: 'all the culture that is more truly native centres around things which even when they are communal are not official – the pub, the football match, the back garden, the fireside and the 'nice cup of tea''. Orwell's celebration of ordinary, commonplace objects, much like H. G. Wells in his early novels (the observations on the proles in *Nineteen Eight-Four* echo the great description of the bar and of 'the plump woman' in Wells' *Mr Polly*), these show in secular form a kind of Puritan pietism. The ordinary is sacred, whether it is a well-laid brick or a blade of grass: a certain attitude of reverence to nature.

Orwell failed to see that the English character might be affected by, or even itself affect, the other national identities. But in 'Notes on Nationalism' (1944) he made an important distinction between patriotism and nationalism. Patriotism is simply a love of familiar institutions and one's own native land, so that anyone who grows up with these values or beliefs, or adopts them as an immigrant, can be a patriot. Nationalism, however, is the belief that one's country or culture is superior to others. The distinction is useful, even if we use different words to make it or want to use 'nationalism' with qualifying adjectives to cover both cases. At least it could lead one to say that patriotism is natural and as such harmless (unlike too many English Left-wing intellectuals who are suckers for everyone else's nationalism while either denying their own obvious Englishness or enjoying rich guilt about it); and also to say that while nations, like persons, are plainly not equal by objective criteria, yet they are, like persons, worthy of equal respect.

It by no means follows, however, that for every nation there must be a state. Such a view is (strong) nationalism as distinct from national sentiment. Or if one must be a nationalist (and certainly in Scotland the word and the feelings associated with it are too important to be surrendered to the separatist SNP), then there is both a strong separatist nationalism and a gentler, open and non-exclusive nationalism. There are multi-national states whose unity does not depend on manufacturing a single national consciousness.[8]

Britishness

The English are now very prone to mistake patriotism for a strong nationalism and to forget that the United Kingdom is a multi-national state. To try to revive the early Hanoverian 'British nationalism' is futile and is to abandon history for mythology. No assertion of such superiority, whether strident, covert or accidental, is acceptable. And we are, indeed, dealing with overlapping, cross-cutting, interactive but none-the-less significantly different cultural identities. If English nationalism is at least a cultural identity, it cannot be shouting in the wind to reprove the Scots for being Scottish (as Thatcher seemed to do, as if it were just a strong provincial modulation of Englishness and need have nothing to do with high politics). Such behaviour is politically provocative and likely to prove

---

[8] A good overview is Walker Connor, 'Ethno-nationalism and Political Instability', in Hermann Giliomee and Jannie Gagiano, eds., *The Elusive Search for Peace: South Africa, Israel, Northern Ireland*, Oxford University Press, Cape Town: 1990. Johannes Degenaar, a political philosopher at Stellenbosch has written a profound series of reflections on artificial one-nation nationalism as integrative forces, as against a pluralist perspective – for example his *The Roots of Nationalism*, Academica, Pretoria: 1982.

self-defeating. Alternatives are not exhausted by the conceptualisation that the present government and the SNP have in common: either the United Kingdom as it is or separation.

It is this confusion of a legitimate if paradoxically under-expressed Englishness with *Britishness* (as Englishness for all) that Tom Nairn and Neal Ascherson acidly call 'Ukanian'.[9] I only differ from them in believing that it is not an inherent aspect of the British state. To prevent this folly cementing itself will need agitation and institutional reform, but the folly was far less in the past than they suggest; and the Conservatives even, as well as the Luberals, once understood this better, through much of the first half of this century, in fact, than the centralising Labour Party.

'British' is a political and legal concept best applied to the institutions of the United Kingdom state, to common citizenship and common political arrangements. It is not a cultural term, nor does it correspond to any real sense of a nation. And nor should it. If in that foreign hotel register I am asked my nationality, I do say 'English'; but if my citizenship, obviously 'British'. To be British demands a kind of loyalty, but a pragmatic loyalty limited to those civic institutions we have in common. (It is rather as Roman citizenship was for peoples outside Latinium). I am a British citizen but I am also English. It happens that I live in Scotland by choice and many of my political and social sympathies are Scottish. If my children had grown up here they could have been Scottish, feeling such and accepted as such. But that cannot be for me at my age; the need for a long period of acculturation is one sure sign of a nation. All this gives me an intellectual and moral conviction that Scottishness is to be taken quite as seriously as Englishness (and both kinds of Irishness too, not to mention that my actual children have a Welsh mother), but taken no more seriously (unless some historical recompense is thought due).

Most Scots I know think of themselves as Scottish and British, perhaps a dual sense of identity, perhaps a more fuctional differentiation. Some make a great bother of this duality and its due proportions, others wear both coats easily. Most wish to see the terms of the Union revised, but are British in the sense that they still want a union. Most modern English, however, have no sense of this duality at all; to be British is simply to be English. The ignorant and irresponsible under-reporting of Scotland in the London media both illustrates vividly and reinforces constantly this self-deception. And the few English who do see this duality in others find it hard not to sound patronising themselves.

John Mackintosh saw both points when he once spoke of 'two ways in which one can feel Scottish':

> One ... is to feel a resentment against the assumptions of superiority, of absolute standards, so evident in the older British universities, in London media circles,

---

[9] Neal Ascherson, 'Ancient Britons and the Republican Dream', *Political Quarterly*, July–September 1986, reprinted in his *Games with Shadows*, Radius, London: 1988; and Tom Nairn, *The Enchanted Glass*, Radius, London: 1988.

BERNARD CRICK

among Whitehall civil servants and so on. The other, when one has been through all these groups and their activities, is to be reasonably confident that the best of what is done in Scotland and by Scots is as good as anything these guardians of proper standards can produce.[10]

And so should the sober Englishman look at the thistle (the leek and the shamrock too). But when he argued the case for devolution, Mackintosh pointed out that it would be all 'self-awareness' but exclude 'nationalist extremism': 'it keeps Scotland in the United Kingdom on the explicit grounds that Scots have a dual nationality; they are English [sic] as well as Scottish'.[11] Surely for once he nods in this minefield of nomenclature. He could have meant what he said: a dual Scottishness and Englishness, but it is a highly questionable claim – even if he were only speaking of himself. He was liked in London and felt thoroughly at ease with the English, but that is not the point. He was so much more Scottish than English, unlike some Scots who spend their working life in the South but visit relatives back North frequently, and become not assimilated but genuinely bi-cultural. Most Scots are not like that. He surely meant 'British'.

Part of John's true Scottishness was his ease in mixing when a constituency MP with all kinds of classes, whereas his London circle were nearly all from the London professional social classes, those involved in maintaining (well or badly) Britishness, indeed, but notoriously uncertain of the many other class and regional modulations of Englishness. And suppose that he meant what he said (the old way to read a text), his claim to be both Scottish and English; this would have implied deafness to clearly Irish minor themes in Scotland, discordant to his Glasgow ears.

More often the English make this confusion. Some years ago a New Zealand historian of political ideas, J. G. A. Pocock, wrote a remarkable article, 'British History: a Plea for a new Subject', an attack on Anglo-centric history as a misreading even of English history and a plea for 'a plural history of a group of cultures'.[12] The new and official National [English] History Curriculum notes the twin difficulty, that English is not British and yet is much affected by the whole context of these islands, but then passes on doing nothing to remedy it.[13] And Keith Robbins, President of the Historical Association, no less, gave the Ford Lectures at Oxford for 1986–87 on a specifically British approach to nineteenth century history. His published chapter on 'The Identity of Britain' is excellent, except that he talked of a 'Britain' of three nations, not Great

---

[10] Henry Drucker, ed., *John P. Mackintosh on Scotland*, Longman, London: 1982, p. 149.
[11] John P. Mackintosh in a pamphlet, *The Case for a Scottish Parliament*, East Lothian Labour Party, Tranent: 1977.
[12] J. G. A. Pocock, 'British History: a Plea for a New Subject', *Journal of Modern History*, No. 4 1975, p. 603.
[13] This author's review of the National History Curriculum and other books on the United Kingdom question, *Political Quarterly*, October 1990, pp. 86–94.

98

Britain, thus excluding Ireland, which sitting as he does in Glasgow made it doubly odd that, in the face of the facts of economic history, he failed to go the whole way. (I completely fail to understand what concept he has of 'integrative' that can exclude Northern Ireland.) Hugh Kearney has given us the only fully integrative account.[14]

After 1920 when the Irish question dropped out of English politics for almost fifty years, both public and official opinion began to lose the old familiarity with 'the United Kingdom question'. After 1950 the end of Empire obviously caused greater psychological problems for the English than for the others. An exaggerated sense of power continued amid visible symptoms of decline. This transformed what had previously been a political virtue into an open wound: the English reluctance to consider a clearly English sense of national identity rather than continue to confound it with a British and, once, an imperial persona. There is now a tendency to put upon the British dimension alone a burden that should have been shared between 'English' and 'British'; but this sharing would have involved for the first time not merely a truly critical self-examination but a far greater empathy for Wales, Scotland and Northern Ireland.

If the distinction can be drawn more clearly, the new immigrants may come to feel more secure – securely British rather than English. (Interestingly people speak of 'Black Britons' not Black English, Welsh or Scottish.) It was the English who seemed (a) to demand of the newcomers that they should become English, and (b) to tell them that it was too difficult. But there is no particular reason why they should become English, unless from individual choice. Like Scots, Welsh and (after all) a majority in Northern Ireland, they could relatively easily and quickly gain a clear British identity – indeed were under some quite proper legal obligation to do so. Enough is enough.

The English ideology

An oddly specific aspect of the English national tradition is usually and unequivocally put forward as British. In times gone by it was needed to ensure the unity of the United Kingdom, but today it begins to threaten that unity: the theory of parliamentary sovereignty.

It is uniquely English. That we are the only country in the European Community without either a written constitution or a Bill of Rights demonstrates this. This does not by itself invalidate it. We English may be right that it is uniquely fitting to British conditions. Once it was. It was born in men's minds out of the philosophy of Thomas Hobbes and the

[14] Keith Robbins, *Nineteenth-Century Britain: Integration and Diversity*, Clarendon, Oxford: 1988; and Hugh Kearney, *The British Isles: A History of Four Nations*, Cambridge University Press: 1989.

experiences of the civil wars throughout the three kingdoms. But its unequivocable assertion in public law was part of the post-1688 settlement, no earlier. Until then everyone had known that power was divided in England between King, Lords and Commons (like 'the trie Estates' in Scotland; and some authorities treated the Church and the Law as quasi-autonomous estates. 'If there had not been an opinion received of the greater part of England that these powers were divided', railed Hobbes, 'the people had never been divided and fallen into this civil war'. But that was the opinion, and the fatal arguments were not about who should wield an unlimited sovereignty but about the relative balance of powers. And, in any case, there were under the same crown, with their own parliaments, Scotland and Ireland. When James I and VI had argued for 'an incorporating union', it was the English Parliament that refused. The Revolution Settlement and the Act or Treaty of Union were crisis measures intended to prevent for ever civil war.

Some Scottish writers need to remind themselves that there are stronger grounds for Scotland's 'Claim of Right' than the belief that Scotland lost its sovereignty through treachery and bribery. (There are democratic arguments, for instance.) In 1707 a majority in the Scottish Parliament, the Scottish Commissioners and almost certainly a majority in the Lowlands (though opinion was divided) saw the urgency for a single overriding authority: to keep the succession in the same hands, to preserve the Protestant religion, to get into the English imperial market, and – very evident as one looks north through Edinburgh streets and sees the Highlands – to preserve peace and order, to end endemic civil war. Federal solutions were discussed but rejected, as too speculative and unlikely in the conditions of the time to provide the security and integration wanted. But most Scots thought that a hard bargain had been struck. All the other important Scottish institutions had been left intact, indeed protected, in the Treaty. There was almost as much difficulty getting the Act through the English Parliament as through the Scottish because the bishops bitterly opposed the intended establishment of the Church of Scotland. The Kirk with its selected ministers and its annual assembly was seen by most as a more representative and national institution than the landowner-dominated and unreformed parliament of Scotland. The law and the local government (which was nearly all the government there was until the nineteenth century) remained in local hands, with the Kirk vastly influential. It seems to me that the irrefutable historical case for a Scottish parliament today is less that Scotland was robbed of one in 1707 but that the authority of the Church of Scotland has withered away, leaving Scotland without any expressive, integrative and policy-making national institution.[15] I am too sceptical of the use of 'sovereignty' as a universal

[15] This author's 'The Sovereignty of Parliament and the Scottish Question' in Norman Lewis, ed. *Happy and Glorious: the Constitution in Transition*, Open University Press, Milton Keynes: 1990.

concept to have much sympathy for either the 'give it back' or the 'there was a uniquely Scottish tradition of popular sovereignty' school of thought. To be a good nationalist and a democratic one does not have to be a bad historian.

There was, of course, always a paradox about the new theory of parliamentary sovereignty. Like its intellectual progenitor, Hobbes' *Leviathan*, it was a gigantic bluff. The potential powers were not intended to be used, except to prevent civil war and to preserve law and order. The eighteenth century state was not strong, it was extremely weak and limited in its functions. Indeed the personification of Hobbes' sovereign-Leviathan had not been some English Tamburlaine but one of his own patrons, Charles II, the author of the Act of Oblivion whose main object of policy was 'not to go on my travels again'. The actions of his brother and successor upset such humane or cynical minimalism, and revived fears of religious persecution and civil war.

Even deep into the eighteenth century the new doctrine was not universally accepted. Blackstone intoned that Parliament 'was the place where the absolute despotic power, which must in all governments reside somewhere, is entrusted by the constitution of these kingdoms'. But the rhetorical exaggeration was deliberate, and everyone must have known it. Even so the young Bentham seized on that passage ten years later in his *Fragment on Government* of 1776 and rudely asked whether Blackstone thought that 'the Switzers and the Germans lack government?' and the great director of the Seven Years War, Chatham, had famously dragged himself to the House of Lords for what proved his dying speech to declare that the Stamp Act was unconstitutional: '. . . that this kingdom has no right to lay a tax upon the colonies, to be sovereign and supreme in every circumstance'. Chatham's view, of course, did not prevail. Burke, while in equal fury against renewal of American taxation, did not deny the rights of sovereign power; he argued the gross imprudence of exercising them:

I am not going into the distinction of rights. . . . I do not enter into these metaphysical distinctions; I hate the very sound of them. . . . Leave [such arguments] to schools; for there they may be discussed with safety. But if intemperately, unwisely, fatally, you sophisticate and poison the very source of government, by urging subtle deductions and consequences odious to those you govern, from the unlimited and illimitable nature of the supreme sovereignty, you will teach them by these means to call that sovereignty into question.

Like many a practical man, or woman, however, Lord North's mind was programmed with unappraised metaphysical distinctions: he said that 'sovereignty cannot be divided', and thus went away the last chance of conciliating the Americans. Our leaders today should consider Burke's argument deeply. Ministers moved with great speed and some over-kill to conciliate Welsh nationalism after 1970 (revealing that Plaid Cymru's priorities lay with the preservation of language and culture by external guarantees more than for Home Rule which—considering that the non-Welsh speaking Welsh are a majority – could actually threaten the language). But Conservative inflexibility over Scotland now leads more and more Scots 'to call that sovereignty into question'.

Pluralism

Blackstone was plainly wrong, and all the English positivist lawyers too. This is important to grasp. It is simply not the case that there 'must in all governments reside somewhere' an 'absolute despotic power'. This view confuses sovereignty with power. Sovereign bodies often lack power, and there can be much power, sometimes more, elsewhere. The theory of sovereignty may have two residual if far from comprehensive applications: (i) to explain and settle jurisdictions: a law is not a law unless it has been passed by a 'sovereign', in our case Parliament (though the sovereign body may, of course, choose to give some other body a superior jurisdiction for defined purposes – as in the Treaty of Rome and the Single European Act); and (ii) to remind that in times of emergency concentration of power is essential and ordinary laws may have to be swept aside if a state is to survive. 'When the very safety of the state is in danger, no consideration of good or evil . . .' said Machiavelli; but the republican took that 'when' very seriously as 'only when'. Otherwise, as John Adams said in 1775, 'sovereignty is very tyranny'.

The confusion of sovereignty with power is common, but mainly rhetorical. Further, there is no necessity behind the belief that the more that power is concentrated the more powerful a state can be. Sometimes so, sometimes not. The United States government has great power, internally and externally, without a doctrine or reality of sovereignty (except in time of war and the specific enjoinment on the President to enforce the laws). Many now argue that in the United Kingdom power is so concentrated in Westminster and Whitehall that policies are not merely unresponsive to regional and local needs, but are difficult to implement. The devolution of decision-making is practised by big companies and armies as a way of applying power; but modern British administration is stuck in a time-warp of Blackstonian concepts.

It is not just the case empirically that the United Kingdom is both a multi-national state and a highly pluralistic society (regions, religions and different ethnic groups cutting across national boundaries even), but that theoretically we all need to see that political power is always pluralistic; Harold Laski went so far to say in his *Grammar of Politics* that 'all power is federal'. To formulate policy there are always different groups to be considered and conciliated, and to carry out different policies different kinds of agencies are needed, and affect the outcomes.

My theory is that the idea of parliamentary sovereignty had an historical origin (it is not a necessary truth about the nature of politics). That origin was at the time of the union of the three kingdoms. It had some function so long as the main business of British (English?) politics was holding the United Kingdom together, and it worked so long as the governing class understood and tolerated the high degree of actual administrative autonomy in the other nations.[16] But it is now actually a threat to the Union. Ireland might have remained within the Union if Gladstone's Home Rule Bill of 1886, essentially federal, had been passed. And the laws and institutions of the EC now make the theory of parliamentary sovereignty not merely an intellectual nonsense, creating misleading perceptions of reality, but an obstacle (as Charter 88 and many others now argue) to any real constitutional reform. We now need institutions that recognise the diversity. We need, in some sense, federal institutions— though in the facts of the case, the very different circumstances of Scotland, Wales and Northern Ireland, it would neither be a uniform federalism nor merely a dressed-up version of English regionalism as the Labour Party now seems to promise, or threaten.[17]

Under political pressure fixed minds can prove flexible. Both the Northern Ireland Constitution Act of 1973 and the inter-governmental *Agreement* of 1985 pledge the British government to legislate for a united Ireland if a majority clearly wish for and formally consent. Sovereignty is at least not inalienable! The *Agreement* also made the exercise of British sovereignty over Northern Ireland subject to consultation with the Irish Government! And it is worth remembering that the old Colonial Office negotiated and freely dispersed federal constitutions to all the old components of the Empire (except to New Zealand, and then only after strong local protests). They understood their business, but federalism was for the lesser breeds within the law, not for the homeland. In the homeland the English ideology thoroughly muddled the concepts of parliamentary government and of the sovereignty of parliament (Mr Hattersley and Mr Major should visit Canada and Australia urgently for a conceptual jolt).

Federal ideas were common in the old Liberal Party and they now enter the discourse of the Labour Party, even if the leaders are still under the fatal spell of 'winner takes all' power (which is also, as Robin Cook points out, 'loser take nothing'). Roy Hattersley is by no means the most conservative in his John Bullish defence of parliamentary sovereignty and opposition to electoral reform or a Bill of Rights; he simply talks about it openly. But I can think of no prominent Labour intellectual outside Parliament who does not now argue for some kind of constitutional reform (except John Griffith). And their theoretical framework is now generally pluralist; both the Leninist and the Webbian or old Fabian sovereign, central state are discarded.[18]

The old informal, conventional constitution has outlived its usefulness. Our lack of constitutional law embroils us more and more with the

---

[16] This author's 'The Sovereignty of Parliament and the Irish Question', in his *Political Thoughts and Polemics*, Edinburgh University Press: 1990, pp. 57–76.
[17] This author's 'Northern Ireland and the Theory of Consent', ibid., pp. 77–93.
[18] For example Mike Rustin, *For Pluralist Socialism*, Verso, London: 1985.

European court and allows a concentration of power that actually restrains the energy of the country. I return to questions of cultural identity. I believe deeply (here I would differ from Christopher Harvie) that the best energy and inventiveness, entrepreneurial spirit as well as the civic spirit, lie in (a great theme of the English novel) 'roots', the provinces and regions, even in England.

We English must come to terms with ourselves. There is so much that is positively good or enjoyably peculiar in our tradition. But we prejudice it by trying nostalgically or sourly to hang on to everything 'that made us great', once-upon-a-time. There is need to shed much dead wood and, above all, not to try to infuse everything that is English into the common property of British. To continue with that bad habit is to make some want to leave home and others, though legally citizens, not feel at home.[19]

[19] Bhikhu Parek argues well for taking 'a plural view of British identity' and that 'being British is not a matter of sharing a body of *values*, for no values are common to all Britons . . .', in 'Britain and the Social Logic of Pluralism' *Britain: a Plural Society*, Commission for Racial Equality, London, Discussion Paper 3: 1989, pp. 58–76.

ENGLISH REGIONALISM: THE DOG THAT NEVER BARKED

CHRISTOPHER HARVIE*

RECENTLY I read in *Die Zeit* about Manchester the rock capital of Europe, while *Der Spiegel* told me that Simon Rattle was making Birmingham into a European metropolis – for symphonic music. In 1990 Germans were treated to articles about 'Glasgow City of Culture' *ad libitum* or *ad nauseam*, so the British provinces seemed rather more obvious than, for the purposes of this paper, they ought to be. But while the Glasgow saga sparked some political follow-up – the first German TV channel ran a long documentary on Scottish nationalism, and *Die Zeit* included Scotland in an article on the collapse of the nation-state ethos – the *politics* of the English provinces were somehow summed up by one of the Manchester rockers saying that his ideology went as far as his trousers. Whatever European salience the English regions have achieved in fashion or entertainment (think of Liverpool in the 1960s), this has never extended to politics. So, to activate decentralisation in England entails overcoming a history and a culture which have – as much as politics and social policy – marginalised it.

The approach of economic and political unity in Europe has revived the ideological regionalism of such as Leopold Kohr and Denis de Rougemont after its frustration in the 1970s, and supplemented it with a brisk 'bourgeois regionalism' which sees the defence-based nation state as getting in its way. The 'semi-federalism' of the major European countries has now created a Council of European Regions at Strasbourg. This has influence with a 'committed' Commissioner, Bruce Millan – who tried to carry Scottish devolution as a member of the Callaghan government – despite (or possibly because of) the hostility of the British government. Even more important, forms of collaboration between neighbouring regions (as in the agreements between Saarland, Luxembourg and Lorraine over transport, environment and education) and between regions with shared economic interests (as in the 'high-tech confederation' of Baden-Württemberg, Lombardy, Rhone-Alpes and Catalunya) are multiplying.[1] But when Baden-Württemberg, for example, originally

* The author is Professor of British Studies at the University of Tübingen, has written widely on British and Scottish social history, is a member of the SNP and author of *The Centre of Things: Political Fiction in Britain from Disraeli to the Present* (Unwin Hyman 1991).

[1] See Denis de Rougemont, *The Future is Within Us*, 1977, Pergamon Press 1983; John Osmond, *The Centralist Enemy*, Christopher Davies 1974; Christopher Harvie, *Europe and the Scottish Nation*, Scottish Centre for Economic and Social Research, February 1989; and

wanted to make East Anglia its British associate, it found none of the administrative institutions which were necessary for cooperation, and chose Wales instead. The situation after the poll tax 'reforms', with education probably centralised, and unitary authorities based on the districts, will be even less plausible. The Manchester rocker had a point. In the Europe of the regions, the English will not be able to see further than their trousers.

Why should this be, and does it matter? In 1982 I wrote a Fabian Tract *Against Metropolis* about centralisation in Britain and how to get rid of it. A Fabian Society referee remarked on the 'unfashionability' of regionalism, and the tract awoke reactions only in Scotland and from the odd veteran of the Common Wealth party. My experience was not unique: political pluralism was cast into the shadows by the devolution *debacle* of 1979.[2] Things have changed. Labour now promises English regional councils, as well as devolution to Scotland and Wales, the whole being co-ordinated through the replacement of the House of Lords by a federal second chamber. Bodies like the Centre for Local Economic Strategies are getting ideas of regional government moving in the North-West. But English history and politics still seem imprinted with a spirit inimical to regional government. The *Political Quarterly* conference for which this paper was written, was effectively dominated by academics from the Celtic fringe, and a poll on the political priorities of Charter 88 members in early 1990 showed decentralisation lagging far behind a bill of rights and proportional representation. The situation could either stay as it is, or become even more centralised.

'Manufacturing' regional identity isn't impossible. The Kilbrandon Commission in the early 1970s found almost as much regional loyalty in England as in Scotland or Wales (perhaps because English regionalism had yet to become a party question and remained at the 'good idea' level).[3] The *Länder* of modern Germany, mostly quite ahistorical and rather unpopular when they were set up in 1949, now have the approval of 71% of the population. And local loyalties in Britain are far fiercer: Labour would never think of sending Gerald Kaufman, say, to run for local office in Newcastle (let alone Aberdeen), but such inter-regional movements are standard practice in the SPD. In Germany, however, the enduring foundations of bureaucracy, educational and religious relationships have been at once uniform *and* decentralised. In Britain tension between the constituent nations and between province and metropolis in England has preserved ancient animosities.

Colin Crouch and David Marquand, eds., *The New Centralism: Britain out of Step in Europe?*, Oxford, Basil Blackwell 1989.

[2] For example, Bernard Burrows and Geoffrey Denton, *Devolution or Federalism*, Macmillan/Federal Trust, 1980, particularly pp. 29–44; Vernon Bogdanor, *Devolution*, Oxford UP, 1980; William L. Miller, *The End of British Politics*, Oxford UP, 1980.

[3] See the *Royal Commission on the Constitution*, *Memorandum of Dissent*, Cmnd 5460-1 of 1973, pp. 26–7.

An ambiguous concept

In British terms, the region is an awkward concept. The definition stems from geography – the approach of the pioneer C. B. Fawcett in *The Provinces of England* in 1919. It is regarded not as a self-standing unit but as an administrative part of the nation-state which, in the eighteenth and nineteenth centuries both suppressed and revived it – for taxation, education and above all military purposes. 'Enlightened despots' and Jacobins alike replaced the local polity of aristocracies, churchman and self-governing towns – diets and estates, cultures like the Breton and Occitanian – with centrally-appointed officials. 'Anti-revolutionaries', such as vom Stein in Prussia in 1808, permitted a greater degree of decentralisation, with elected councils on the 'British' pattern. But both systematically devolved central departments to a local level of *Commissariats* and *Regierungspräsidien*: miniature versions of Paris and Bonn, or of Helsinki or Oslo. Save in Ireland, Scotland since 1885 and Wales since 1964, there has never been such a tradition here. English regionalism has been traditionally 'strong' (in the greater amount of government administration devolved to councils) and 'weak', in the sense that all negotiations with central government have had to go to Whitehall. Thus English MPs have, unlike their Welsh or Scots colleagues, rarely seen themselves as regional tribunes.[4]

This low visibility has misled many historians – even academics with a close interest in provincial history, like Kenneth Morgan in *The People's Peace* (1990), and Harold Perkin in *The Rise of Professional Society* (1987) – to discount local politics. In their day, Marx and Engels were equally uninspired in analysing the impact of culture and administration on class politics, and never explained why the revolutionary spirit of 1848 was absent in 'industrialised' Britain and Belgium and at its bloodiest where industrialisation scarcely existed – in Hungary and Southern Italy. But much of it could be put down to the impact, or lack of it, of local government. Reform could be postponed in agrarian societies until the boil of discontent burst, but in the new industrial areas opening up around the coalfields, a concentrated and 'rootless' working population required control by military and police authorities, and an administrative system which could cope with public health disasters and mass-unemployment. In Britain such a system was in place – displacing earlier religious and status-derived responsibilities – by 1848.

At this stage English *ad-hockery* performed as well as the Napoleonic system. Between 1830 and 1870 English borough councils changed from privileged corporations to something much more systematically 'interventionist'. But there were two drawbacks. The first was that the new

---

[4] See J. F. MacDonald, *The Lack of Political Identity in English Regions*, Strathclyde University: Centre for the Study of Public Policy, 1979, p. 11.

urban society failed to follow the old geography and, very often, the local government seat was different from the population centre. The second was that there was no over-arching philosophy. Benthamite reform implied units larger than the traditional parish – notably the Poor Law Unions (1834) – but these restricted local authorities to executing the rigid economic guidelines of a powerful central office, enforcing its will by a travelling inspectorate. Although similar structures were used for public health (1848) and education (1870), the large unit was not maintained: 'the future growth of our local government system was deformed by a rash of small units which we are still (1971) trying to abate'.[5]

The Benthamite programme provoked a backlash, articulated by figures like Toulmin Smith, David Urquhart and the Anti-Centralisation Union, 1854–7, although it was really as a result of the administrative incompetence of more traditional bodies in the Crimean War that the Benthamite General Board of Health was closed down in 1854. Thereafter the ideology of British local government drifted. Powers were gradually concentrated in the elective County Councils, set up by the Conservative government in 1888. The semi-federalisation of the country, proposed by the 'Radical Programme' of 1885, was never followed up.

When the concept of regionalism became current in the 1880s, it accompanied the 'triumph' of the unitary nation-state and it had a somewhat derogatory tone. The *OED* records 'that unfortunate "regionalism" of Italy' as an early usage (1881) in *The Manchester Guardian*, typical enough in being directed at one of Europe's less-successful nation-states (Spanish regionalism made a similar early appearance). In the early 1900s it became more positive, with the growth of pluralist political theory, whether of a New Liberal, Guild Socialist, Young Fabian or neo-Catholic sort – represented respectively by Harold Laski, G. D. H. Cole, H. G. Wells and G. K. Chesterton. This was not co-terminous with nationalism, which is self-referential, but was a 'qualified sovereignty' response to the challenge posed by Irish Home Rule to the centralised British constitution. Its last outing was in the Speaker's Conference on constitutional reform held in 1919–20, and the failure to hold Ireland to home rule effectively swept it away.[6]

The culture of English regionalism

Paradoxically, this political collapse was accompanied by a literary and ideological identity which regionalism had never previously enjoyed. The next decades were full of proposals for provincial government by the likes of G. D. H. Cole, W. A. Robson, the Town Planning Institute, and Political

[5] W. Thornhill, *The Growth and Reform of English Local Government*, Weidenfeld and Nicholson, 1971, p. 7.
[6] John D. Fair, *British Interparty Conferences*, Clarendon, Oxford, 1980, pp. 224–241.

and Economic Planning. This activity, however, concealed a complex ideological parentage. Fawcett's *Provinces of England* was a by-product of the 'reconstruction' ethic of World War I but the man behind it, indeed the foremost exponent of the regional ideal, was the geographer-polymath Patrick Geddes, in his *Cities in Evolution* (1913). Geddes was quite un-English. He showed aspects of Victorian liberalism, literary positivism and of the Fabian planning of his disciples Patrick Abercrombie and Raymond Unwin: that road to municipal collectivism which was the executive face of the welfare state. But he stood apart from the English literary-humanist tradition; not just as a Celtic literary nationalist, but in following the Scottish tradition of 'civic virtue' inhering in the *polis*, and the inter-connection of internal and external federalism.[7]

If we look at the origins of this ideology, as disciples of J. G. A. Pocock have done, we find it defining itself, as the 'right government' of the small political unit, precisely at the time when England produced the critical cultural artefacts of its own national identity, Shakespeare's plays and the King James Bible. In *Scottish National Consciousness in the Age of James VI*, Arthur Williamson has stressed the continuity of this localist ideal in Scots political theory, compared with the 'protestant imperialism' of the English – continuing in Andrew Fletcher, Adam Ferguson and John Galt. But by 1815 it was being dismembered and reintegrated into a radically different 'English example'.[8]

This provided a corollary to continental Mazzinian nationalism and, as a war-generated ideology, took as axiomatic the relation between patriotism and fighting.[9] Perhaps the most 'English' moment of the nineteenth century was the Volunteer movement of 1859, with its scratch regiments of artisans, railwaymen and professional gents, ranged against putative French aggression following on the Crimean War. The Scots were equally bloodthirsty, but for other reasons: their mercenary and militia traditions. Even someone as sensitive as Graham Wallas, in *Human Nature in Politics* (1908), saw the test of nationality as being prepared to die for one's country. This idea of the nation went on to convince free-traders and Fabians alike that economic utilities, such as railways, ought to operate in the context of, if not be owned by, the nation-state. The former were always advertising their patriotism; the latter saw 'municipalisation' as a means to a national end.

The English 'patriotic-bourgeois' ethos was a combination of culture,

---

[7] Helen E. Meller, 'Patrick Geddes: an Analysis of his Theory of Civics, 1880–1904' in *Victorian Studies*, March 1973, pp. 291–315. I have attempted to outline a 'Scottish' tradition of political thought in the nineteenth century in 'Enlightenment to Renaissance' a paper given to Cambridge social historians in May 1989.

[8] Williamson, op. cit.; John Donald, 1979, esp. pp. 5 ff; and see George Elder Davie, *The Scottish Enlightenment*, Historical Association, 1971.

[9] See Tom Nairn, *The Enchanted Glass: Britain and its Monarchy*, Radius 1988, especially Chapter 2 'The Nation'; and Linda Colley, 'Whose Nation? Class and National Consciousness in Britain, 1750–1830' in *Past and Present* No. 113 (1985).

'good manners', and romantic historical consciousness with a well-developed civil society and robust if minimal government machine. And it was derived less from Burke than from the qualities formulated in the modernisation of Scottish society in the eighteenth century and then given a wider audience by the writings of Scots philosophers and publicists, notably the Mills, Scott and Carlyle. Scott in particular reflected both the change from status to contract, and the insecurity which stemmed from a society dependent on the 'cash-nexus'. His prototype of social settlement was the transformation of the Scottish border from a lawless 'debatable land' to an example of 'improvement' and 'cultivation', of a demotic but still securely deferential sort.[10] The message was even more tellingly put over by his neighbours the British 'clerisy' – Wordsworth, Coleridge, Southey, Thomas Arnold, William Whewell, Carlyle, 'Christopher North'—based in the English north-west, an area of high literacy, local grammar schools with scholarships to the old universities, small 'independent' farmers, and conservative populist politics: a reassuring combination of *Gemeinschaft* and civil society. Coleridge, Arnold and Carlyle drew deeply on the German notion of the superiority of 'cultivation' over 'civilisation', which identified centralisation with the liberal, Protestant left, and 'particularism' – whether in Ireland or Bavaria – with the mainly Catholic right. 'Lake District' regionalism rejected particularism; it projected a national identity through a regional example.

Nineteenth-century progressives discounted regionalism in the national histories that they organised. Italian urban republics or German imperial free cities were stigmatised as decadent, and more-or-less crazy militarists and racists were legitimated as actors in episodes of 'natural' development. Regionalism was ridiculed as 'Balkanisation', although this was in fact a miniaturised and generally malevolent version of Bismarckian national egoism. This distorted and continues to distort our comprehension of regionalism.

Other British regions were given the Lake District treatment and turned into politically-innocuous cultural divisions of the national community. Largely through print-capitalism, regional 'authenticity' emerged, as in – 'Yorkshire' and the Bronte industry, and of course 'Wessex' and Thomas Hardy. But not even the Webbs would have fitted Mayor Henchard of Casterbridge into any thesis about local government! Behind both, perhaps, stands John Ruskin, with his combination of 'civic virtue' – crystallised in his version of Venetian civilisation, but owing a lot to Carlyle – and downright reactionary anti-modernism. These popular metropolitan projections mirrored native growths, such as the Lancashire dialect poets, Hartley's *Clock Almanacks* in Wakefield or the dialect verse of William Barnes in Dorset, which themselves reflected the 'international' development of a phonetic shorthand in the 1830s. William

---

[10] See Christopher Harvie, 'Scott and the Image of Scotland' in Alan Bold, ed., *Sir Walter Scott: the Long-Forgotten Melody*, Vision 1983, pp. 17–42.

Donaldson has claimed in his remarkable work, *Popular Literature in Victorian Scotland* (1985) that vernacular literature, far from being parochial, could be progressive and cosmopolitan in its range of reference. Similar arguments were being made at the time for Nynorsk in Norway, Icelandic and Finnish.

In Britain, however, the political dimension was weakened by two things: firstly the urban and fanatical loyalties created during and after the 1870s by Association Football (significantly Irish nationalists 'politicised' sport at this same time and outlawed 'English' games); and secondly that symbiotic exploitation of rural sentimentalism and overseas English-speaking markets, called in Scotland the 'Kailyard', facilitated by the Copyright Agreement with America in 1891.[11] Regional *Gemeinschaft* novels, pawky, sentimental, and didactic, were often written by highly politicised, metropolitan literary men – Hugh Walpole, Arthur Quiller-Couch, Silas K. Hocking, Francis Brett Young. They appealed to a nonconformity now figuring in national politics, imperially-conscious and less bound to its local, democratic roots.[12]

Both these developments reflected a weakness of provincial urban leadership. I don't think that Engels, for example, was ever conscious of Manchester, in which he lived for some thirty years, as a *regional* capital. He saw it more as a sort of internationalised epiphenomenon of industrialisation. Effective 'bourgeois regionalism' pre-supposed an interventionist nation-state *and* a local bourgeoisie prepared to remain local. This was unlikely among the beneficiaries of the 1832 Reform Act, whom the public schools, the Empire and the 'self-government' of the professions rapidly locked into a 'British' identity.[13]

The British regional ethos created in 1885–1914 was an intriguing amalgam of upper-class elitism, 'print-capitalism' and one element of the Scottish civic consciousness – much more conservative than Geddes – which had been peripatetic during the nineteenth century. Thomas Chalmers' *Christian and Civic Economy of Great Towns* (1823) influenced the Charity Organisation Society and, through Arnold Toynbee the elder, the university settlement movement. The latter linked the professions to social reform and the Labour movement. With a population becoming urban at the same pace as that of the United States, 'civics' became a central concept of industrial society along with 'pragmatism' and 'progressivism'. The great city was seen as a source of opportunities as well as problems. In Britain its ideology was firmly anchored in the administrative and not-particularly-democratic approach

[11] See Christopher Harvie, 'Behind the Bonnie Briar Bush: the Kailyard Revisited', in *Proteus*, No. 3, 1978.

[12] See Carola Ehrlich, *The "Dialectable Duchy": Regionalism in the Novels of Sir Arthur Thomas Quiller-Couch*, Tübingen MA thesis 1988.

[13] Martin Wiener, *English Culture and the Decline of the Industrial Spirit*, Cambridge 1981, omits the question of elite migration from the provinces, but see Philip Waller's study of Liverpool, *Democracy and Sectarianism*, Liverpool University Press 1981, pp. 276ff.

of the Christian Socialists, the Positivists and the Charity Organisation Society; and it contained a strongly anti-urban element, which went right back to the 'Lake District', through the influence of Ruskin on Octavia Hill, one of the founders in 1896 of the National Trust. When one wants to assess contemporary regionalism as a political force, compare the resources of any of its pressure groups with those of the National Trust!

There were exceptions, but in the long term these have only proved the rule. There was a revival of culture in 'New Liberal' Manchester, which before World War I came close to rivalling London: C. P. Scott and his remarkable team at the *Manchester Guardian*, Rutherford, Weizmann, Alexander and Tout at the University, the Gaiety Theatre, the plays of Stanley Houghton and Harold Brighouse, the novels of F. C. Montague and the early artistic career of L. S. Lowry. Even after the impact of the depression, Manchester culture was still lively in the 1930s, producing much of the political theatre movement – Joan Littlewood, Ewan MacColl, Sidney Bernstein – and with Namier and A. J. P. Taylor at the university. The comparison of this with our contemporary young Mancunian contemplating his trousers, too zonked out to make it to the Coronation Street theme park, let alone to Professor Marquand's lecture room, is evidence enough of the problems that we face.

Regionalism and the Left

If the socialist commitment to Utopia militates against local identity, this may help explain the paradox that the regional government ideal is weak in a Labour movement which was in its origins regional. 'We retain,' as Anthony Crosland wrote in 1974, 'an amazing sense of class and little sense of community.' Sir Halford MacKinder, as a geo-politics expert, was one of the first theorists of a provincial restructuring of Britain. But he noticed in *Democratic Ideas and Reality* (1919) that in his Glasgow election campaign of 1918 the class politics and industrial self-government offered by the Soviet revolution cut completely across any local loyalties on the part of the red Clydesiders he was up against. If this was the case in an area in which Labour had always had a strong local identity, the weakness of regional reform elsewhere in Britain seems explicable enough.

Kenneth Morgan remarks of the former London County Council Herbert Morrison in *Labour People* (1985) that he managed simultaneously to protest about the 1945–51 Labour government's inroads on local autonomy, while embodying 'the centralising force of nationalisation'. To Labour, regionalism had bourgeois Fabian fingerprints all over it, and appealed little to that 'Municipal Peter the Great' type of politician who didn't care what the council was or did as long as he ran it. Reforming local government has always seemed, in the absence of a 'great idea', like swimming in treacle. Little progress is made in a sticky and intrigue-laden atmosphere. Part of this may also be the systemic malfunctions embodied in Harvie's law which states that: 'the most opportune time for regional government reform varies inversely with its political utility'. No Labour government ever puts it at the top of its priorities, therefore after the usual 'soundings' have been made it will come after a couple of years of office, when the Tories are picking up seats like Abertillery, and of course most of the big cities. Labour councillors will be, by definition, hostile to any change which infringes their power – often exerted like something in the Eastern Europe of old, and the government won't want to do its opponents a favour. So the result, if result there is, is minimal and apologetic. Really drastic change only comes when the government has nothing much to lose (this usually applies to the Tories), and the alternative, for local magnates, is much, much worse. Which is why Scotland – and to some extent Wales – have in the past had more thorough-going reforms. In 1929 and 1974 Scotland was put through the mill, partly, one suspects, because the alternative was home rule. And home rule has been to local councillors, at least until very recently, what garlic is to vampires.

The other anti-regional force was the decline of industrial England. Fawcett's *Provinces of England* included rather a touching scheme for 'a few hundred miles of new branch-line railway' which could 'complete' the geographical improvement of his twelve provinces. Schemes for transport improvement were also linked to regional government reform in the later, flashier and – unhappily far more influential – Buchanan Report (1963); but Fawcett's plan had reflected a 'steam age' North-South balance tilted in the former's favour. The North's apparent prosperity was hit by overspecialism in the war years, and never recovered, not just because its *ethos* was frozen in the 'depressed area' typology of the 1920s, but because its local elites, economic or cultural, ceased to carry much clout. Hugh Gaitskell, in part inspired by reading D. H. Lawrence, went to teach in Nottingham in the mid-1920. The place gave him 'the feeling and fact of stagnation' and the university seemed 'indolent and depressed and almost becoming provincial'. By contrast, London had 'so much vigour and better taste and better intelligence and more personality in the atmosphere'.

Academics – usually dying to get back to Oxford, Cambridge or London – perhaps presented too substantial a profile in provinces whose industrial elites were in decline. These were little 'assisted' by subsidised migration after 1928, or by the Special Areas Commissioner created in 1933, who provided much evidence for Wal Hannington's spirited polemic *The Problem of the Distressed Areas* (1937). The fact that the Scottish Commissioner rapidly liaised with the Scottish National Development Council promoted by the shipbuilder Sir James Lithgow, and helped create Scottish Economic Committee, extending the Scottish Office's remit into the economic sphere, emphasised, not for the last time, that the claim to nationality was more than an emotional crutch.

The literary 'image' didn't help. For a time in the 1930s the influence of

D. H. Lawrence, boosted by shots of feminism and socialism, might have produced something more authentic *and* politicised, but this wasn't helped by the deaths of those two individualistic left-wingers Winifred Holtby and Lewis Grassic Gibbon in 1935. *South Riding* was the first and only work of serious fiction about local politics in England, although the theme has been important in Scotland (John Galt) and Wales (Gwyn Thomas).[14] But in 1935 the 'patriotism' of the Popular Front shackled imaginative writers to the defence of Eng. Lit. Thereafter provincialism was permitted, along the lines laid down by T. S. Eliot in *Notes towards the Definition of Culture* (1948), to echo selective cadences of the 'English mind'. Solid north-country common sense from J. B. Priestley's Bradford, end-of-the-line bleakness from Larkin's Hull, a collection of neat daguerrotypes of bandstands and cemeteries in Betjeman. Priestley in *English Journey* (1934) called for a federal system, and some such ideas were raised by the radical movement he helped form in 1942, Common Wealth, but of politicised regionalism on European lines there has been in England scarcely a trace.

George Orwell, significantly, equated centralisation with his benign version of socialism. In his industrial Iliad *The Road to Wigan Pier* (1937) there is no discussion at all of regional self-government, and although a system of decentralised administration was in fact set up in the late 1930s, to function in the event of invasion or of London being incapacitated through bombing, this had little influence on peacetime organisation in England. (The socialist in charge of it in Scotland, Tom Johnston, went on to become that country's most successful ever Secretary of State.) Despite Common Wealth, initiatives from Robson, Cole, and even Webb (and even with Labour-led London County Council after 1934 as a useful prototype), the Attlee government expropriated the property of local authorities – gasworks, electricity works, hospitals – and increased their duties as executives of central government. It ignored their reform.

The tinkering which followed, illuminated by Ealing Comedy episodes like the defence of Rutland, did not prevent drastic descents on British councils over the next twenty years by tightly-knit political economic pressure groups. We are still living with the traumas inflicted by Beeching, Buchanan, and system-building in the 1960s. Perhaps, as a reaction to this, there was a growing consensus that regional authorities were essential. Both the Redcliffe-Maud Commission (1964–9) and its dissenting member, Derek Senior, tackled the issue of strategic, physical and educational planning by recommending five English provincial councils, either indirectly-elected or (in Senior's case) appointed. A very similar scheme came from the Peacock-Hunt note of dissent to the Kilbrandon Report. But neither was embodied in the Act of 1972 or in the Labour Government's schemes for devolution, despite Lord Crowther-Hunt

---

[14] This theme is further developed in Christopher Harvie, *The Centre of Things: Political Fiction in Britain from Disraeli to the Present*, Unwin Hyman 1991.

being initially in charge of these.[15] Instead water and many health service powers were hived off to appointed bodies. Professor George Jones commented: 'in the absence of any provincial or regional level the crucial decisions on the regional framework or structure of land use will be in the hands of central government civil servants.'[16]

More insidiously, local government retreated from public esteem and awareness, something accelerated by the decline in the English (though not the Welsh or Scottish) local press, which no longer interested itself in providing detailed information on council meetings. The shift of the *Manchester Guardian* to London in 1957 was emblematic of this, as were the revelations of corruption on a huge scale in the Poulson case of 1973 which brought down the one recognisable 'regional' figure in British politics, T. Dan Smith, the Labour leader of Newcastle City Council, and member of the Redcliffe-Maud Commission. Oddly prophesied in John Arden's 'mystery play' *The Workhouse Donkey* (1963), the Poulson affair led to a brief flurry of interest on the part of novelists and playwrights. There was Margaret Drabble's *The Ice Age* (1978), David Hare and Howard Brenton's *Brassneck* (1974) and Melvyn Bragg's *Autumn Manoeuvres* (1978), but no lasting intellectual engagement in reform. In fact, the more robust provincial literary radicals, the Yorkshireman Arden and the Liverpudlian John McGrath, cleared out, to Ireland and Scotland, respectively.

In the 1970s and 1980s in Catalunya, Lombardy or Bavaria regional autonomy was *not* socialist but essentially a phenomenon of the post-national European bourgeoisie, negotiating new linkages between multi-nationals, European institutions and local enterprises. This sort of arrangement should – *pace* James Bulpitt's notion of 'central autonomy' – have endeared itself to English Tories, but so drastic was the concentration of economic power in England, the closure of traditional manufacturing industries, and the sheer power-obsession of the Thatcher *regime*, that no analogous movement surfaced. Instead the initiatives came from the Left. In the 1980s a young and highly articulate Labour leadership in the Greater London Council and in one or two of the metropolitan authorities set up by the Local Government Act of 1972, for example West Midlands and South Yorkshire, pioneered schemes of social, cultural and environmental reform, and even made local government momentarily glamorous. These efforts were squashed by Thatcher in 1985, but they resembled some of the 'red-green' alliances which were altering German cities in the 1980s without making them lose their commercial attractions.

[15] *Royal Commission on Local Government*, Vol. 1 (1969) Cmnd 4040, p. 165; and Note of Dissent, Vol. 2, Cmnd 4040–1, pp. 138–43.
[16] George Jones, 'The Local Government Act of 1972' in *Political Quarterly*, 1973, p. 159.

What is to be done?

This late-flowering activism, as well as the quest for a means of solving the House of Lords problem, can be seen behind the Labour Party's current proposals. But such commitments are no more than a first stage, and their chances of progress after any granting of autonomy to Scotland can't be assessed as very promising. So, what is to be done? Like Mackinder, Fawcett and Geddes, I regard a strong sense of local identity as essential to a bourgeois civil society – let alone a social democracy. Such a state of affairs is general in Europe (except possibly in South Italy) and notably absent in provincial England. Philip Larkin's angry high-Tory forecast of 1973:

> It seems, just now,
> To be happening so very fast;
> Despite all the land left free
> For the first time I feel somehow
> That it isn't going to last,
> That before I snuff it, the whole
> Boiling will be bricked in
> Except for the tourist parts –
> First slum of Europe: a role
> It won't be so hard to win,
> With a cast of crooks and tarts . . .

has been brought about by his own party. The appalling decline of British manufacturing industry and the diversion of resources from research, development and training into the retail, property and recreation sectors makes regional reconstruction more and more difficult, while the deracination of the British *grande bourgeoisie* forebodes a South American situation where the elite loots the populace and lives an 'off-shore' hard-currency-sustained life behind guards and barbed wire in Dulwich or straightforwardly abroad.

Yet the reconstruction of provincial England is going to be complex, and requires changes in central government as well. Particularly useful would be a Whitehall broken up in favour of agencies on the Swedish model, with its first-line administrative offices at provincial level. Given modern communications, is this more difficult than shifting entire executive arms of Whitehall offices to Swansea or East Kilbride? Such steps would also aid the decentralisation of company headquarters from the City of London to the regions. Full regional representation in European institutions would be a valuable counterweight to the strengthened Commission which must challenge the multinationals. It could also help create a socially-responsible low-resource consuming style of 'market socialist' or 'principled capitalist' enterprise along the lines of the John Lewis Partnership or the Bosch Foundation in Germany.[17] As to powers, I stick to my formula in *Against Metropolis* which was also Max Nicholson's in *The System* (1967), that no function presently devolved to Edinburgh, Cardiff or Belfast should be retained in London. The details of the political machinery are in that forgotten Fabian pamphlet; I think they're as good as anything subsequently proposed.

How does this change come about? Through revolution. I use this noisy word to gain attention, but I am also mindful of the observations of my former Edinburgh colleague, the international lawyer Tony Carty, who was commissioned in the 1970s by the Highlands and Islands Development Board to examine a similar example of institutionalised injustice, landholding in the Scottish highlands. 'It is an old joke among lawyers', he later wrote, 'that there is no law relating to land reform. Most radical land change in the world occurs through revolution. The lawyers simply come in to tidy up afterwards'.[18]

Much European devolution has been post-catastrophic: in Germany in 1945–9 and indeed in 1990; in Italy after Mussolini; in Spain after Franco. The Charter 88 poll suggests that reform by persuading existing power groups doesn't look at all promising. Moreover, the collapse in property values may actually enhance centralisation by lessening the economic motives for getting out of London. Will a decent 'herbivore' government get so far along the road of constitutional reform, and then confront a very nasty economic situation when the carnivores, as usual, repatriate their funds? Provincial devolution then becomes a *faux frais*, a luxury whose achievement can indefinitely be postponed. But what we're after is a bourgeois revolution and the bourgeois have always been a notably unsentimental lot. Enough of them seem sufficiently browned off with the Thatcherite *debacle* to favour the measures of groups which she pushed into active resistance: something peaceable but as effective as the strategies which toppled the Communist regimes in the East.

Here is a possible timetable. It is very likely that, whatever happens in England, the Conservatives will be reduced to a level in Scotland at the next election at which government is impossible. The experience of inter-party cooperation in the Scottish Constitutional Convention makes it likely that informal pacts will be created to budge the last majorities. My guess is that there will then be forty-odd Labour MPs in Scotland, with perhaps a dozen or so nationalists and the present number of Liberal Democrats. If the Conservatives win in Britain as a whole but on a minority vote, those MPs will inevitably create a Scottish Constituent Assembly. It would formally secede, pending dicussions on the renegotiation or repeal of the Act of Union, emphasising its power by the interdiction of tax revenues and oil supplies. The resulting emergency would be

[17] See David Marquand, *The Unprincipled Society*, Fontana 1988, especially Chapter 8.
[18] Tony Carty, 'The Highlands and Islands Development Board: a Vehicle for Land Reform in Scotland?' in Irene Evans and Joy Hendry, eds., *The Land for the People*, Scottish Socialist Society 1985, p. 40.

sufficent to generate an all-British constitutional convention: not least by provoking a revolt among Conservative dissidents sufficient to give a working majority for a 'government of national unity', which can introduce a package of constitutional reforms on the necessary scale.

If the result is a Labour regime, the risk is that constitutional reform will seize up after Scottish devolution has been carried. The need will be for a bogeyman sufficiently fearsome to push constitutional reform to the head of the political agenda, and keep it there long enough. Again, Scotland will be the necessary fulcrum. A nationalist opposition will rapidly put pressure on a Labour-Liberal administration in the Scottish parliament: Tam Dalyell's 'slippery slope'. The result, again, will have to be some sort of all-British convention – or Scottish secession. Melodramatic? Perhaps, but if successful European regionalism seems to have a lot to do with the energy and self-confidence of the civic-minded *bourgeoisie*, then cast an eye over the rhetoric, and the actions, of Britain's Liberals before 1832....

AUTONOMY IN SPAIN: LESSONS FOR BRITAIN?

TOM GALLAGHER*

THE claim is still occasionally heard that the British experience of state formation has been so exceptional that no worthwhile lessons can be drawn from other European countries. A look at Spain suggests that this is an unnecessarily dismissive statement. Both countries find themselves on the margins of Europe, their distinctiveness reinforced by formidable natural barriers. At different times in their history their rulers have been confronted by strong centrifugal challenges based on memories of former statehood, different social systems, or linguistic or religious distinctiveness which have often come to a head during periods of weakness or crisis in the life of the state.

Managing states whose outward geographical unity concealed enduring regional tensions proved to be a taxing role. During the periods of imperial expansion which Britain and Spain both enjoyed, separatist pressures abated. But the loss of overseas possessions resulted in a loss of state cohesion, and challenges to the legitimacy of the state were mounted by peripheral regions impatient at being shackled to declining centralised polities and which felt that their future lay in being self-governing entities in their own right.

The timing of flare-ups in the centre-periphery relationship has varied as has the strategy of the central state in seeking to contain them. But in the 1970s it looked as if both Spain and Britain were prepared to respond in similar fashion to regionalist pressures which had been released, in the one case by the dissolution of an authoritarian Spanish state and, in the other by the collapse of political consensus—the elites at the heart of the British state had come to disagree about the ground-rules for managing an increasingly unwieldy democracy. Plans to grant differing measures of Home Rule to Scotland and Wales and what might loosely be defined as their Iberian counterparts, the historic nationalities of Catalonia, Euskadi (the Basque Country) and Galicia were drawn up. In the event, it was Spain, a state which had been firmly unitary for the previous 150 years, which managed to transform itself into a more decentralised polity. In Britain, despite the much-vaunted empiricist tradition of its rulers which had previously enabled gradual adjustments in the face of regional dis-content, institutional resistance at the heart of the state and the chronic disunity of those proposing devolutionary change combined to leave the

* The author is Reader in Peace Studies at the University of Bradford. He is currently studying the impact of nationalism in post-communist Europe and comparing the transitions to democracy there with those in southern Europe.

powers of the central state untouched by 1979. There followed a reaffirmation of the unitary state principle in the 1980s which in turn produced festering discontent, particularly in Scotland, where radical legislation was enacted in what was widely seen as a bid to erode those aspects of institutional autonomy on which devolvers had rested their case for self-government.

A cycle of conflict

In Spain where the might of an implacable state had been used to subdue the unruly Basque region, a cycle of conflict steadily escalated in which those who had been denied an outlet for their nationalist feelings finally turned to violence to express their frustrations. The long-running war of insurgency in the Basque Country has been the outcome of the central state's withholding both the means of self-expression and the exercise of responsibility to regional movements with substantial support. The most intransigent elements have completely renounced all aspects of Spanish identity and have become engrossed in a sporadic guerilla war whose appeal derives from inflicting pain on the representatives of the Spanish state rather than in securing a free Euskadi. In Northern Ireland the same hallmarks are displayed by the IRA whose irregular soldiery are not so much interested in a united Ireland but in the business of fighting for this increasingly distant goal. British and Spanish governments, confronted with a legacy of misrule left by unwise governments of differing degrees of intolerance, have felt obliged to make concessions to violent nationalist pressures. Indeed more has arguably been conceded in the case of Ulster to a nationalism augmented by violence than to the constitutional and peacable agitation seen in Scotland even though it is possible to argue that the latter possesses greater historical legitimacy as well as broader electoral support.

In its treatment of Scotland, London government can learn much from the disastrous failure of the Northern Ireland government after 1920 to recognise the legitimacy of an opposing political tradition and offer it the means to pursue its aspirations through the outlet of constitutional politics. Similarly, British power-holders might ponder over the colossal misreadings of history which prompted General Franco (whose rule was nearly co-terminous with that of the Ulster Unionists) to consider that his mission was to unite Spain around its centre by suppressing all regionalist aspirations. Such a misreading of history often occurs where a ruler seeks to mobilise an evocative past in order to overturn an unsatisfactory established order. (Mrs Thatcher's attempt to seek legitimacy for policies that broke with the post-war consensus by tracing their origins back to a Victorian era, one in which Britain's prosperity was supposedly derived from a minimal state in harmonious equilibrium with free-wheeling capitalism, is just one particularly bold example.)

Franco's defiantly centralist outlook was based on a supposed link between unity and greatness in the sixteenth century. The union of the crowns of Castile and Aragon had created the first real nation of Europe, united more than two centuries before the union of England and Scotland, and nearly four centuries before the unification of Italy or Germany. If Spain was to be great again, the example to follow was the centralised Spain of the Catholic monarchs, Ferdinand and Isabella.

This view was based on a misreading of Spanish history.[1] The marriage of Ferdinand and Isabella in 1469 had been a dynastic union. Political unity did not come for over two centuries, by which time Spain was in serious decline. During the period of greatness, Spain was never a unitary state. Aragon (which included Catalonia) retained its coinage, laws and system of land tenure as well as constitutional system that allowed a local parliament considerable power. The approval of this parliament was needed before Castilian troops could be sent through its territory. Meanwhile the Basques retained a very real measure of independence down to the nineteenth century: they were exempt from military service and their Assemblies could decide what taxes should be paid to Castile.

Until the eighteenth century it is possible to argue that Spain was a confederation of loosely connected states. The eight centuries' long struggle against the Moors had provided the basis for unity, as had the clear geographical definition of the Iberian peninsula. Absorption with Spain's imperial mission overseas meant that commitment to a united Spain remained a largely abstract vision.

This was perhaps shown most clearly in the neglect of communications.[2] Spain has twelve ranges of mountains which run on a north-south axis. Any journey from Madrid involves crossing between two and three of them to reach the populous and more prosperous coast. This rugged terrain has been a formidable barrier to the movement of people, goods, and ideas and it frustrated the centralising instincts of Castile. Communities and regions were thus isolated both from each other and the country as a whole. Strangely centralisers have never tried to create an efficient network of communications to extend their control: Franco ignored the possibilities of a modern network of railways and roads. Parallels exist with the Britain of the 1980s where the centralising tendencies of the state have not been accompanied by major capital projects, such as a fast-rail link from the north to the Channel Tunnel, which could integrate faltering provincial economies more closely with the metropolitan heartland.

The strong regional variations in Spain induced by climate, geography, and poor communications led to the growth of strong local patriotism. The instability of nineteenth-century Spain widened the gulf between Madrid and the provinces. The new class of politicians influenced by the French

[1] D. Gilmour, *The Transformation of Spain*, Quartet, London 1985, pp. 106–7.
[2] R. Graham, *Spain: Change of a Nation*, Michael Joseph, London 1984, pp. 81–3.

121

revolutionary tradition felt any expression of regionalism to be reactionary, and saw the provinces as there to be taxed and subdued: they dealt
with them via intermediaries, usually the most unpopular figure—the local
boss or *cacique*.

Movements for autonomy

Bad government produced intense local frustration which burst into
periodic violence. In northern Spain movements for autonomy were
incubated by Carlism, an ultra-Catholic agrarian creed which rallied
traditional interests against the modernising, centralist, and secularising
trends of important liberal ideas. The earliest manifestations of Basque
and Catalan nationalism were based on the clerical sentiments of the
peasantry or the urban middle-class. But economic factors broadened the
base of the regional challenge to the dead-hand of centralised rule.

Catalonia was the only part of Spain which by the middle of the nineteenth century possessed a modern bourgeoisie with bourgeois values. Its
prosperity was based on textiles and on a commercial agriculture stimulated by inheritance laws that, unlike the rest of Spain, allowed primo-
geniture. The loss of Cuba in 1898 in which Catalan industrialists had
large interests, provoked an explosion of anger against Madrid. Their
complaints rested on the incompetent way the affairs of the country were
handled by Madrid, its neglect of commerce and trade, and the fact that
Catalonia with one-eighth of Spain's population, paid one-quarter of its
taxes but got back only one-tenth of the total budget. By the 1900s, the
largest party in Catalonia was the Lliga Regionalista based on the
autonomous sentiments of the middle-class.

The Basque National Party (PNV) was already in existence as a reaction
against the loss of Basque privileges. Its progress was slower as Basque
industrialists and financiers tended to ally themselves with Madrid. But in
both cases fully-fledged nationalism was clearly a response to industrialisation in peripheral areas where memories of a semi-independent
existence were still fresh and where distinctive linguistic and cultural
traditions increased the sense of alienation from the centre.

The two pillars of Castialian autocracy, the military and the Madrid
bureaucracy, refused to make concessions to the forces of regionalism
even when, as in Catalonia, they could claim to speak for a majority of the
population. When parliamentary government collapsed in the early
1920s, General Primo de Rivera imposed centralised rule, convinced that
'a quarter of a century's silence about the regions . . . and Spain will have
been freed from one of her greatest perils'. But the uneven economic and
social development of Spain, with a backward conservative centre
refusing to give any ground to an economically advanced periphery,
exacerbated separatist leanings and made the 1930s an explosive decade.
Separatism was seen as a more insidious and dangerous foe than

Communism by many among those in the threatened privileged interests which in 1939 would emerge triumphant from the civil war.

Regional sentiments were ruthlessly suppressed and any remaining vestiges of practical autonomy were curtailed except in one Basque province, Navarre, which had sided with Franco in the civil war and, as a reward, was allowed to retain many of the fiscal and municipal powers which all the Basque provinces had once possessed. The excesses and cruelties of Francoism bred a violent response and, by the late 1960s, the actions of ETA, the Basque guerrilla movement, were destroying the myth of the authoritarian regime's inviolability. By killing Franco's designated successor in 1973, ETA short-circuited the ailing leader's plans for an orderly succession. Upon his death in 1975 his successor, King Juan Carlos, realised that his survival, and that of the restored monarchy, depended on coming to terms with the popular groundswell for democracy.

Transition to democracy

The transition to democracy succeeded for a number of interlocking reasons. Franco had presided, however uneasily, over important economic and social changes which made a continuation of authoritarian rule increasingly unrealistic. Indeed, the last fifteen years of his rule when the Spanish economy enjoyed the greatest period of expansion in its history, also witnessed possibly the most profound changes in Spanish society since the expulsion of the Jews and the Arabs before the seventeenth century: the majority of people ceased to depend on the land, there was a rapid transfer of people to the cities, and centuries of relative isolation were replaced by a drive towards closer integration with Europe. Franco had left behind a powerful old guard or 'bunker' but it found itself daunted by the prospect of having to subdue a complex, modern society; the two individuals at the helm of the post-Franco state, the new Head of state, King Juan Carlos, and Adolfo Suarez, the man he appointed as Prime Minister in 1976, proved able to appease and isolate the old guard while convincing popular forces that restoration of democracy was on the agenda.

Without the emergence of a gifted opportunist like Suarez who had the nerve and the insider knowledge to set about dismantling the authoritarian regime, the process could not have been accomplished with so little upheaval. Perhaps in Britain if pressure for a democracy based on active citizenship achieves the momentum that the desire for democratic renewal achieved in Spain in the 1970s, a well-placed and shrewd Suarez-like member of the political establishment will emerge to smooth the path towards full-scale reform of the system. A foretaste of what could happen may have been provided in the biggest constitutional upheaval of the post-war period: the ending of Northern Ireland's self-governing status by the

Conservatives, hitherto the champions of the Unionist cause. William Whitelaw, the gravedigger of the old Stormont system, had all the attributes, high rank in the masonic order, distinguished army service, and a family steeped in Orange tradition, to forestall a violent backlash from the Unionist ultras.

Regional autonomy was at first low on the agenda as the Franco state was liquidated. In 1977 after the first free elections since before the civil war, Spain found itself being governed by the Union of the Democratic Centre, a liberal-Christian Democrat party composed of opposition moderates and young middle-ranking state officials prepared to replace Francoism with a European style democracy. The failure of the party to make electoral headway in Catalonia persuaded Suarez of the need to recognise the region's special status.

Catalan consciousness had shown no signs of diminishing as the Barcelona area witnessed spectacular economic growth which drew in migrants from Andalucia and Castile, so that by 1980 40% of the population was non-Catalan in origin. For a common front against dictatorship had emerged in the 1970s drawing in Catalan nationalists and immigrants who felt no inclination to identify with the centralist dictatorship, especially one whose propaganda had eulogised the frugal, devout peasant of Castile while its economic policies were depopulating the region. There were difficulties and delays but considering the centuries of antagonism between Catalonia and Madrid, it is remarkable how smoothly obstacles were dealt with; by 1980 it was possible to establish an autonomous government in Barcelona. Central government had refrained from exploiting the social tensions arising from a large immigrant population living alongside an indigenous population acutely sensitive of its own native culture and the persecution it had received in the previous forty years; and armed separatism was not a complicating factor because a highly pragmatic political force, 'Convergence and Unity', spoke for the bulk of the nationalist electorate. It emerged as the largest party in the first regional elections of 1980 and in the following two contests it won outright majorities to govern Catalonia through the 1980s.

The route to Basque autonomy was far more problematic since the democratic era saw an intensification of ETA's campaign of violence against the Spanish state in a bid to create an independent Euskadi or Basque homeland. For too long Suarez saw the Basque problem as one of public order. A bold gesture of conciliation that could have isolated ETA from its mass support, such as a broad amnesty or even recognition of the Basque flag, was not forthcoming – perhaps for fear of provoking the military *ultras* into outright revolt. Precious time was lost before the Government realised that the only chance of bringing peace to the region lay in the creation of an effective autonomous government controlled by Basque nationalists. Tough negotiations were dragged out in 1979 between Suarez and Carlos Garaikoetxea, the leader of the PNV, the largest and least militant of the Basque parties. The statute agreed upon gave the Basques a larger measure of self-government than any other region was to receive. Euskadi argued successfully on historic grounds for the right to levy and collect all taxes except custom duties and taxes on petrol and tobacco. While Spain's other autonomous communities are financed under a block grant arrangement, Euskadi, basing its case on its historic rights, argued for a method of financing that gave it more control of its revenue. The Basques were also given the right to set up their own police force and to control their own radio and television stations (the latter being a big concession in a land where the party running central government has imposed strict conformity on what can be broadcast.

The ambiguous approach

In retrospect, there is a strong case for suggesting that Spain's leaders did not really appreciate the importance of what they were setting in motion. There was no clearly thought out theoretical approach or even step-by-step policy but a series of initiatives in reaction to pressure of events, often dictated by short-term tactical considerations. The picture was no different in Britain where the devolution proposals of the mid-1970s were a response to nationalist pressure rather than a recognition of the need for a coherent strategy of institutional rebuilding.

The ambiguous approach to the new shape of regional Spain and the powers it could acquire was reflected in the 1978 Constitution. Article 2 refers to 'the indissoluble unity of the Spanish Nation, the common and invisible fatherland of all Spaniards, and recognises and guarantees the right to autonomy of the nationalities and regions'. The term 'nationalities' is not defined and appears nowhere else in the constitution, it being a device which allowed the Basques and Catalans (and later the Galicians) to feel that their status as historic entities was being recognised.[3]

The constitution allows for a decentralised Spain divided into 'autonomous communities', a term which had no precedent in Spanish constitutional law. Two levels of autonomy are recognized, one to meet the demands of the historic nationalities which enjoyed strong traditions of autonomy, the other to encompass those regions in which the desire for self-government had hitherto been absent.

It has long been suspected that the impetus behind 'decentralisation all-round' lay in the need to appease influential elements of the military. They feared that singling out the Basques and Catalans for special recognition was taking a big step towards the dismemberment of Spain. The slow

---

[3] A definition of the two terms by Oscar Jaszi, the Hungarian sociologist, as he felt they applied to east-central Europe at the end of the Hapsburg period, may well apply to contemporary Spain: '"nation" means a fully mature nationality which has reached its complete independence as a state-building organism; "nationality", on the contrary, means a struggling national entity which under the sway of a dominant nation has not yet reached its complete independence'. O. Jaszi, *The Dissolution of the Habsburg Monarchy*, University of Chicago Press, Chicago 1927, p. 26.

complicated route mapped out for those other regions (who could only achieve autonomous status after a period of five years in which at least two-thirds of local provincial councils show a clear majority in favour) suggests that the political draughtsmen may not have envisaged autonomy extending into every region.

Nevertheless, it soon became clear that there was no part of Spain which wanted to be excluded from the autonomy process. The tide of social change which had transformed Spain into a consumer-orientated society with a large middle-class had not undercut loyalty to the *patria chica* (the little fatherland) which in the turbulent periods after 1800 had often eclipsed wider loyalty to a state, and a state, moreover, which to many Spaniards had appeared as artificial or threatening. The prospect of seeing powers won back from Madrid to a more accessible tier of government was such an attractive one that no council in any of Spain's 39 provinces held out against the autonomy process. Discontent from provincial and municipal governments would emerge later as powers were lost to the '*Autonomias*', but what is striking is the way that local patriotism took precedence over the powers of municipal and provincial government.

Could Britain follow?

Would local self-assertion be sufficient to drown the protests of municipal power-holders if Britain went down the same road of wholesale decentralisation? In Scotland, where national self-consciousness and disgruntlement with central control is comparable with feeling in Catalonia and Euzkadi, this may well prove to be the case. The large regional councils which emerged in the 1970s did not become a focus for loyalty and affection because of their unwieldy and anonymous character (nobody is going to perish on the barricades for 'Central' Region). Moreover, the biggest unit, Strathclyde Regional Council has given demonstrable backing to the Scottish Constitutional Convention in its bid to create a self-governing parliament with entrenched powers.

England, however, lacks any tradition of political expression in the regional sense. Below the central state, the countries were the chief focus of political identity and when local government reorganisation abolished them in the 1970s as the units of government, the new structures did not engage the loyalties of voters in anything like the same way. To reconstitute the counties in any scheme for regional government would probably turn out to be a costly exercise resulting in the duplication of services. In those parts of Spain where, as in England, identification with town or district was not accompanied by an over-arching regional consciousness, strenuous efforts were made to prevent the proliferaton of 'autonomias' based on single provinces. Some, like Asturias or Murcia, were based on a province either because the province was a compact entity or because it did not prove possible to link up with adjoining areas, and they have turned out to be a success. But it proved difficult to know what to do about Castile, the sparsely populated tableland comprising much of the Spanish interior. It was felt to be simply too big to be an 'autonomia' in its own right and it was rather arbitrarily divided into Castile-Leon and Castile-La Mancha. Discontent with this arrangement is evident by the graffitti in favour of a separate Leon. Attempts to carve out similar artificial units in the English South and Midlands might induce a similar sense of displacement.

History has been ransacked to find precedents that will enable continuity with a submerged past to be claimed by the autonomous communities. Castile-Leon traces its identity back to the sixteenth-century revolt of the independent towns and communities of this part of Spain against the centralising designs of Charles V. Perhaps if future English regions promote themselves as assiduously as former industrial towns have been able to do, by reinventing themselves as heritage centres, dimly remembered events such as the Monmouth rebellion or the Pilgrimage of Grace will emerge in order to provide a focus of identity.

Inevitably the rather makeshift character of some of the regions enabled the central bureaucracy to maintain and even expand its powers and influence rather than see them curtailed which was the hope of the more idealistic drafters of the autonomy statute. Government departments in Madrid used the excuse of improving links with and between the regions, especially the weaker ones, to carve out a role which justified maintaining the old high rates of expenditure and staffing which had made the Spanish bureaucracy an object of criticism.

The resilience of the central Spanish state placed the 'autonomias' that claim to be nation-based very much on their guard. They have insisted that past tradition of self-rule mean that they deserve preferential status. The control over their own finances accorded to the Basques and the leeway given to Catalonia in regard to cultural and education policy is a sign that their distinctiveness has been recognised. Similar demands are likely to be made in those parts of Britain where nation and state are not identical. A tradition of statehood, the survival of distinctive institutions, as well as a form of administrative devolution, all combine to make many Scots feel that they are deserving of powers of self-determination significantly greater than those likely to be given to the English regions. Such assertiveness has been the cause of resentment or else incomprehension in an area like the North-East of England where impatience with the performance of the unitary state has given demands for regional government a sharper edge than elsewhere. Local politicians have tended to see Scotland as simply another declining industrial region which (having already done better in terms of assistance from the central exchequer), has a flimsy case for advocating entrenched powers of self-government. Parts of Spain have seen a similar response to the demands of the Basques and Catalans for self-determination.

Different time-schedules

The establishment of an unwieldy form of decentralisation, falling short of federalism but extending beyond administrative devolution which allowed for different degrees of autonomy and different time-schedules in which it could be achieved, was a recipe for conflict. The most serious challenge to this untidy formula came not from the historic nationalities but from Andalucia, the largest of the designated regions, containing one-sixth of the Spanish electorate. A nationalist movement emerged which in the 1979 election won five seats in the Spanish parliament. Notwithstanding this, the Suarez government decided that Andalucia must embark on the slower route to autonomy.[4] Its status was not clearcut: a region which had a distinctive culture derived from the Moorish period but one that had never been an historic entity in its own right and which, since the Reconquest, had been an extension of Castile populated mainly by Castilians.

Andalucia was the prime example of how regional consciousness began to stir in the face of the political transformation of Spain. It may have also been a defensive reaction to the homogenising tendencies of mass culture in the wake of the region's exposure to tourism. Suarez's decision that Andalucia should follow the slow route to autonomy unless a majority of the electorate in each of its eight provinces voted otherwise in a referendum held in 1980 provoked uproar. Despite the state media's refusal to give any publicity to those in favour of Andalucia being treated as an historic region, the angry Andalucians turned out in larger numbers than either the Basques or the Catalans had done and voted over-whelmingly in favour of rapid autonomy. However, one province—Almeria—failed to meet the requirement that half the electorate must vote positively and the result there invalidated all the rest. Andalucia could not proceed to establish an autonomous government even though nearly two-thirds of the five million electorate had gone to the polls. Meanwhile, in Galicia, later in 1980 the autonomy process could go smoothly ahead even though there was only a 28% turnout in the referendum, owing to its status as a historic region.

If cumbersome ground-rules were to produce such a farcical outcome in any process enabling the countries and regions of Britain to acquire self-government, they could well fatally damage the whole enterprise given the range of interests in the media and the structure of metropolitan power likely to be hostile to any meaningful transfer of power. In the event, the Andalucian muddle hastened the collapse of the ruling UCD and contributed to the resignation of Suarez at the start of 1981; in February

---

[4] An illuminating account of the autonomy process has been given by a former Suarez minister who resigned over the treatment of Andalucia in 1980. See Manuel Clavero Arevalo, *Espana' desde el centralismo a las autonomias*, Planeta, Barcelona 1983.

Spain's democracy only narrowly averted being topped in a *coup* led by officers appalled at the multiple assaults on the unity and integrity of their Spain.

The Calvo Sotelo Government concluded that the brakes would have to be applied to the process of regional autonomy to avoid further attacks on the state itself. Following a summit to discuss regional autonomy to which no Basque or Catalan leaders were invited, the main Madrid-based parties used their combined parliamentary votes to pass in July 1981 the Organic Law on the Harmonisation of the Autonomy Process. LOAPA sought to claw back powers already agreed with the autonomous communities and to force their parliaments to look to the central government for the ratification of their laws in areas where they could initiate legislation. It was met with huge protests in Catalonia and the Basque Country as ethnic parties tried to block its implementation. Eventually, the Constitutional Court held that certain provisions did violate the constitution and that LOAPA could not be implemented. This was a rare concession to regional sentiment from a body which has more usually reflected Madrid-based opinion.

However, Spain was in a state of flux in the early 1980s which culminated in the collapse and disappearance of the ruling UCD and the election to office of the centre-left PSOE (Spanish Socialist Workers Party) in 1982. The prolonged weakness of the parliamentary right has enabled it to be twice re-elected, though with a diminishing share of the vote. During what has become the PSOE era in Spain, one region, Andalucia, has acted as the chief power-base of the government. It is the home not just of Prime Minister Felipe Gonzalez but of leading party officials who mounted a successful assault on the central power structures of their own party and who, once in office, continued to operate in such a clannish way that they were soon unkindly described as 'the Seville Mafia'.[5] Playing such a pivotal role, it is not surprising that Andalucia has done well in the allocation of government resources and in the location of major prestige projects. Despite the aura of modernisation that surrounds the Gonzalez administration, patronage has been extended or withheld in the age-old Spanish manner by a government far more concerned with wielding the state machine to its own advantage than with fulfilling its pre-election promises to overhaul and reform a cumbersome and often self-serving bureaucracy.[6]

As PSOE has increasingly come to occupy a moderate political position (its attachment to Thatcherite economics makes it more conservative than its ill-fated predecessor, the UCD), one of the few ways it has kept faith with its marxist heritage is by remaining strongly centralist in outlook.

[5] PSOE's centralist outlook is well-conveyed in the definitive study of the party in the 1936–87 period by Richard Gillespie, *The Spanish Socialist Party*, Clarendon Press, Oxford 1988.

[6] For the way in which modernist rhetoric sits uneasily alongside old-fashioned political practices in PSOE, see the chapters on Spain in T. Gallagher and A. N. Williams (ed), *Southern European Socialism*, Manchester University Press, Manchester, 1989.

TOM GALLAGHER

Regionalism has been decried as reactionary and pre-modern. Refusal to make further concessions to regional sentiment was just one of the ways in which a Government burdened by a radical past sought to demonstrate its fitness to rule in the eyes of the still powerful military. In the first PSOE term, transfers of power to the Basque government, which had already been agreed, were blocked. By the mid-1980s the Basques and Madrid were locked in a tussle over the financing and administration of the region's social security and social insurance schemes. For a long time the Socialist government insisted upon a uniform system of unemployment provision and health care. Eventually when autonomy was finally obtained in these areas, the welfare provisions introduced by the PNV-dominated coalition turned out to be in advance of what existed in the rest of the country: the ruling Socialists in Madrid had turned their faces against a strong safety net for the unemployed leaving the running to the Christian Democrats.[7]

Mutual distrust between a purposeful government which views the distribution of power as a threat to its own authority and regions which have drawn upon strong local consciousness to provide effective rule, has soured the relationship between centre and self-governing periphery. The challenge to PSOE's electoral dominance has mainly presented itself in regional terms since the Government's rightward drift means that difference between the chief Madrid-based parties are now very slight. In 1986 the Government's securing of a Yes vote in a referendum to decide on Spain's membership of NATO was undermined when the Basque Country and Catalonia voted against inclusion in the western military alliance. In the 1989 general election PSOE lost its overall majority in part thanks to the increase in support for regional or outright nationalist parties, more of which are represented in parliament than anywhere else in Europe. The failure of the centre-right to form a single unified party and ruthless attempts by the central apparatus of PSOE to quell dissent by enforcing conformity at all levels of the party, have allowed regional parties to be outlets for dissatisfaction; and they may have prevented frustrations with an increasingly autocratic style of rule from spilling over into more destructive courses.

The EC dimension

The tug of war between the Madrid government and the regions intensified following Spain's admission to the European Community in 1986. Madrid's insistence on centralised economic policy co-ordination, so that Spain can derive the best advantage from EC membership, has run into resistance from the historic regions anxious to keep control over their

---

[7] C. Ross, 'Basque Lessons For Scotland', *Radical Scotland*, No 43, February/March 1990.

local economies. Conflict soon surfaced over the collection of VAT. Madrid argued that it was such a complicated tax that only central government could levy and collect it. But the Basques insisted that the strong measure of economic control allowed by their statute of autonomy gave them the right to levy and collect VAT on all firms domiciled in their autonomous community.

All the Spanish autonomous regions have an office in Brussels and enjoy observer status with the Community. The Basque Country and Catalonia, in particular, are aware of the benefits opening up for their areas since Spain joined the EC. Geographical proximity to the main EC markets and the weight of existing industry gives them advantages other parts of Spain lack: much of the foreign investment that flooded into Spain after 1985 has been in the Bilbao-Zaragosa-Barcelona axis that includes both regions. The welter of regulations emanating from the EC has interfered with the operation of the autonomy statutes often down to the minutest detail. Controversy has raged about who should implement the Brussels directives preparing the way for a single European market, an argument which the central state seems to have won. The Spanish government has also insisted on maintaining control of the EC regional fund, thus preventing the autonomous communities from having a determining role in the manner of its allocation. Its track-record in Andalucia poses a question-mark over its claim to be an honest-broker, but difficulties lie in the way of the autonomous regions forming a solid front to gain some leverage over a vitally important source of revenue that will only flow for a limited period. Solidarity between the autonomous regions has been notable by its absence in the 1980s. The most powerful ones, Euskadi and Catalonia, have been slow to make common cause with the others, which are mainly Castilian in outlook, perhaps because of a fear that this will diminish their claim for recognition as distinct nationalities. As a result, inter-regional associations to deal with common problems such as pollution, or inter-regional cartels to confront multi-nationals so that they do not play one region off against another, have been slow to emerge.

The region best-placed to forge an alliance against the centralised tendencies of Madrid is Catalonia. It is home to Spain's most powerful nationalist movement, Convergence and Unity, which has run the Catalan autonomy government since its inception and has worked relatively smoothly with the large Castilian-speaking population in its midst. Catalonia has participated in inter-regional initiatives in the EC and champions the concept of Europe of the Regions, whereby decision-making runs from sub-national to supra-national bodies with the nation-state no longer being the pivotal arm of government. However, its failure to overcome historical rivalries with other regions so as to forge a powerful Iberian coalition that might breathe life into the concept, suggests that 'Europe of the Regions' remains a rhetorical device for a sub-national unit like Catalonia keen to carve out its place in the new Europe.

Possible examples of such rhetorical shadow-boxing were the motions passed by the Basque and Catalan parliaments at the close of 1989 that only their respective electorates can limit or define the amount of self-determination they should have: moreover in deciding what their relationship with the rest of Spain should be, total independence was not to be excluded as an option. The background for such an initiative was exasperation with the restrictive interpretation of the scope of autonomy emanating from the Gonzalez government as well as a desire to be identified with the independence movements building up in the former Baltic States, where similar statutes were being proclaimed.

The least-known of Spain's stateless nations was staking a claim for recognition in the new Europe emerging from the collapse of authoritarian rule. Thanks to the emergence of Manuel Fraga, the populist conservative, as president of Galicia's autonomous community in December 1989, the remotest of Spain's historic nationalities began to figure more prominently in Spain's constitutional debates. Galicia's rich cultural heritage and widely-spoken language (Gallego being related to Portuguese), have been the basis of its claim for separate status. Political nationalism has been weak and divided, perhaps because this poor region, known for high rates of emigration, lacked the strong economic base which proved to be a catalyst for nationalism in turn-of-the-century Barcelona and Bilbao. Nevertheless, despite having served in a Franco cabinet, Fraga seems determined to acquire as much self-government for his ill-favoured region as possible. This ex-centralist has embraced the symbols of Galician nationhood with gusto and in 1990 made an official visit to neighbouring Portugal which evoked criticism that he was pursuing his own foreign policy. Comparisons with the late Franz-Josef Strauss, whose populist conservativism enabled Bavaria to enjoy a considerable degree of autonomy within the Federal German state, are increasingly heard.[8]

Constitutional reform?

If constitutional reform, leading to the break-up of the Westminster-Whitehall axis becomes a distinct possibility in Britain, the Spanish experience is bound to be utilised by both opponents of change and its advocates: it has been such an ambiguous process that it contains lessons that both centralisers and reformers can press into service on their own behalf.

A glance at British political arrangements reveals that a number of the elements that have complicated the decentralisation process in Spain are also present: well-entrenched central interests reluctant to see a diminution of their powers; regions that lack a distinctive identity and whose

[8] See J. Gibbons, 'Spain's Bavaria: the 1989 Regional Elections in Galicia', *ACIS*, Vol. 4, No 2, Autumn 1990.

weakness may enable the central state bureaucracy to maintain its influence even in the institutions of a legally decentralised polity; a recent tradition of pursuing an *ad hoc*, short-term approach to decentralising power which, because of built-in ambiguities, leads to the risk of the whole process being short-circuited; tensions between already existing local tiers of government and those proposing Parliaments or Assemblies based on historic precedent or the particular needs of regions or former state territories (Scotland); and an undeclared civil-war in an area containing a population of mixed loyalties where heavy-handed state measures have had the effect of pushing one segment into protracted revolt.

In 1989 a delegation from the Scottish Constitutional Convention were guests of the government of Euskadi. During their fact-finding mission, they were impressed by the progress made over a relatively short period in setting up an efficient form of government which was accessible to the population in a manner new to Spain. It is unclear where the unravelling of a state like Spain's grounded firmly on the unitary principle will ultimately lead. Will the outcome be a fully federal state? or for a long time to come will the autonomous process continue to be an untidy affair reflecting the uneasy compromises that have been worked out between central governments and vigorous regions on the margins of the state no longer prepared to endure subordinate status? Whatever the outcome, the Spanish experience offers many lessons for reformers keen to redistribute power on a more rational and effective basis so that there is little likelihood of the democratic absolutism that marked the 1980s returning as a governing style in the future.

EUROPE AND THE REGIONS

DAVID COOMBES*

Economic integration by means of the European Community was initially expected to lead in time to a political federation encompassing most of Western Europe, but it has also been viewed as possibly encouraging claims for regional autonomy within existing states and re-uniting communities now divided by national frontiers. Integration and disintegration of established political authority may, in other words, be seen as complementary.

Like most conjecture about European integration, however, political debate on this aspect is often confused and is liable to raise false expectations. The consequences of European integration for the present system of nation-states are far from self-evident. In particular, economic integration does not necessarily lead to political federation. This is one of the main lessons—and a painful one for many political scientists—of the past experience of the European Community. Indeed, a large measure of international economic integration has been occurring in Europe and much more widely without any substantial changes in political structures or even in the strength of national identities. European federation is a process that is still necessarily unfolding and uncertain.

Moreoever, the claims and pretensions made on behalf of regional or local communities within existing European nation-states vary greatly in both their economic and political significance. They range from separatist or irredentist nationalism to the utilitarian defence of local or provincial commercial interests. To lump them together as some common species of 'regionalism' can be altogether misleading.

These complex issues have, however, acquired major practical significance as a result of certain important recent developments in the European Community. In particular, the European Community has in the last few years adopted a series of new measures and procedures in an attempt to deal with evident economic inequalities between different regions. This particular development is not by itself as exciting as sometimes seems to be assumed either by autonomist political movements or by ordinary regional and local authorities. In the first place, the European Community still has no genuine common regional policy. In the second place, even it if had, this would not necessarily favour de-centralisation of political authority within the states, let alone any revision of established national boundaries. On the other hand, when taken together with other developments, the Community's largely unsuccessful search for a regional policy

* The author is Professor of European Studies, University of Limerick, has published numerous books and articles on British, European and international politics, and served as a private consultant to the EC on various subjects, including most recently local development.

does have potentially far-reaching implications for territorial structures of political authority.

Integration and disparity

The first and the earliest development we need to consider is the European Community's own recognition that economic disparities across space present a major predicament. A division of the Community between richer and poorer areas, corresponding largely to a geographical distinction between centre and periphery, first became evident in the mid-1970s and has persisted ever since. It has among other things intensified demands for special measures of public intervention to assist those regions that apparently benefit less from increased economic integration and may even be worse off as a result of it.

Consequently, regional policy, which had previously been a marginal aspect of European affairs, became a much more politically-charged issue. The response to regional inequalities in the common market has, in fact, had more to do with appeals to sectional interest, political doctrine or ethical standards than with economic analysis.

Economic analysts face all kinds of difficulties in trying to estimate regional differences in economic performance in the Community, not least because they have to rely on existing political (and national) definitions of what constitutes a region and these are usually arbitrary from an economic (and a European) point of view. For some years now the Community has used a definition of peripheral areas proposed by academic geographers on the basis of a variety of economic and social indicators. In the present Community of twelve the areas concerned (on the basis of 1983 data) cover over 40 per cent of the Community's surface, contain 20 per cent of its population but produce only 12 per cent of its gross domestic product (GDP). Economic activity in the same areas tends to be highly dependent on agriculture and they have far higher rates of unemployment than the Community average.[1]

However, it is primarily in terms of economic divergence between member states themselves that 'spatial disparity' has come to be treated by the Community as a problem demanding special actions at a European level. One of the main factors contributing to the problems of the disadvantaged areas was the series of world economic recessions that, along with other more or less contingent trends and events, produced general circumstances unfavourable to sustaining economic growth in the Community as a whole. Another factor was the enlargement of the Community's membership, successively in 1973, 1981 and 1986, to include new states with very different economic conditions from those of the original

---

[1] See D. Keeble, J. Offord and S. Walker, *Peripheral Regions in a Community of 12 Member States*, Commission of the European Communities, Brussels, 1988.

135

six members. The latter had all experienced a remarkably rapid expansion up to the end of the 1960s. They have even managed to sustain a modest rate of economic growth since, though with much higher rates of unemployment. Nevertheless, the fact that the more prosperous states were better equipped to cope with the effects of world recessions, while the common market was being extended to those in an economically weaker position, only strengthened suspicions that spatial disparity may be endemic to economic integration.[2]

Indeed, some economic theorists maintain that spatial disparity between central and peripheral areas is an inevitable consequence of the removal of barriers to economic movement across political frontiers and that its causes are essentially 'structural'. The centre or 'core' of a common market is, for example, assumed to benefit disproportionately through its better access to consumers and suppliers, its attraction of mobile labour and capital, and its greater capacity to exploit technological innovation and economies of scale. The disadvantages of the periphery are expected to get correspondingly worse.

Certainly, the regional problems envisaged by such a model of economic change are different in kind from the short-term adjustments normally expected from innovations like the European common market or even changes in technology, wider patterns of international trade or consumer preferences. However, as with many economic theorems, a long-term causal or 'structural' relationship between integration and spatial disparity is extremely difficult, if not impossible, to establish with any certainty.

The 'core/periphery' model is often used to ,ecommend nationally autarkic policies as the only defence available to the weaker regions. This kind of prescription has had some influence, especially in the 'core/periphery' model's original application to the problems of less-developed Third-World countries.[3] However, the same assumptions should presumably apply to economic integration at any level—not just in the European Community or world-wide but also within nation-states themselves. If the model's assumptions are consistently applied, even a self-sufficient national economy would still contain disadvantaged peripheral regions, while if these regions were independent nations, they would in their turn generate their own internal disparities. This kind of geographical determinism is, therefore, of little practical use for policy makers trying to remedy the effects of regional disequilibria.

---

[2] Disparity between member states is normally measured in terms of Gross Domestic Product (GDP) per inhabitant. Taking this measure for the Community of 12 to equal 100, in the period 1984–6 four states appear exceedingly worse off: Greece scored 57, Spain 72, Ireland 64 and Portugal 52; Luxembourg (126), Denmark (116), Germany (115) and France (111) appear very much better off.

[3] The relevant theoretical approaches are expounded and analysed in: H. Armstrong and J. Taylor, *Regional Economics and Policy*, Philip Allan, Oxford, 1985; S. Holland, *The Uncommon Market*, Macmillan, London, 1980, pp. 49–65; D. Pinder, *Regional Economic Development and Policy*, George Allen & Unwin, London, 1983.

An alternative approach is to consider how the consequences of economic integration can be satisfactorily managed. Those who put their faith in a mixed economy believe that suitably corrective forms of public intervention certainly can and should be used to mitigate the worst effects of spatial disparity, especially if the evidence suggests that they are otherwise unavoidable. They do not necessarily deny that regional disadvantage in a common market should be seen as a consequence of more deep-seated economic and social factors. However, they would expect appropriate measures of public policy to bring the beneficial effects of economic integration to all regions eventually. This 'mixed-economy' approach is the one that has usually tended to prevail both at national and European level in the Community.

The 'harmonious development of economic activities' is one of the fundamental objectives of the Treaty of Rome, which defines the method of achieving this objective (in its preamble) as 'reducing the differences existing between the various regions and the backwardness of the less favoured'. The Treaty does not simply provide for the liberalisation of trade and factors of production but also for a whole series of possible safeguards and interventionist measures: the common customs tariff, the common agricultural policy, rules against monopolistic and other restrictive practices, procedures for justifying state aids (especially when intended for regional development), the European Social Fund (ESF) and the European Investment Bank (EIB).

The fact that the European Economic Community went so far was highly controversial and displeased advocates of free trade. But it also reflected a delicate balance among regional economic interests defended by the original member states. Without some special safeguards to protect those interests (including especially the common agricultural policy, with its special attractions for France and, to a lesser extent, the ESF, promising advantages especially to Italy) the Community would certainly not have succeeded in establishing a customs union among the Six. However, in the changed international economic conditions of the 1970s and 1980s, and with the accession of new members with different economic interests to protect, the initial design of the late 1950s was clearly in need of reform. Moreover, some aspects of the partial economic order negotiated during the 1960s turned out to create more problems than they solve: in particular, the common agricultural policy (CAP) has itself contributed both to spatial disparity[4] and to new conflicts of interest between member states.

Nevertheless, the Community's reaction has been mainly conservative. Most of the member states' governments have been reluctant to give the Community additional powers to implement 'structural' measures, which might be expected to interfere with their own responsibilities for public management of economic affairs. The preference of the governments of

---

[4] See Commission of the European Communities, *Study of the Regional Impact of the Common Agricultural Policy*, Regional Policy Series No. 21, Brussels, 1981.

many states for 'monetarist' policies during the 1980s strengthened resistance to any substantial increase in the financial resources available to the Community for public intervention; by the mid-1980s the Community was, in fact, in a major financial crisis of its own. The problem of economically backward regions also to some extent came to be overshadowed by that of the general decline of growth rates and a critical increase in rates of unemployment for the Community as a whole (from 2 per cent at the beginning of the 1970s to almost 11 per cent in 1986). The natural tendency for governments to seek their own solutions to such economic problems vitiated the aim of removing preferential and protective barriers to trade and contributed to widely diverging price levels and rates of inflation. It was, in fact, these aspects of 'economic divergence' that most pre-occupied the Community at the beginning of the 1980s.[5]

For the past ten years the whole process of European integration has been under review and as a result the economic objectives of the Community have been largely renewed. The focus is now on two overriding and intimately connected aims: the abolition of remaining non-tariff barriers to free trade among the present twelve member states, chiefly by means of the highly-publicised 1992 programme; and, ultimately far more ambitious and significant, the establishment in phases of an economic and monetary union (EMU), based on centralised management of money markets with a federated system of central banks.

Effectively, then, the European Community is being reconstituted: the inaptly named Single European Act is already in place and the member states are currently negotiating a further set of amending treaties for EMU. However, this process is no more and no less than a long-delayed logical extension of the course of economic integration on which the original Community set out but for which inadequate legal provision was initially made. It is, in particular, now much more readily acknowledged that this course cannot be effectively followed, and the anticipated benefits cannot be gained, without a much greater measure of economic convergence.

'Convergence' is central to all the Community's policy statements explaining the advantages of further integration and how they are to be realised.[6] It is still far from clear how, on the one hand, 'convergence' as a *means* of realising intensified economic integration relates, on the other hand, to 'convergence' as an *end*. There are various ways of eliminating differences between national economic policies, depending on the price

[5] See M. Hodges and W. Wallace (eds.), *Economic Divergence in the European Community*, George Allen & Unwin, London, 1981.

[6] See Commission of the European Communities, *European Economy*, 'The Economics of 1992', No. 35, March 1988, 'The Economics of EMU', special issue, 1990, and 'One market, one money', No. 44, October 1990; Commission of the European Communities, *Report on Economic and Monetary Union to the European Council by the Committee chaired by J. Delors*, Brussels, 1989; T. Padoa-Schioppa, *Efficiency, Stability and Equity*, Oxford University Press, Oxford, 1987.

that it is considered justifiable or possible to expect the weaker members to pay. The result of integrating formerly separate national economies (by persuasion or force) may not, however, be convergence in real terms. Convergence in terms of EMU would entail, *by definition*, that states relinquish a whole range of remaining instruments that have previously been used to correct spatial disparities, including the power to fix nominal rates of exchange. To the extent that spatial disparity did, therefore, persist in an integrated European economy—whether between states or between regions within states—something else presumably would have to be done about the consequently unemployed human and physical resources. In earlier periods of history, the option was often to resettle weaker populations as slave labour and to requisition waste land for agricultural purposes. Emigration and tourism may be the more humane modern equivalents.

If, however, the general objective is, indeed, to improve the material conditions of life prevailing, say, in the West of Ireland or Thrace to a level comparable to those in, say, Hampshire or Baden (and to do so without any major reduction in the civic status of the populations concerned), then a whole series of unresolved questions arise about the economic changes this would entail and how they could be usefully facilitated, if at all. It may seem, therefore, all the more surprising that the governments of even the economically weaker member states have gone along with both the internal market and the EMU (which is in most respects its corollary) as much as they have. An explanation of this apparent peculiarity of political judgement will be offered next, but first we should note its likely consequences for regional interests alienated or divided by existing states.

Clearly, those interests—along with all others—can expect to become far less dependent on existing national authorities for their economic welfare, as state governments are divested of further instruments of economic and monetary policy. They must at the same time, however, expect to become far more dependent, other things being equal, on competitive economic forces and on their own capacities for responding to them. Regional communities that have already attained a relatively high degree both of economic advancement and of political autonomy (such as Flanders or Catalonia) might well view these future prospects of European integration favourably. Others that are less well endowed, however, (such as Northern Ireland or Crete) might well take a less optimistic view of their prospects in a wider market in which national governments have less scope to adopt protective measures. Whether and how far the Community itself manages to influence either view, and in ways that encourage the break-up of existing nation-states, have much to do with the interpretation of the causes of spatial economic inequality that the Community decides to adopt.

Economic and social cohesion

The second development to be considered arises from a series of decisions over the past five years that have significantly increased the Community's capacity to adopt an interventionist regional policy. Those decisions have important consequences for regional and local communities in all the member states, though more particularly for those considered least capable of adapting to economic change by their own efforts.

In the first place, although economic liberalisation is still the Community's primary objective, the previous vague commitment to 'harmonious development' has been upgraded by the addition of a new title to the EEC Treaty: 'economic and social cohesion'. This explicitly provides for financial intervention by the Community from its own resources for 'structural' ends. Economic and social cohesion is, therefore, now enshrined in the Community's basic law as a fundamental principle, an essential counterpart to the internal market without frontiers. Its real significance is, however, legal and political rather than economic and social. Indeed, it was formerly adopted by the Single European Act (SEA) in 1986 largely thanks to the negotiating skill of Greek and Irish representatives, helped by Portuguese and Spanish participation in the framing of the SEA as prospective new members.

It is still far from obvious what kinds of public intervention at a European level should, or could, be genuinely structural in effect. The primary responsibility for taking measures to deal with unacceptable spatial disparities (that is, to ensure 'harmonious development') rests as it always has with the member states themselves. Although 'aids granted by states' with an economic purpose are generally prohibited by the common market regime, the Commission may—and normally does—exempt approved national programmes of regional development from this rule (in accordance with articles 92 and 93 of the EEC Treaty). However, the Community's own legal framework, even as now revised, does not prescribe any particular definition or solution for the structural causes of regional inequalities in a common market. Nor do the amendments made by the SEA endow the Community with any substantially new powers to implement a common regional policy. The financial instruments to which they refer already existed, including the European Regional Development Fund (ERDF).[7]

The so-called 'structural funds', which constitute the main arm of

---

[7] Article 23 of the Single European Act defines the structural funds as the ESF, the ERDF and the Guidance Section of the European Agricultural Guidance and Guarantee Fund (EAGGF). Together with the lending operations of the EIB and the so-called 'new Community instrument' these make up the 'structural instruments'. The 1989 budgetary appropriations for the funds (in commitment expenditure) were, respectively: ECU 3.5 billion for the ESF; ECU 4.5 billion for the ERDF; and ECU 1.5 billion for the Guidance Section of EAGGF.

Community intervention for purposes of economic and social cohesion, form part of the Community's own budget. Expenditure from these funds is made by the Community's Commission in accordance with the budgetary allocations approved jointly on an annual basis by the Council (consisting of representatives of state governments) and the European Parliament. However, the funds can be used only for the purposes and in the ways specified in prior Community legislation, which in this case has to be adopted unanimously by the Council (on a proposal from the Commission and after consultation of the Parliament).

For the most part the funds can be used only to make partial contributions to public expenditure in the states themselves on application from the national governments concerned. They are chiefly intended to subsidise specific types of public works (to improve the physical infrastructure of regions or localities) and public services (mainly of vocational training and employment), though they have increasingly also subsidised new investment by private as well as public undertakings intended to modernise and otherwise adapt existing methods of production, especially in agriculture.

Strictly speaking, the funds are intended to compensate for additional public expenditure incurred as a direct consequence of spatial disparities that persist in spite (or because) of the common market. In effect, they serve as a limited means of re-distribution of financial resources between the governments of member states. More recently they have been rather crudely employed as a kind of payment on the side to those states otherwise most reluctant—and justifiably so—to accept the further opening of markets that the SEA was primarily intended to bring about.

Nevertheless, the status of regional policy at a European level has been notably re-inforced. And this represents a partial victory for those in the Commission who had complained for many years about the frustrations of trying to adopt a genuinely structural approach without the appropriate means—or the authority—to do so. The Commission successfully seized on an opportunity created by dissatisfaction on all sides to propose an overhaul of the whole system of intervention intended for 'structural' purposes. Although 'system' is probably still too generous a term to describe it, the result substantially increases the potential direct influence of the Community, and of the Commission in particular, on economic activity at a regional level, though mostly within the regions defined by the states themselves as being the most disadvantaged.

Reform of structural funds

The SEA provided for a reform of the structural funds, but it did not deal at all with two other inter-connected issues vital to its success: the methods of financing the Community's budget and reform of the common agricultural policy. Other important recent decisions have temporarily settled these issues in a package that included new provisional legislation for reform of the structural funds. The fact that this settlement is only of temporary effect and rests on delicate political compromises is a typical reason why the instruments of positive intervention available to the Community are still essentially limited.

The first of these decisions concerned the methods of financing the Community's budget and provisionally resolved a financial crisis that had built up over several years for a combination of reasons. Because of the redistributive effects of both revenue and expenditure, certain member states had become regular net contributors to the budget. On these grounds they objected to the tendency of Community expenditure to increase each year; the UK government forced the issue in 1985 by threatening to withhold Community revenues collected in its jurisdiction (an act which would have been illegal). It had always proved impossible to control expenditure on the Community's common agricultural policy, which accounted for between 60 and 75 per cent of the total budget, because this was pre-determined by a guarantee to maintain prices (and so also farmers' incomes) artificially in relation to fluctuating and unpredictable world market conditions. As agricultural expenditure had tended to grow in aggregate without benefiting all member states equally, so it had become impossible to meet other demands for Community expenditure, such as those for increased use of the structural funds, without, that is, finding new sources of revenue. By 1986 the overall level of expenditure from the Community's budget was such that existing sources of revenue were fully used up.[8] However, unlike most national governments, the Community is unable on its own authority either to create new sources of revenue or to run a budget deficit. This fundamental limitation remains, but the immediate financial crisis was resolved in 1988 by a package of measures designed to provide adequate resources for the ensuing five years.

The second decision was taken as a condition of these emergency financial arrangements. In an unprecedented step the Community adopted an 'inter-institutional agreement', which came into force on 1 July 1988 and virtually fixed allocations of expenditure for the period 1988–92 with the aim of providing 'budgetary discipline'. A vital part of this agreement is a commitment to hold expenditure on the guarantee activities of the CAP within a very confined ceiling. At the same time allowance is made for a substantial increase in expenditure on the structural funds. Consequently, these are expected to double in amount over the five-year period from ECU 7 billion to ECU 14 billion at 1988 prices.[9] Even allowing for the additional costs of catering for the accession

[8] Article 201 of the Treaty establishing the EEC. The Community's 'own resources' consist of all receipts from the common customs tariff and from agricultural import levies, receipts from a fixed percentage of the VAT (now 1.4 per cent) and a 'fourth resource' of special national contributions.
[9] Inter-institutional agreement on budgetary discipline and improvement of the budgetary procedure, *Official Journal of the European Communities*, No. L 185/33, 15 July 1988.

of two new member states in 1986, this increase reflects a major shift in the Community's whole approach in favour of 'structural' intervention rather than mere income support as in the CAP. Implementation of the agreement will mean that total expenditure from the structural funds will have risen from 1.2 per cent as a proportion of the budget in 1970 and 19.6 per cent in 1985 to 25 per cent by 1993. The relative influence of the Community's 'structural' policies in the member states' own expenditure decisions will also be significantly increased.[10]

Even so, the Community's budget will remain miniscule in comparison to typical national budgets, reaching no more than 1.2 per cent of total estimated Community GNP by 1992. It is not yet intended, therefore, to use the budget as either a mechanism for effecting significant inter-regional transfers on a lasting basis or an instrument of macro-economic policy.

However, the third set of decisions, on new regulations for the structural funds, give much greater weight to the Community in deciding how the money is to be distributed.[11] There is now a general priority to use the funds collectively for purposes of regional policy and specifically for 'promoting the development and adjustment' of the economically weakest regions. These are, in effect, the peripheral regions on the Community's western and southern margins. They include three states in their entirety, Greece, Ireland and Portugal, most regions of Spain, the Italian Mezzo-giorno, Northern Ireland, Corsica and the French overseas departments. These 'objective no. 1' regions should receive roughly 60 per cent of the funds available in the period 1989–93 and the rate of assistance that can be provided for these priority regions is significantly increased.

This priority has clearly been influenced by the geographical explanation of spatial disparity, though it also reflects the political demands of the recipient states. A relatively new category of problem regions is also included as a secondary target of financial intervention: those 'seriously affected by industrial decline' (measured chiefly in terms of rates of unemployment) scattered throughout the Community. In addition, special measures are provided for the development of economically and socially backward rural areas and for special categories of the unemployed. But the overriding concern is with the geographical and political aspects rather than with broader economic and social causes of inequality.

The new regulations also increase the Commission's influence on how the money from the structural funds is spent. This intensifies a trend over several years towards more discretionary use of the funds. In order to claim most of the subsidies now available each member state concerned has to submit a long-term regional development programme for the

[10] The structural funds are expected over the period 1989–93 to represent 2.3 per cent of GDP in Ireland, 2.9 per cent in Greece and 3.5 per cent in Portugal, see *European Economy*, No. 44, October 1990, p. 230.

[11] The relevant legislation and administrative procedures are set out in Commission of the European Communities, *Guide to the reform of the structural funds*, Brussels, 1989.

Commission's prior approval, which takes the form of a 'Community support framework' detailing the specific kinds of assistance that may be granted. This process must, in principle, involve representatives of all the various interested parties, including regional and local authorities, as must the subsequent procedures for 'monitoring' the implementation of the national programmes. This requirement has proved, not surprisingly, to be at the same time the most attractive from the point of view of regional interests themselves but also the most difficult to get member states' own central governments to observe in more than the letter.

Especially where the 'regions' concerned constitute entire states, the participation of regional and local interests seems to be in practice no more than consultative, while there has been considerable misunderstanding and disagreement between those governments and the Commission in this and other respects. There is, on the one hand, reasonable anxiety that direct dealings between the Commission and regional interests within the states might create havoc for the management of public expenditure (with all the implications for macro-economic policy that would entail). On the other hand, the Commission itself is simply not equipped with either the manpower or the legal and political authority to manage the efficient allocation of financial resources in response to the claims of local corporate interests.

There are, indeed, inherent shortcomings in the Community's whole approach to regional policy that arise partly from its very reliance on the structural funds as a method of public intervention. These will persist, in spite of the reforms now in place, and will have to be faced again, at least when the present arrangements come up for renewal in 1992, if not before, in view of the progress now being made towards EMU.

Above all, there are the overriding but still unsatisfactorily resolved questions pertaining to the Community budget—both how it is financed and how its resources are allocated and distributed. The structural funds, even as now expanded, are unlikely to be sufficient in quantitative terms to secure the weaker member states against all the possible repercussions of economic change consequent on the 1992 programme, let alone the prospects of EMU. Even if some reliable and objective measure were available of what would be sufficient in this sense, it is unlikely that all the states' governments could be convinced to accept it as an alternative to a new round of pragmatic bargaining, in which some would be bound to expect to come off better than others. More important is the question whether, even assuming a new deal on allocations to the existing structural funds can be struck, this is a suitable method of providing a re-distribution of resources.

Even if an increase in this spending were politically feasible, there must be a limit to what satisfaction national governments can derive from further subsidised public expenditure on roads, industrial sites, tourist facilities, telecommunications and even vocational training, as well as a limit to what projects of these types they can reasonably invent to claim

144

Community funds. From an economic and social point of view, of course, the limits of such 'structural' actions are even more apparent and more ludicrous in the breach. They also seem unavoidably to create additional responsibilities for national administrations, without necessarily altering the existing political and legal relationships between central and local authorities. The long-term value of increased Community 'regional' expenditure is, therefore, disputable in terms both of economic and social returns and of political expediency.

Certainly, the principle of economic and social cohesion implies far more than the use of the structural funds and extends to all spheres of Community policy as well as bearing directly on the policies of member states themselves. What it means in such a wider context, however, has not been articulated. This is a very serious shortcoming as the Community and its member states face the prospects of managing an integrated economic space, in which by the end of this century the state governments could be reduced to fiscal instruments in any attempt to treat unacceptable economic hardship anywhere in their own jurisdictions. Given the stress on economic convergence and monetary stability in the present official scenarios for EMU, even fiscal instruments cannot be expected to give much flexibility on their own.

It may be that the only genuinely structural approach is to hope that increased freedom of movement in a massive common market brings about desirable economic changes naturally. Almost by definition, however, this view implies a radical transformation in the existing relationship between public authorities and local communities, with the latter finding themselves dramatically more exposed. The concept of cohesion, indeed, makes no sense unless its political connotations are spelled out.

Federalism and regionalism

The last two relevant developments will be considered together and far more briefly. In combination they offer the only practical solution of the predicament for regional policy to which European integration seems inevitably to lead.

The first of them is the recently renewed prospect of some genuine movement towards political unification in Europe, at least among the present member states of the European Community. Not since the end of the second world war have so many prominent political personalities, including heads of government, been so willing to talk and act convincingly in terms of federation. This is partly an indirect consequence of the fundamental changes in world politics and, more particularly, in central and eastern Europe, that have now led to an end of the Cold War. It is also a direct consequence of the restored sense of confidence in economic integration inspired by the revival of the European Community in the 1980s. But it should be seen, additionally, as a recognition of the

145

basic shortcomings of the Community as a mere economic confederation of otherwise sovereign states.

The fundamental reason why the problem of spatial disparities in a common market has proved so intractable is that economic integration cannot bring the benefits expected of it, or be made compatible with the needs of public management, without a corresponding, if not a prior, adaptation of political institutions.

A genuine regional policy, in the sense of a concerted effort by public authorities to eliminate the causes of spatial economic inequalities, is possible only in a political union. One of the main reasons why it cannot exist in a mere confederation is that, as we have seen in the experience of the Community, there is no central authority capable of employing or controlling the instruments of public management that are necessary to design or implement such a policy. Ultimately, measures of subsidisation intended to recompense the participating states' own central authorities, however generous and however well backed by attempts to co-ordinate national programmes, cannot provide a solution to the underlying causes of economic inequality in a common market. They may temporarily relieve the symptoms and be a political device for keeping the confederation together. In the longer term, however, they are unlikely to serve even these limited purposes, partly because they give rise to inefficiency and partly because they make unreasonable demands on the generosity of the states which are net contributors.

The fact is that predictions based on economic theories of the liberalisation of trade are not sufficient on their own to justify European integration as an end of public policy. Political choices always have, and always should, prevail. Economic analysis cannot provide a reliable explanation of the causes of spatial disparity in an integrated economy, but public policy must continue to be concerned with the undeniable tendency of economic activity left to itself to threaten certain regions with possibly endemic economic decline or under-development. The fact that public policy does continue to concern itself with such outcomes is clearly demonstrated in the persistent tendency of the member states of the European Community to adopt a range of measures of their own, including both non-tariff barriers and fiscal and monetary instruments of macro-economic policy. The consequence, intended or not, has been to frustrate the aim of economic integration enshrined in the Community's basic law.

But there is no guarantee either, especially in view of wider international economic and technological changes, that by adopting these alternative protective measures the existing nation-states can eliminate the problem of spatial disparity by themselves. There is, in fact, good reason for supposing that they exacerbate it, at least in the longer term. They deprive all parts of the Community of increased benefits of greater economic efficiency and international competitiveness; and not all the states concerned are strong enough to pursue their own economic policies in the

146

face of international fluctuations without excessive inflation, mass unemployment or both.

If the governments of the Community's member states have now accepted the need for a genuine common market, this is, indeed, partly because the shortcomings of the present customs union and common agricultural policy became so apparent. In this sense, there is a certain irreversibility in the process of European economic integration. On the other hand, it has also become apparent that to obtain tolerable economic stability in a genuine common market, especially one with the free movement of capital, there must be much greater co-ordination of national economic policies than has existed up to now. The Community's current (and longstanding) priority in this respect is to promote greater monetary stability within the common market; even—perhaps especially—the weaker states see advantages in that objective. In fact, most of the states' governments seem now convinced that the present economic confederation must adopt a common monetary policy with a common institution to direct it, with or without a common currency as its central instrument. They also recognise, though with much less certainty as to how they would intend to manage the outcome, that such a step must effectively deprive the states concerned of much of their remaining scope to pursue independent macro-economic policies.

The decisions regarding EMU, therefore, are clearly also decisions about political unification and this has been acknowledged in the convening of an inter-governmental conference in December 1990 to decide measures of political union. Under that heading the states' governments seem, as in the past, to be mainly concerned with issues of foreign policy and security; this is appropriate enough, since no political union could conceivably exclude such matters. Nevertheless, the present Community falls far short of the requirements of a political federation in two other crucial respects.

On the one hand, a genuine federation would require political institutions that gave at least legislative power to elected representatives of all citizens, regardless of their nationality. That power could not be confined, as it now virtually is in the Community, exclusively to the executive branches the various states. On the other hand, a genuine federation would also be expected to assume responsibility for any residual problems of economic and social deprivation not adequately treated by public authorities at other levels. In other words, it would among other things have to have its own budget, which it would employ on its own responsibility for redistributive and other purposes and for which it would be accountable to the politically representative institutions.

The significance of these pre-requisites of a European federation will become clearer, if we consider another and final development. This is the apparent growth in West European states of what tends nowadays, unsatisfactorily, to be called 'regionalism'. Encompassed in this term tend, in fact, to be a whole mixture of political tendencies, administrative reforms and economic and social changes that have recently and widely challenged the centralised and bureaucratic nature of authority in the modern nation-state. The exact nature and practical consequences of this phenomenon are difficult to determine. When states establish distinct 'regional' units of government within their jurisdiction, this is as likely as not to be mainly for the convenience of central administration rather than for the granting of political autonomy to local communities. 'Regionalism' as political doctrine verges on the absurd, failing to distingush between the contrary values of national separatism or irredentism, on the one hand, and the general de-centralisation of state authority, on the other.

In fact, as we have already seen, the 'regions' considered pertinent to European regional policy are in some cases sovereign states. In other cases, however, they are not. The status of Northern Ireland is particularly anomalous in this regard and in a way that might have been expected to lead to more political controversy. Although considered equivalent in economic terms to the Republic of Ireland, as a 'priority region', Northern Ireland does not, however, have the same political status as the Republic, which is a member state of the Community in its own right. Indeed, in view of the strength of separatist tendencies in places like Scotland, Catalonia, the Basque country, Sicily and so on, many regions must be wondering why they do not share the political status now afforded to Ireland, Greece and Portugal. On the other hand, their status as economic regions of the Community is equally disputable from the perspective of distinctive regions and localities within those member states. It may, indeed, impede effective treatment of crucial spatial disparities, especially since these same states have the most centralised and concentrated political systems in the Community.

However, if barriers to inter-state economic activity are virtually to disappear, and especially in the framework of EMU, sovereign statehood must otherwise lose most of its normal economic advantages. In this respect nationalist separatism is actually deprived of much of its economic rationale. At the same time, there will be less economic reasons for political authority within states to be centralised. Indeed, local communities will need more resources and more initiative of their own—both political and economic. Opportunities for direct political representation at a European level must consequently be seen as all the more important for those communities, whether central or peripheral, as must the capacity and the willingness of public authorities at a European level to adopt economic and social policies compatible with their interests. It is in the context of federalism, therefore, and probably only in that context, that 'regionalism' begins to make sense as a coherent doctrine of political change.

Conclusions

So long as the process of economic integration in Europe is treated as compatible with the continued sovereignty of nation-states, economic and social inequality between regions cannot be avoided. Possibly, as some economic theories seem to suggest, they cannot be avoided anyway, except at excessive costs in terms of economic efficiency. Possibly, economic integration, of which the new legal order being gradually put in place by the Community is only one aspect, leads inevitably to the deprivation or exploitation of some regions by others. Regional policy is in any event of doubtful efficacy as a palliative or a cure.

As often as not regional policies demand a far greater measure of centralisation than is compatible either with good administration or with the demands of regional and local interests. What now passes for regional policy in the European Community is in effect nothing much more than a valiant attempt to co-ordinate certain types of public expenditure in the member states, including a preponderant element of political bargaining in which the financial policies of central governments are usually the decisive factor. The Community still does not have any better intelligence than national governments themselves as to what the structural causes of regional inequalities are or how to treat them effectively.[12]

These weaknesses are, however, endemic to the present stage of confederation and they make further economic integration in that political framework at best a mixed prospect for aggrieved or divided territorial communities. If the same framework is retained, then the best economic option for some regions might well be secession within the existing Community. Assuming the other member states were prepared to recognise them, those regions could then play their full part as member states in the horse-trading over financial transfers. Some communities might for similar motives benefit from shifting their allegiance to other, smaller states that are already recognised in their entirety as 'regions'. Such an outcome might, of course, produce political and economic chaos and would certainly worsen the existing long-term predicament of the European Community's so-called regional policy.

If, on the other hand, the Community were transformed into a federation, then the causes of regional discontent might be removed with less disruption and more efficiently. This presumes, however, that national sovereignty is an inadequate defence against the undesirable effects of economic change. It also presumes that a European federation would have representative political institutions with the power to implement their own economic and social policies.

In other words, a truly federal European union would have its own

---

[12] On the inherent limitations of regional policy, see Wayne Parsons, *The Political Economy of British Regional Policy*, Croom Helm, London, 1986.

responsibilities, particularly of a financial nature, to guarantee the provision of public goods such as education, health and social security and even some forms of transportation and energy supply at equivalent standards throughout the union. There would also, therefore, have to be a substantial federal budget, which would in turn give the union significant influence in fiscal policy as an instrument of macro-economic management. People in all regions might have something to gain from this. But there would be particular advantages for those now dependent on centralised national administrations that, for good or bad reasons, do not make adequate public provision or do so at a cost, for example in high taxation, that may impede self-generated economic development. The European Community does not yet seem sufficiently prepared to face up to issues of this kind.[13] However, notions like convergence, cohesion and even regional policy do not offer a viable alternative. Given the current pace and emphasis of economic integration, it is high time that the political order at both European and national levels be adapted to take account of its consequences.

[13] Some modest proposals of this kind were discussed in The MacDougall Report of 1977: Commission of the European Communities, *Report of the study group on the role of public finance in European integration*, Brussels. See also: National Economic and Social Council, *Ireland in the European Community*, Dublin, August 1989, pp. 395–445.

THE ROAD TO CONSTITUTION

J. M. ROSS*

SUPPORT for the abandonment of the United Kingdom's unwritten constitution, based on the unrestricted powers of the Crown-in-Parliament, seems to be making some headway. Suggestions for provisions to be included in a new, written, constitution are numerous, specific and enthusiastic. But the debate on how to bring about a written constitution has so far been less active and much less specific.

Can we envisage, in the foreseeable future, a situation in which the agreement and promulgation of a comprehensive written constitution becomes a political practicality? If not, is there an alternative way forward? Let me discuss these questions and put forward the case for creating special constitutional machinery for the handling of constitutional issues; for defining what these issues are, but leaving decisions on these issues to evolve over time. This would not preclude a full written constitution, but would evade the necessity to attain agreement in the near future on many of the contentious issues that would have to be dealt with in a full constitution. It provides for a step by step approach, with considerable constitutional security for each step as it is achieved.

Effective gradualism

There is no historical precedent for the creation of a complete new constitution other than in circumstances of actual or prospective collapse of state authority. This is not just an accident of history. A new constitution implies not merely radical change but comprehensive, simultaneous radical change. That kind of change is inherently improbable without either a severe, widespread and longstanding disillusionment with the existing state, or a discontented minority able and willing to use violence. There is some, and probably increasing, disillusionment with the British mode of government, but, with the doubtful exception of Scotland, it does not look like approaching the degree of disillusionment hitherto needed to destroy one form of government and replace it with another. There is no sign of a violent minority able to threaten the existing state.

There is a thought in some quarters that the impact of membership of the European Community on the exercise of national sovereignty will create a climate of opinion receptive to a new constitutional pattern. However, the effects of European pressures are likely to be mixed and in

* As a civil servant Jim Ross played a substantial role in framing the Scotland Act 1978. Since retirement he has been active in the Campaign for a Scottish Assembly, writing several influential articles in *Radical Scotland*.

the short term may be counterproductive. For an appreciable further period they will produce confusion in the mind of the electorate, and confusion is at least as likely to drive people back on traditional shibboleths as to encourage them to new adventures, the more so as the limits placed by Europe on British initiative are likely to be obvious sooner than the benefits of British influence on European initiatives.

A government with the will to promulgate a written constitution, with a parliamentary majority for its specific provisions, plus the legislative time and the freedom from competing crises to drive it through, is not impossible—but highly improbable. There is another reason for taking things by stages. The idea that a new constitution is needed is still confined to a small minority, few of whom are near the top of either of the two main parties. Even that minority has so far concentrated largely on certain aspects of constitutional practice. Any systematic list of the issues to be covered in a comprehensive constitution would show large and important matters to which hardly any thought has yet been given.

What is worse, there is a risk that many of the enthusiasts for constitutional change have got their priorities wrong. It is true that, by comparison with other advanced countries, the British citizen is short of written rights and often suffers in consequence. But in practice he suffers much less from this deficiency of the British state than from the steady slide of the United Kingdom down the league of social and economic success to an extent that cannot be explained by loss of empire and international influence.

That slide cannot be attributed to a failure to analyse its social and economic causes. There is vast documentation, official and unofficial, to show that these causes were accurately perceived. It cannot reasonably be ascribed to stupidity of British politicians in choosing policies. They are plainly no more stupid than others and there has never been much wrong with their social and economic objectives. The only reasonable assumption is that Britain suffers from an institutional sclerosis which adversely affects the choice and frustrates the impact of policy. The United Kingdom Government, or the Crown-in-Parliament if one is to be pedantic, has limitless power and total responsibility in the constitutional sense. But except for matters of high politics it has never sought, or learned, to use the power except in a regulatory sense. It leaves all the work to somebody else, local authorities, quangos or whatever. But because these workhorses are created by statute or the prerogative, unlike the old magnates, and because all statutory and prerogative responsibility flows back to Westminster, it doesn't give the bodies doing the work the constitutional status, stability or confidence to do an effective job. In Britain the centre doesn't do things locally, rarely allows the locals much scope to do things locally, and doesn't allow the locals to have a hand in anything the centre does.

As a result, British Government is relatively unsuccessful in achieving its social and economic objectives. This analysis of the British disease is a subject in itself. Until it is fully addressed and conclusions drawn about its implications for the drawing of a written constitution, it is much too early to be thinking of the promulgation of such a document.

Altogether, the case for gradualism in an approach to a written constitution needs exploration because we are almost certainly going to have to fall back on it whatever our inclinations.

The obvious form of gradualism is simply to pursue a series of specific constitutional demands (Bill of Rights, proportional representation, etc.), in the hope that they will all eventually be met and will form a constitution. This could be done either opportunistically, by pursuing whichever appeared to have adequate support at a given time, or systematically, by defining the most significant and urgent and concentrating on them. There is an argument as to whether tactical emphasis should be put on the achievement of rights or on the machinery for the exercise of power. Both have their place. Any machinery of power, however balanced, may have curious results if it does not operate within a framework of rights. But rights will be of limited value if they do not run with the grain of the machinery on which they depend for implementation.

If we must have priorities, it seems wise to put the machinery first. Without it, we run the risk of 'plus ça change . . .'. Where legislation runs against the grain of constitutional machinery, the machinery is more likely to erode the effect of the legislation than the legislation to change the character of the machinery. The prospective impact of Bills of Rights, Freedom of Information Acts etc., has to be judged accordingly. Well-judged changes in machinery, on the other hand, may promote the achievement of rights.

Further, nothing can be irreversible, but under the present British constitution even the most treasured rights are all too easily reversible. Bearing in mind that, since the Liberal administration of 1906 no party other than the Conservatives has achieved two full consecutive parliamentary terms of government or more, and that no party has less incentive to improve British constitutional machinery, the protection of what advances are made is therefore no less important than making the advances themselves. Finally, if it is correct, as suggested above, that institutional sclerosis is the root cause of British failure to progress adequately, it follows that an immediate onslaught on the central mechanics of the British state is the top priority in opening the way to improvement.

Need for new machinery

The clearly discernible flaws of present British machinery of government are:

(i) the Cabinet and specifically the prime minister have too much power;

(ii) the House of Commons as a collectivity under the thumb of the government has too much power, but individual MPs or groups of MPs acting independently of Party have too little;

(iii) the citizens have too little power to influence the government which acts in their name;

(iv) there are no procedural distinctions between the important and the unimportant (the question of adhering to the Treaty of Rome may be dealt with more summarily than a scheme for the registration of dogs);

(v) the machinery makes the worst of the two worlds of centralisation and decentralisation by concentrating all power at the centre but nearly all work and most responsibility elsewhere with local authorities or other bodies.

Ideally, we may want a changed House of Commons, a reformed Second Chamber and a wider ranging structure of decentralised, constitutionally secure, elective bodies, not to mention an improved judiciary and other such. But these imply a whole series of difficult political controversies of uncertain duration and outcome. It would be useful to identify a single mechanical change, economically expressed in legislation, which would make a contribution to the correction of the flaws listed above and give promise of continuing improvement thereafter.

I suggest a single draft Bill, which need be of only ten clauses or thereby, plus some schedules which could also be quite short. The Bill would draw a distinction between constitutional and policy issues. The machinery for dealing with the latter would be left untouched, but new machinery would be devised for the former. First, issues to be regarded as constitutional would have to be defined. Let's assume the following to be constitutional issues:

the liberty, personal security and rights of free speech of the citizen, rights of participation in government and rights of information from government;

the freedom of the press, television and radio and rights to publish;

the powers, rights and duties of representative assemblies;

the systems of voting for members of representative assemblies;

the frequency of elections to representative assemblies and the procedure for calling elections.

If and when the Bill became an Act, new legislation affecting any of the issues listed above would have to follow the procedures laid down in the Act and existing legislation dealing with these issues could be made subject to it. Any doubts as to whether new or existing legislation fell within the 'constitutional' definitions above would be resolved by the Judicial Committee of the Privy Council. Matters could be referred to that Committee by the government or through a motion put down by 100 or more MPs.

If an existing statute were declared constitutional, it would be possible for 100 or more MPs to force a referendum as to whether the electorate wished that statute to be amended. If the vote favoured amendment, the government would be required to set up a royal commission to report on amendment. Following the report, the government would not be obliged to legislate, but if it did not it would be seen to be ignoring the result of a referendum.

Any constitutional legislation reaching the statute book, whatever the earlier procedures, could be the subject of a referendum asking the electorate to say whether they were content with it, unless the legislation had passed with a majority of two thirds or more in the House of Commons. An adverse referendum would not oblige the government to repeal the legislation in question, but if it did not it would again be undeniably flouting public opinion.

What would such a Constitutional Statutes Bill do if it were enacted? It would detract appreciably from the power of the government, it would give substantial power to large groups of MPs not necessarily acting on a party basis, and it would give the electorate a voice on specific issues of importance, instead of being confined to an occasional vote on the basis of a muddling manifesto. It would give an additional power to the judiciary, in the form of the Judicial Committee, but the power would be a narrow, specifically legal, one with little scope for value judgements.

Some concrete examples may be useful. If the proposed Bill had been in force when the recent Official Secrets Act was passed, the government would have acted in the knowledge that the Act would have to run the gamut of a referendum. In the context of a Constitutional Statutes Act, the Treaty of Union between Scotland and England could be declared a constitutional issue and much else could follow.

The Constitutional Statutes Act as described would also serve as a form of entrenchment, by creating special difficulties in the way of repeal or amendment of established rights, individual or collective, in face of popular disapproval. A particular stimulus for the idea of the Act was the need of a form of entrenchment for any legalisation setting up a Scottish parliament. Any amendment or repeal of the Constitutional Statutes Act itself would also be subject to the procedure laid down in the Act.

The Constitutional Statutes Bill, which already exists in draft, is more complex than has been revealed here, though not much, and its provisions are obviously open to much debate and further refinement. There may be better ways of achieving the essential objective; an early change of constitutional procedures bringing with it a built-in encouragement to constitutional improvement and an obstacle to constitutional malpractice. But that objective should be the priority of those seeking general constitutional change.

Gathering political impetus?

There are two current political factors with which the proposal for a Constitutional Statutes Act can be linked. It is widely agreed within the Scottish Constitutional Convention that there must be a mechanism for entrenching the scheme it puts forward for a Scottish parliament. The Constitutional Statutes Act could meet the need without a complete constitution or hazardous attempts at immediate reform of existing institutions such as the House of Lords.

The idea of a Constitutional Statutes Act can be pressed on the basis that it would effect clear constitutional improvement immediately, without prejudicing the prospects of a written constitution or any specific feature that might eventually be built into that constitution. Any written constitution ought to be put through procedures such as those described above rather than left to the vagaries of present parliamentary procedures. Above all, one can legitimately ask the question, what are the reasons for *not* having a Constitutional Statutes Act? Given the poor performance of British machinery of government over the last three generations or more, in what way is government better—or as good—without such a statute or something like it?

TOWARDS A
CONSTITUTIONAL
EQUATION?

JAMES CORNFORD*

THERE are two distinct arguments in progress about the future of the
United Kingdom. The first concerns the national question to which most
of the contributors to this volume have addressed themselves. The second
concerns the constitution more generally. It is the relationship between
these arguments that I propose to consider. The first necessary observa-
tion is that the national question is one of profound indifference to most
Englishmen. If they think about it at all Englishmen regard nationalism in
Scotland and Wales as a harmless eccentricity and in Northern Ireland as a
nasty aberration. But it is not important.

Considering that the creation of the United Kingdom was a central issue
of politics over five hundred years and remained a major preoccupation of
government well into this century, a brief explanation is required. Ireland,
for all that the settlement was messy and the business unfinished, has
receded from centre stage: the threat to the Protestant succession is gone
and likewise the security problem in the Western Approaches. Conflict
over land tenure is no longer a central political issue and the rump of Irish
representation in the House of Commons, though it may yet prove
important in a hung parliament, is hardly even a shadow of the great
Parliamentary Party before 1914. The number of Irish within the United
Kingdom was drastically cut by partition, but there has also been a major
shift in the demographic weight of the constituent nations over the last two
hundred years: England has increased its share of the population of the
United Kingdom from roughly 60 to 80 per cent. Although this change is
not precisely reflected in parliamentary representation, with the departure
of the Irish, England dominates Parliament. More recent electoral
changes have reinforced the importance of English politics. With the
decline of the Labour Party in the South East of England and its
continuing success in Scotland and Wales, support for the major parties is
increasingly polarised. There are fewer marginal seats and these are
concentrated in London and the English Midlands. The Conservative
Party does not need to address the special interests of the Scots, the Welsh
and the Irish. The Labour Party will not win by doing so.

On the other hand the costs of union to the English appear to be
containable and, despite the effects of the dispute in Northern Ireland on

* The author is director of the Institute for Public Policy Research and Literary Editor of
The Political Quarterly.

the mainland, acceptable. The Scots are over represented at Westminster, which under the present electoral system favours the Labour Party in Scotland. Any moves towards greater independence for Scotland within the United Kingdom will bring this question firmly onto the agenda. The other costs of the union are difficult to disentangle. The Scots have used their weight, especially under recent Labour governments, to secure favourable treatment regarding expenditure on functions administered by the Scottish Office; and so to a lesser extent have the Welsh and the Northern Irish. But there are passionate disputes about the distribution of other public expenditure such as Ministry of Defence contracts, the distribution of public employment and the benefits of tax expenditures like mortgage interest relief, not to mention the Petroleum Revenue Tax. It can also be argued that the equalisation effects of transfer payments under Social Security which apply across the United Kingdom are far greater than any special treatment given to the smaller nations.

Nevertheless any attempt to address the national question by constitutional measures within the United Kingdom will put these questions of representation and benefit on the agenda of English politics and remove them from the decent obscurity which they have lately enjoyed. If there are to be changes for Scotland, Wales and Northern Ireland, they will entail changes for England too. The National question will have to be linked to the constitutional question.

Litany of complaint

There is a now familiar litany of constitutional complaint: of an electoral system which seriously distorts representation, excludes middle opinion, and threatens to perpetuate rule by the largest minority party; of a Parliament which is dominated by the executive through control of its procedures and the disciplines of party, patronage and the Press, and which therefore fails to scrutinise effectively the conduct of government or to play any constructive role in legislation; of a national administration which practices excessive secrecy and against whose actions there is inadequate redress; of a local government which is at once the dependent of and the scapegoat for central government and which enjoys little support either in Parliament or among the electorate; and of a police force which has been used increasingly in a political role, which has little accountabilty, which has absorbed more and more resources while crime rates rise, and whose reputation for probity has been sadly dented.

For each of these ills there is a specific: electoral reform, more powers for Select Committees and a reformed Second Chamber, Freedom of Information, the restructuring of local government (again) and devolution, a Bill of Rights or incorporation of the European Convention on Human Rights, and other proposals for the statutory protection of privacy, the control of the security services, the strengthening of employment rights and of anti-discrimination measures brought together in Labour's *Charter of Rights*. What has emerged over the last three or four years is a growing interest across the political spectrum in bringing these together. This reflects a common understanding of the underlying problem which is best expressed in Dunning's famous motion of 1780:'The power of the executive has increased, is increasing and ought to be diminished'.

A more recent and less succinct statement of the problem may be found in *The Scottish Claim of Right*, July (1988):

> The English Constitution provides for only one source of power; the Crown-in-Parliament. That one source is now mainly embodied in the Prime Minister, who has appropriated almost all the royal prerogatives. . . . In fact, if not in theory, the Prime Minister is Head of State, Chief Executive and Chief Legislator, and while in office is not circumscribed by any clear or binding constitutional limitations. Against this there is in the United Kingdom not a single alternative source of secure constitutional power at any level.

Political power there certainly is. Even if it works through the Gothick Constitution of the Conservative party, the electorate has the last word.

This is not *constitutional* power, however, and it is the belief that restraints on the executive and on the centralisation of power must be given constitutional rather than political force that has become a common theme of reformers. The need for the entrenchment of rights both for individuals and for devolved governments implies a constitutional document. This has been for long the view of the Liberal Democrats and their predecessors and has been given outline expression in their Federal Green Paper No. 13: '*We the People . . .' Towards a Written Constitution*. It was the theme of *Charter 88*, which has evoked such a remarkable response. It is at least implicit in the proceedings of the Scottish Convention. And it has been given an interesting dimension in recent work of the Institute of Economic Affairs as a protection against the encroachments of the European Community.

There are differences of interest and emphasis between these various bodies. But just as there is a common diagnosis of the constitutional problem, so there appears to be emerging a similar model of the future constitution. In the first place, it is unionist: it assumes the continuing existence of the United Kingdom and insofar as it addresses the national question does so as a question of decentralisation or devolution. In other respects it is also conservative. There appears to be no market for republican ideas. The monarchy is preserved, though there are proposals to subject the prerogatives of the Crown as exercised by the Prime Minister to greater Parliamentary control. There are no proposals to separate the executive and the legislature: the executive will continue to be drawn from Parliament. There will be cabinet government, collective and individual responsibility of ministers, with all that implies for the conduct of Parliamentary business. Parliament will retain its ultimate supremacy: the powers of subordinate tiers of government will be prescribed in specific terms and the reservoir of legislative power remains with Parliament. Devolved powers will not touch those subjects essential to the continuing existence of the United Kingdom as a common market—trade, commerce, taxation, social security, and as an international actor—foreign affairs, defence, security.

But the balance of forces within Parliament will be changed by the introduction of some form of proportional representation and by the replacement of the House of Lords with an elected second chamber with enlarged powers. Equally important both the rights of individuals and the powers devolved to subordinate tiers of government will be entrenched: that is to say it would require special Parliamentary procedures to change them. It might involve also the consent of those affected, whether bodies or persons, through ratification of amendments, referenda and so forth. Finally entrenchment would mean a much enlarged constitutional role for the judiciary both in litigation about individual rights and in interpreting the extent of legal powers of various authorities and questions arising from conflicts of law between them. This would require at least the establishment of a constitutional court and possibly an overhaul of the methods of recruiting, appointing and managing the judiciary.

The Scottish question

This agenda is so far removed from the everyday concerns of British politics that one may well question whether it deserves serious consideration. The reason for thinking that it does lies in Scotland. There is of course a general case for devolution or decentralisation, which is accepted by constitutional reformers, whether this takes the form of constitutional protection for local government or the establishment of regional institutions similar to those of one or other of our European neighbours.

Neat solutions require neat problems: where the national question meets the constitutional question things are anything but neat. The United Kingdom is not a nation state, but a state which embraces four identifiable 'national' units. One of these, England, dominates the union by reason of its size and population (four-fifths of the whole). One of the smaller nations, Wales, has been administered for four hundred years or so as part of England. Another, Scotland, has enjoyed a large and increasing degree of administrative devolution and retains independent national institutions. The fourth, Northern Ireland, until recently enjoyed a large degree of political devolution, which has been withdrawn because its continued presence within the United Kingdom is disputed. These differences of size, of institutional development and of political climate make it difficult to imagine a coherent constitutional settlement. Many may feel that if it works don't fix it. Northern Ireland plainly doesn't work but is small and remote enough to be treated as a special case.

Scotland is another matter. Though dissent is expressed within constitutional bounds, Scotland presents an acute case of the general problem that large parts of the United Kingdom are ruled by a government for which most of the electors did not vote. The governing party in the United Kingdom holds only 10 out of 72 Scottish parliamentary seats and has recently had no more than 20 per cent support in opinion polls. The Government's policies are deeply resented and there has been a strong revival of the demands for political devolution which failed to be carried in the 1970s, and substantial support for the Scottish National Party, in by-elections and in the opinion polls, whose policy is independence in Europe. The movement for devolution now commands support from a wider and more influential body of people, including the Scottish TUC, the majority of Scottish local authorities and the Churches as well as the Labour and Liberal Democratic parties. The Scottish Convention in which these bodies have been represented has been engaged in developing its own views on the future of Scottish political institutions, rather than waiting for some dispensation from London. As a result the Conventions demands go well beyond the shabby damage control operation of the 1978 Scotland Act. The argument now concerns not simply what powers to devolve but how to entrench them.

The Scottish Labour Party, the largest party in Scotland, is also the major force in the Convention and is committed to major devolution. The UK Labour Party has accepted this commitment as the price of the Union, since without its Scottish members it has no prospect of commanding a majority in Parliament. Neither the Convention nor the Scottish Labour Party (nor the UK Labour Party) has confronted the critical constitutional question: how is Scotland's continued representation at Westminster to be justified—the West Lothian question. It is not constitutionally coherent nor will it be politically acceptable to other UK parties for Scotland's seventy MPs to vote at Westminster on matters for which they have no responsibility.

One possible answer would be to reduce Scottish representation at Westminster in the way that was done for Northern Ireland before direct rule. This does not answer the constitutional question and would probably not work politically because of the greater number of Scottish MPs who would still be involved. The anomaly would be too large. Nor could it be overcome by the suggestion in the Liberal Democratic constitution that Scottish members (or others) should not vote when matters devolved to Scotland but not to other parts of the UK were under discussion in Parliament. The withdrawal of significant numbers of MPs for particular business would be likely to change the party balance in Parliament in such a way as to make it impossible for the Government to carry its business. Treating Scotland as a special case is unlikely to work for long. Hence the attraction of using Scotland as a model not only for Wales and Northern Ireland but for England or its regions as well.

This is not an option which will have any appeal at all to the present government. If anything the tendency of their policy is the opposite. The developing argument within the party is over the continued existence of anything that can properly called local government, at least in England. One possible response to the political disaster of the poll tax is to go further down the same route: to remove from local authority control both education and community care (and possibly the police?). Community care would be transferred to the National Health Service. Education, either through mass opting out of schools from local authority control or through a specific education grant tied to a detailed national policy, would equally cease to be a responsibility of local *government*. And the local authority as a means of local administration could be replaced by a direct agent of central government. This might happen if the county councils, which nobody seems to love, were to disappear. Their education departments, no doubt in streamlined form, could come directly under the Department of Education. The remaining district authorities would then concentate on the efficient delivery of a limited range of local services.

This is partly a political fix, a way of bringing the poll tax down to an acceptable level. But it has much more serious constitutional implications, which are reflected in the use of the term community charge in the first place. A charge is made for services rendered: a tax is levied for collective purposes, without necessary regard to individual benefit. The Jacobin tendency, pronounced in the attitudes of Mrs Thatcher, rejects the legitimacy of institutions intermediary between the people and their elected government. We do not know how far these ideas have gained at the expense of the traditional liberal belief in local self government, which has until now been an important strand in the thinking of all political parties, or at least an ideal to which the major parties thought it prudent to pay homage, even as they attempted to prescribe their own national policies on local authorities of a different persuasion or to control their expenditure. The rhetoric of partnership and the practice of non-intervention have long been abandoned. Local government burdened with increasing responsibilities by central government is not trusted to carry them out.

It is unlikely, to say the least, that a Government with such attitudes to local self-government will see the national question as an opportunity for general decentralisation or devolution. On the contrary, the national question is seen as a question of management, or to put it more grandly as a problem of traditional statecraft. Northern Ireland is to be coaxed back to 'normality' and eventually into some form of mutually accepted condominium with the Republic. Wales, in spite of passionate local controversies over culture and language, is a success story. It has benefited, as Scotland did, from having a Secretary of State in the Cabinet, fighting Wales' corner in Whitehall; and also from a territorial department of central government in Wales, pulling together the threads of policy and engineering a degree of cooperation between central government, local government and other public authorities and the private sector. The Conservatives are not alone in preferring to leave things as they are.

Scotland presents a more difficult problem. There are at least two possible responses for a centralist government: to call 'the Scots' bluff or to make further concessions to Scottish sentiment for a political price. In the first place one can imagine a new Conservative Government, elected with even less support and fewer seats in Scotland, responding to the resulting uproar by offering a referendum in which the options were independence or the status quo. The argument here is that there is no coherent or acceptable half-way house between separation and the continued primacy of the UK Parliament. The assumption is that the Scots, faced with this choice, would keep ahold of nurse. The alternative, meliorist, strategy would be to offer the Scots an Assembly, to create in effect an autonomous region on the Spanish model, but at the cost of losing special representation in the Cabinet, reduced representation at Westminster, possibly with an opt-out provision for non-Scottish business (which would prove much less of an embarrassment to a Conservative than a Labour government); and also a less advantageous treatment in the distribution of public expenditure.

The dilemmas

There would be political advantages in an old style Northern Ireland solution, whatever the constitutional problems. The question is whether such a settlement, imposed as it would have to be, would have much chance of stability. Once there is an elected assembly to speak on Scotland's behalf, the terms of the union will be a matter of continuous reinterpretation and legitimate dispute. It is impossible to predict the constitutional outcome of a debate which is seen politically in terms of Scotland versus the Rest.

These constitutional dilemmas are more acute for the Labour Party. It is already committed to a Scottish Assembly, without changing the basis of the present bargain; and that commitment has been given detailed expression. Donald Dewar's 1987 Scotland Bill and subsequent drafts produced for the Scottish Convention, which take the constitutional argument further, have been based on careful thought and much hard work. The latest versions that I have seen set out what is a quasi-federal relationship between Scotland and the United Kingdom, including the fundamental notion that any statute establishing an Assembly should have a special status as a *constitutional* statute: that is a statute which would require special Parliamentary procedures to amend. Some Scottish constitutional lawyers have long argued that this is in fact the status of the Act or Treaty of Union. No alteration in its terms should therefore be made by ordinary statute. If it is to be replaced, then it should be by an equally binding settlement in which the conventions of the English Constitution do not prevail. These are deep waters.

Labour also has plans for assemblies for Wales and Northern Ireland and for some form of elected bodies for the English regions. These have

163

not been worked through in the kind of detail of the Scottish proposals, but one may presume that the plans for Wales and Northern Ireland would be close to those for Scotland, allowing for major differences in administrative and political circumstances. In the absence of anything equivalent to the Scottish Convention, it is difficult to know how much these commitments reflect opinion within and without the party itself and whether constitutional thinking in Northern Ireland and Wales shares any of the radicalism of the Scots.

The proposals for the English regions certainly do not: they bear a strong resemblance to those of the Minority Report of the Royal Commission on the Constitution, which advocated the creation of the elected regional authorities to take over the regional responsibilities of central government. To those would be added a few strategic functions of local government, following the abolition of the county councils and the introduction of a new system of most purpose authorities based on the present district authorities and metropolitan boroughs. There are two sources of political pressure for this programme: one based on a concern for regional economic development and the need to have more active and responsive authorities at a regional level to coordinate local, national and European economic initiatives. The other reflects concern in the conurbations, and especially London, about the absence of any strategic authority to deal with land-use planning, transport, and other functions which cannot be effectively handled either by boroughs individually or through informal cooperation. The position in London is particularly serious, given political divisions among the boroughs and the powers of unsympathetic and uncoordinated central government departments over the city as a whole. A recent report to the London Regional Labour Party began to put together the case for a strategic metropolitan authority with many of the functions that regional authorities across the country might also have.

Is there a case for a grand design? It should be said at once that there are powerful arguments against doing anything more than is strictly and politically necessary. These apply with particular force to the proposals for England. Critics point to what they regard as the 'ignis fatuus' of reorganisation: the notion that you can resolve or even address problems by institutional change. Local government is still reeling from the changes enforced on it over the last ten years. The last thing it needs is another upheaval. What is needed is a period of calm, of consolidation, a restoration of partnership between central and local government, based on agreed policies and adequate funding. There is nothing which a regional tier of government could do, which could not equally well be done by such cooperation. Sort out the poll tax, and concentrate on those areas of policy, like education and housing, which require urgent attention. If you must make a bargain with the Scots, sobeit. Otherwise constitutional change is a diversion, consuming time and political energy much better spent on the *real* business of government.

164

Epur, se muove. If the first step has to be taken, others will follow: and you might as well have a clear idea of where you are going and why. The constitutional changes proposed for Scotland are radical and in principle incompatible with current constitutional conventions. If they are enacted, with or without adjustments to the Union bargain, they will prove unstable and unacceptable either to Scotland or to the rest of the United Kingdom, particularly England. There is a general case for the decentralisation of government, quite apart from the need to give greater expression to national identity. Scotland, Wales and Northern Ireland, despite its troubles, are better served by their departments than is England by Whitehall. Ministers and Civil Servants are closer to their constituencies, more familiar with and to the people with whom they have to deal in local government, in the health service, in education and in the public and private sectors of industry. There is a better chance of coordination within the departments themselves, even if it is not always achieved. It is easier to launch initiatives, to experiment, to reconcile interests, to persuade, to reach agreement. Even opponents are better understood. At the same time it is a commonplace that ministers in Whitehall are overwhelmed with detail, submerged by a flood of minor decisions, while Parliament struggles in vain to digest the mass of legislation driven through it. We hear much less these days about overloaded government: but it is not clear that the new mood of confident assertiveness has actually produced a better performance.

A general decentralisation on the Scottish model would relieve central government of much domestic responsibility, particularly for the delivery of services, and allow it to concentrate on major economic policy, taxation, social security, trade, foreign policy, defence and all these matters as they relate to the European Community. Government and Parliament would have a much better chance of becoming effectively involved in the development of the Community, if they could let go of some of their domestic preoccupations. They could tackle the fear of imposed uniformity from above if they were less intent on imposing uniformity below. The best way to avoid the late-Victorian nightmare of piecemeal disintegration is to think in advance of the general settlement to which individual decisions may impel you.

A general settlement?

The moral of these exhortations is as follows:

1 Treat Scotland on the understanding that it is to provide the model not only for Wales and Northern Ireland, but for the regions of England also. Some functions to be devolved to a Scottish Assembly such as the civil and criminal law and the administration of justice, could also be devolved to Northern Ireland, but not to England and Wales. In other respects do not devolve to Scotland matters you could not contemplate devolving to the

JAMES CORNFORD

English regions. A high degree of symmetry is essential to a coherent settlement.

2 Make a proper job of devolution: that is devolve legislative competence to the Assemblies, set out clearly what are the limits to that competence and provide an impartial mechanism, i.e. the courts, for settling disputes about that competence. Do not retain powers for the central government to interfere directly in devolved matters by a *political* override, as was provided in the 1978 legislation. There will of course prove to be overlapping interests and responsibilities, but separate powers should provide a basis for collaboration rather than conflict in dealing with them. Quasi-federation requires quasi-federal arrangements.

3 Do not devolve powers to establish or administer taxes. Powers of taxation are not necessary: what is essential is a guaranteed entitlement to a share of revenue. In the United Kingdom as elsewhere, any scheme of devolution will require a large measure of equalisation between regions. This can best be achieved by raising all taxation, except perhaps a local property tax, on a UK basis and distributing the revenue through an entrenched formula. This formula should be simple, robust and transparent. The tax most readily assigned for national/regional purposes would be the personal income tax, representing at present about 25 per cent of central government revenue. Reassignment of this revenue among the nations and regions on a population basis would roughly meet current expenditure on Scottish Office functions across the United Kingdom. The system could be made a little more sophisticated by allowing national/regional governments to vary the standard rate of income tax within limits in their own area and thus to vary their own revenue at the margin. Such a system would not favour the Scots and would be strongly resisted by them. This is not an argument against it. It would probably favour the poorer English regions. To work at all the formula would have to be set with an agreed adjustment mechanism and *not* annual renegotiation. The more complex it becomes the greater the opportunities for fudging and for central government interference.

4 Devising boundaries for the English regions has been a favourite parlour game for nearly a century. No pundit produces quite the same results, though some have clearly taken more trouble to establish clear criteria than others. Many are derivative either of their more determined colleagues or of administrative boundaries drawn up by various public authorities and industries, which are equally diverse. Since devolution is a political enterprise the primary consideration should be some sense of identity, actual or potential, rather than calculations of administrative convenience or ideal size. In some parts of England, the North East, Yorkshire, East Anglia, the South West, it may be a case of expressing an existing identity. In the South Midlands and South East it may mean discovering a latent identity—or even inventing one. And again, if these

166

hard choices are to be made, they had better be set in aspic. The lesson of local government here and abroad is that continuity, political tradition, identity and loyalty are more important than logic or convenience.

In all these matters, functions, competence, revenue and boundaries, there is a common factor: they need to be set out clearly and un-ambiguously and they need to be protected from unilateral change by central government. They need in fact to be incorporated in a written constitution. The circle closes.

APPENDIX
THE GUARDIAN: TWO
EDITORIALS*

1. Who we are and what we ought to be

CONSTITUTIONS should be built to last. Unfortunately, although the case
for constitutional reform has been a recurrent theme of British politics in
its agonised post-imperial phase, most of the many piecemeal attempts at
change have been either administrative failures, as in the tragic case of
local government, or political failures, as with devolution.

In spite of these experiences, there is still a widespread and entirely
justified view that this country's constitutional arrangements are less
appropriate now than they have been at any time in the democratic era.
But that may owe as much to a failure of understanding of the kind of
country we inhabit as to a failure of political will to change it. Accordingly
we shall look in two leader comments, today and tomorrow, first at the
problem of British national identity, and then at the possible shape of a
new constitutional settlement.

The two themes belong together because the choice of the best type of
constitution is inseparable from the settled understanding of who we are.
There will be no new constitutional settlement until we resolve that
troubled sense of identity. Since the French Revolution, Europeans have
organised themselves in nation states based often, though not always, on
common language and cultural identity. National identity, as people
throughout Central and Eastern Europe have asserted, is the fundamental
underpinning of a people's willingness to be governed as one. This is not
an antiquated form of consciousness but a modern one.

In this country, it seems, such ideas are not so easily applied. This is not
because we are different from other Europeans, as many like to believe.
Nor is it because our institutions are of special antiquity, although they are.
It is because we do not live in a nation state like France or even Germany.
Instead we have multiple identities; for us, the unfortunate parallels are the
Soviet Union or Yugoslavia (though without their liberal constitutions) or
perhaps Spain. We are a state without a nation; we are nations without
states. We are citizens of a United Kingdom of separate but unequal
countries, but we do not think of ourselves as Ukanians.

We more readily recognise ourselves as British, but this, typically,
remains a pragmatic self-image, which is one reason why most of us feel no
sense of identity with Ulstermen, Falkland Islanders or Gibraltarians but

* The editors gratefully acknowledge the permission of *The Guardian* to reproduce these
leading articles of 8 and 9 May 1990.

will cheer unequivocally for John Barnes or Nigel Benn. It means that, whatever our local origins or emotional loyalties—be they Chingford, Chapeltown or China—we accept the permanence of the English domin-ated constitutional settlement of this island.

Even so, there are many sorts of British. They salute many different flags, as well as none at all. Only the white English, and not all of them either, can easily elide all these levels into one seamless and unproblematic identity—and often with distressingly racist and violent results. Many Scots, by contrast, seek to have no other identity than as Scots, bridling at the very idea of themselves as British. Smaller minorities also have equally proud visions of themselves as irreducibly Welsh, Irish, Manx or Cornish. These identities are distinctly national in ways which proud people from Yorkshire, much less proud people from Berkshire, will never know.

Any new constitutional settlement which ignores these factors will be built upon uneven ground. Perhaps that is inevitable, and we must just make the best of it. Britain is not, after all, a country which can easily be redistributed into federal Länder or administrative departments on the German or French model. We therefore have to decide whether to accept the unevenness of the ground, by designing constitutional arrangements which privilege the national minorities even more than they (the Scots especially) are privileged under the existing system, or whether to level the ground and design a constitutional system for Britain which treats us all as equal Britons. The national question is the starting point for reconstruc-tion of the British constitution.

Politically, the vital decision lies with the Scots. The Scots are by far the largest and most important of the national minorities living in Britain. They possess their own institutions. They are the only ones who could realistically make a fist of separation from Britain, the more so because as members of the EC, they are already part of the new administrative Europe. There is, in fact, nothing to stop Scotland becoming an inde-pendent nation except the Scots themselves. It is therefore time that the Scots decided the question of independence, which they should do in a referendum. The outcome, though, would not just be an historic choice for Scotland. It would also be decisive for the future of the country they would leave behind. Any regionalisation of British government depends crucially upon whether Scotland is in or out.

There is no reason in equitable principle why such an option should not also be open to other national minorities in this country. In practice, however, it is hard to imagine any of them—even the Welsh—choosing independence, especially as long as their separate cultural identity is properly respected and nurtured and as long as local government is given a meaningful role once again. Respect and nuture of minority cultures is in no way necessarily antagonistic to or incompatible with the maintenance of the English-dominated settlement. This is as true of the Third World minority cultures in this country as it is of the minority cultures which we tend to think of as indigenous.

Northern Ireland is a special case, partly because it is the only part of the United Kingdom which is territorially disputed by a foreign power, partly because the British would actually quite like to be rid of it and partly because its right to secede, at least in principle, has already been conceded by the holding of a referendum. Nevertheless, it is part of the United Kingdom unless and until its inhabitants choose otherwise.

The goal of this self-examination must be to transform Britain into a modern nation state on the European model. The nation state is the most dynamic and effective embodiment of political identity in the modern world. Many illusions on that score have been challenged and sometimes dispelled by recent events in central and eastern Europe. But it is part of the British talent for collective historical self-deception that we fail to see the parallels in the USSR and Yugoslavia for our own predicament.

Not that the nation state reflects everything that we are or embodies everything which we wish to be. The nation state is not fixed for ever in history as the exclusive focus of collective identity. Ask a Shetlander or a Liverpudlian. Or ask the inhabitants of any village, rural or urban, in the land. Simultaneously, we are each of us members of an archipelago of different communities defined by an interplay of such factors as geography, class, race, education, religion, ability, politics, age, children, work and sex. We tend to think of these as small, often highly localised communities. But they are also very large, international communities too. We are English, but we are also Muslims, we are gays, we are unemployed, we are Europeans.

Finally and most important, the nation state is neither the irreducible embodiment of our collective identity nor its most appropriate protector. These limitations are as observable as they are also desirable and inevitable. Two centuries ago, Kant argued that to envisage civil society at all is to envisage world civil society. Today we must also recognise that we cannot have citizenship in the full sense, in one country any more than we can have free markets or socialism in one country either. Britain's problem is that it is not a nation. But there are mutltinational problems too, and they require multinational remedies. That is why today, for example, there are many levels to our need to strengthen the European dimension of our identity; the need is partly idealistic (it would be nice to control our lives together), partly pragmatic (it would be wise to do so), partly empirical (we do it that way anyway) and partly political (if we want to do it effectively, we need to get a better grip on it).

European idealism is fine, up to a point. But the pressing need for constitutional reform to incorporate the European dimension is based upon the daily reality of the European identity, not some misty internationalist vision. Our new constitution must therefore be based upon many considerations and apply many principles. But it must be bedded in the reality of the material circumstances of identity as well as embodying an overall theory of how power can best be controlled. It is a big task and there will be no second chances for those who get it wrong.

The immediate reason for getting it right is the most important of all. The evidence of the Thatcher years, building on lessons from previous eras under governments of all parties is that we stand in real need of better democracy, better justice and a richer culture of citizenship. These are not abstract refinements or academic daydreams, things which can be infinitely postponed to a more convenient time at the end of the rainbow. They are pressing present needs, essential to the reconstruction of effective civil society in Britain in the aftermath of its continuing sub-version by doctrinaire possessive individualism.

There is a second imperative, in one sense contradictory, but essentially linked. Urgent legislation is very frequently bad legislation, and certainly incomplete legislation. If Labour actually comes to power at the next general election, it will arrive committed to a very piecemeal and unplanned approach to such change. The word at Westminster, for instance, is that Labour intends to legislate for Scottish devolution in its first year of office. Other reforms, some of them as yet no more than impromptu asides from Mr Roy Hattersley, may follow later, if in fact they follow at all. All previous experience, not least that of the way the Callaghan government handled devolution more than a decade ago, cries out that this approach would not only be ineffectual but destructive. Constitutional changes requires something better: a coherent strategy of institutional rebuilding deploying tested theories and grounded in reality, not a patch-up job of running repairs. Tomorrow, we examine the course that this urgent but comprehensive constitutional reconstruction ought to take.

2. Building bricks for a better Britain

In an ideal world, any new constitution would be written on a clean sheet. Such, indeed, is the firm intention of many of the proponents of constitutional reform in this country today. It is, however, a fantasy. This in no way means that a written constitution is undesirable. On the contrary. But a reform of this scale can only be embarked upon, let alone implemented, with enthusiastic public support.

Where is that support in Britain today? Even to the most optimistic inhabitants of today's lively and growing ghetto of reformist enthusiasm, it must surely be obvious that public opinion as a whole is only minimally engaged. And the problem goes further. Among the politically active, there is still nothing like the degree of cross-party involvement which ought to be a precondition for something so far-reaching. To put it simply, most Tories aren't interested—not while they are in power, anyway. Even in the awakening Labour Party, it is still not a mass issue either.

This is not an objection of principle. It ought, nevertheless, to provide a cautionary and disciplining context for those who plan the necessary programme of reforms. In practice, the opportunity to reconstruct a nation's institutions arises only when the comprehensive destruction of an older order creates a sufficiently widespread demand and need for a fresh settlement. Britain does not face such a situation, nor is it foreseeably likely to do so.

There is a second stubborn reality. If we are serious about coherent radical constitutional change we cannot leave out of the debate the future of the monarchy. After all, the hereditary monarchy is at the apex of the structure of British constitutional arrangements. It is literally our sovereign power. Yet modern British society has patently failed to confront this question. It remains a taboo political subject and republicanism, despite modest revivals, is less discussed in Britain in the 20th century than it was in the 19th. This omission does no credit to the British political culture. Until this dimension is faced, talk of a written constitution embodying a dynamic new culture of British citizenship seems unduly optimistic.

This is not, therefore, an ideal world in which balanced and rational new designs can be neatly substituted for corrupted and barnacled old ones. What is vital, however, is that this conclusion does not encourage the belief that the only alternative is a hotch-potch of marginal constitutional reforms which won't cause uncontrollable political waves. Constitutional reform must still be conceived, enacted and developed as a coherent programme.

The overarching objective of all constitutional change must be the modernisation of British civil society so that more citizens can increase their liberty and what Ralf Dahrendorf calls their 'life-chances'. By so doing, they can play a more active, informed and equal part in their own government, at all levels, but especially at the level of the nation state with which they identify. This can be achieved by gradualist political means; indeed, there is no alternative. But it must be a tough-minded, even ruthless, gradualism. Every project must be part of a broad reforming scheme governed by the principle of modernising democracy in Britain.

At its heart should be two great and complementary objectives. The first is to limit and modify the existing system of unconditional parliamentary sovereignty. This has been the principal means by which the existing constituion has allowed the Thatcher governments, like their predecessors, to abuse liberties on so lavishly. This objective must be achieved by simultaneous action on three fronts: electoral reform, parliamentary reform and making Parliament more accountable to law.

The aim of electoral reform must be to allow citizens to elect a Parliament which more truly and fairly represents both the geographical spread and the political balance of opinion in the country as a whole, at the same time providing a stable government which can use the power of the state to carry out the appropriate wishes of the majority. This cannot happen under the existing first-past-the-post system, which satisfies neither aim fully. But neither can it happen under a system which is so relentlessly proportional that it makes any aspects of healthy political life impossible, as is now the case in Israel.

The necessary cultural breakthrough at this stage is to accept the principle of the need for electoral reform. It is less necessary to make an immediate commitment to a particular means. There are many possibilities, none of them perfect. One attractive model, combining both small single member constituencies and majority victories, might be based on the French system. French voters have the opportunity, on a constituency basis, to vote first for the party of their choice and then, if no one secures more than 50 per cent of the votes, to choose between the two strongest candidates, thus ensuring that the winner is always supported by a majority. A single chamber elected along these or comparable lines, and subject to the supervision process suggested below, would be a much fairer Parliament than the unrepresentative assembly we have at present. (It should go without saying that the existing House of Lords, based on heredity and patronage, should play no role at all in any reformed structure.)

But electoral reform is not enough. Parliament itself needs to be reformed, so that it can do its job better. In part this is a material question: the long overdue provision of appropriate salaries, staff and facilities for MPs, perhaps involving a move from the inadequate Westminster premises. But the culture and procedure of Parliament need to be more critically reviewed too, in order to raise the level of invigilation and debate and to reduce reactionary and obscurantist practices which alienate Parliament from the people. Parliament supposedly exists to pass laws, to control the executive and to act as a truthful forum of national debate. At present it only does the first of these things. Too many MPs are in hock to a party patronage system which stifles independence and encourages self-censorship. Some of this can be done by new rules of procedure, strengthening the power of individual MPs at the expense of party managers, by further empowering select committees, and by devising a more rational form for standing committee scrutiny of bills, making greater use of independent expert testimony. Other changes—such as the recruitment of many more women MPs, more sensible hours, and a more realistic workload—are not really constitutional questions, though they are absolutely part of modernising the parliamentary system.

Even so, a modernised and reformed Parliament, more fairly elected, still needs to be under greater constraint of the rule of law. Today, parliamentary sovereignty has become a means by which the majority party is able to confer vast areas of devolved power and discretion upon ministers—especially the Prime Minister—and civil servants in ways which Parliament is powerless to control. It is not untrue to describe it, as Lord Halisham did until his own party won power, as elective dictatorship. Electoral and parliamentary reform will do something to constrain these tendencies, but they will not be as effective as a Bill of Rights, based upon the European Convention on Human Rights, which clearly sets out the governing principles of a modern society. This would provide a yardstick against which a standing constitutional commission, not exclusively composed of lawyers, could assess and comment upon proposed legislation and against which, ultimately, the courts would be able to judge it.

We should not be afraid of the role of the law. It has become a reflex reaction at this point in the constitutional debate to object that the judges, with their class and educational background, cannot be trusted to be objective. Very well: in that case, we must reform the judiciary, as part of the necessary modernisation of the legal system. In the last analysis, the rule of law arbitrated by independent judges is preferable to—and certainly less corrupt than—the rule of the party, the whips and the caucus.

So the second great objective of constitutional reform must be to destroy the needless centralisation off which the rule of party feeds. The centralisation and lack of accountability of decision making in Britain is unrivalled in almost any nation in Europe today, including those in the East. But whereas many European nations, East and West, are a least attempting to become less centralised, Britain is moving in the opposite direction.

In part this is a reflection of the dominance of London in British life, which is one reason why the possibility of moving the administrative capital and Parliament out of the South East, perhaps to York, needs to be taken seriously. To a much greater extent, though, it is an embodiment of the protective self-interest of the British ruling class, which is imprisoned within an ancestral administrative citadel of its own construction.

There are two principal ways of breaking up this monopoly. The first is to take powers away from the centralised state which are more appropriately exercised elsewhere—at a more local level, or at a more international. The second is create a system of public accountability in which all powers—local, national or international—are open to independent scrutiny and influence.

The need for a properly conceived devolution of power within Britain could be justified solely on the fact that the existing system is now such a mess. The most important criterion for reform, however, is still a relatively simple principle: that collective functions should be administered at the level where they can be most effectively controlled and efficiently organised. There is, obviously, a danger of creating too many wasteful layers of decision-making; nevertheless, it is clear that most functions can be best administered either at international, national, regional or local level and that appropriate forms of democratic accountability need to be matched to them.

This distribution of functions between the different levels of government can be a very pragmatic exercise. Monetary policy, for instance, is now largely an international matter. Higher education, by contrast, is generally a national concern. Most public transport is a regional subject. But provision of parks and libraries is a local matter. None of these is an absolute, of course; each relates in various ways to the others. But we have lived for too long in a system predicated on the belief that only the national is truly legitimate. The essential task for the future is to establish the legitimacy of a network of levels of decision making.

Much of this network will be a natural expression of the contours of peoples' understanding of their own identities. Some of it, however, will not. There is a readier understanding of what regional government might mean in Newcastle, say, than there is in Oxford. At all levels, efforts must be directed to creating incentives to make the system dynamic and responsive: here an enhanced role for mayors in cities, perhaps; there the direct election of the European Commissioners. Annual elections, at least at the more local levels, might be a meaningful stimulus.

Underlying all these ideas, though, must now surely be the recognition that the existing system is a failure. Individual rights against the state have been eroded. Traditions of local and minority autonomy are being squandered as we watch. While others set the international governmental agenda, we wrap ourselves in the Union Jack and rage at the world outside. Attempts to mitigate and illuminate the processes of government and administrative decree have mostly become broken reeds. Doubtless there are still those who see this tangled jumble of bogus assumptions, self-regarding conventions and hostility to change which conceals one of the most élite systems of power in any democracy as the positive embodiment of the British—though they really mean English—genius. The real alarm, though, is that so many others so clearly feel powerless to change it and remain inertly indifferent to the call for reform. The most pressing task, therefore, is to rouse them.

INDEX

Act of Union (1707), 2, 100
Anglo-Irish Agreement (1925), 74
Anglo-Irish Agreement (1985), 69,
    75–7, 86, 103
Anti-Centralisation Union, 108
Anti-Corn Law League, 28
Arnold, Thomas, 110
Ascherson, Neal, 97
Assembly of Welsh Counties, 60
Autonomy, *see* Regions and
    Regionalism

Barker, Ernest, Sir, 93n
Basques, 119–20, 122, 124–5, 128
Barrow, G. W. S., 38, 38n
Basque National Party (PNV), 122
Beer, Samuel, 36
Bentham, J., 101
Bevan, Aneurin, 2
Bill of Rights, 19–20, 103, 173
Birch, A. H., 27n
Blackstone, William, Sir, 101–2
Blake, Robert (Lord), 93, 93n
Bogdanor, V., 106n
Briggs, A., 28n
British Social Attitudes Report (1990),
    70–2
Britishness, 3–6, 69, 90–1, 96–9, 168–
    71; *see also* Englishness
Brown, Alice, 47n
Buchanan, G., 41
Burke, Edmund, 3, 92, 101
Burns, Robert, 3, 40, 44
Burrows, Bernard, 106n

Campaign for a Scottish Assembly, vii,
    48, 49, 49n
Cannadine, David, 5
Carlyle, Thomas, 110
Carty, Tom, 117, 117n
Catalonia, 122–4, 131–2
Catholic Church, 73–4
Celtic identity, 2–3, 57–8, 80–1
Central Office of Information, 90
Centre for Local Economic Strategies,
    106

Chalmers, T., 111
Charity Organisation Society, 111–12
Charles II, King of Great Britain, 101
Charter 88, vii, 76, 103, 159
Chatham, William Pitt, Earl of, 101
Chesterton, G. K., 108
Christian influences, 16, 50, 70–3, 75,
    80–1, 100
Christie, Campbell, 53
Church of Scotland, 41, 100
Citizenship, 109–12, 154, 171
Claim of Right for Scotland, A, 49–50,
    100, 159
Clark, Jonathan, 1
Cobbett, William, 92
Cobden, Robert, 27, 30
Cole, G. D. H., 108, 114
Coleg Harlech, *see* Harlech
Collins, Gerard, 23
Colls, Robert, 94n
Commission of the European
    Communities, 137n, 138n, 141,
    143, 143n, 144, 150n
Common Agricultural Policy (CAP),
    10–11, 14, 137, 142–3
Connor, Walter, 96n
Conservative Party (UK), 46, 56, 117–
    18, 157, 163
Constitution of Ireland (1937), 85
Constitution of Spain (1978), 125
Constitutional reform, vii, 55, 76,
    102–4, 116, 132–3, 151–3, 158–60,
    171–5; entrenchment, 154–5; and
    Scotland, 48–54, 160–3; and United
    Kingdom, 103–4, 165–7, 171–5
Constitutional Statutes Bill, 155–6
Constitutional Steering Committee, 49
Convention of Scottish Local
    Authorities, 50
Cook, Robin, MP, 103
Council of European Regions, 105
Council of Ministers, 17, 19
Crick, Bernard, 82, 98n, 100n, 103n
Crosland, Antony, 112
Crouch, Colin, 30n, 106n
Crowther-Hunt, Lord, 114

177

INDEX

compared, 8–12; of Parliament,
109–13, 151–2
Spain, 119–33; transition to
democracy, 123–6; lessons for
Britain, 126–7; differing time-scales,
128–30
Spanish Socialist Workers Party
(PSOE), 129, 129n, 130
Stalin, J., 27
Statute of Westminster (1931), 8
Stevenson, R. L., 40
Stokes, E. T., 91n
Stone, Norman, 1, 3
Suarez, Adolpho (Prime Minister of
Portugal), 123–4, 128
Swift, Jonathan, 3

Tawney, R. H., 94
Taxation, negative view, 166
Terrorism, 87
Thatcher, Margaret, MP, 1, 6, 40, 46,
47, 78, 86, 96, 115, 120
Thomas, Dylan, 3, 58
Tocqueville, Alexis de, 94
Town Planning Institute, 108
Toynbee, Arnold, 111
Treaty of Rome (1957), 7, 102, 137
Treaty of Union (1707), 18, 44, 90,
100, 155, 163
Trevor-Roper, Hugh (Lord Dacre),
91n

Ulster, *see* Northern Irish
Ulster Unionist Party, 72

Ukanian, 66, 97; *and see* Nairn, Tom
Union of the Democratic Centre
(Spain), 124, 128
United Kingdom, nature of, 4–6, 55–6,
91
United Nations, 84
Urquhart, David, 108

Voltaire, 93

Wales, *see* Welsh
Wallace, William, 138n
Wallas, Graham, 109
Weber, Eugen, 32n
Wells, H. G., 95, 108
Welsh, 56–67; obsession with state,
65–7
Welsh Development Agency, 61
Welsh Office, 60–1, 64–5
West European Union (WEU), 10, 23
Western Mail, 61
Whitelaw, William (Lord), 124
Whyte, John, 70, 72
Wiener, Martin, 111n
Wilson, Gordon, 47
Wilson, Woodrow, 28
Wood, Ian, 42n
Wordsworth, William, 110
Worsthorne, Peregrine, Sir, 4

Yeats, W. B., 3

181